BREAKING

THE 10

This graphic novel is also available as an e-book.

ISBN 978-1-68112-021-8
© 2016 Seán Michael Wilson & Michiru Morikawa
Library of Congress Control Number: 2016906542
1st printing July 2016

Volume 1

Sean Michael Wilson
Michiru Morikawa

nbm GRAPHIC NOVELS

Nantier • Beall • Minoustchine

NEW YORK

Chapter 1

'Thou shalt not steal.'

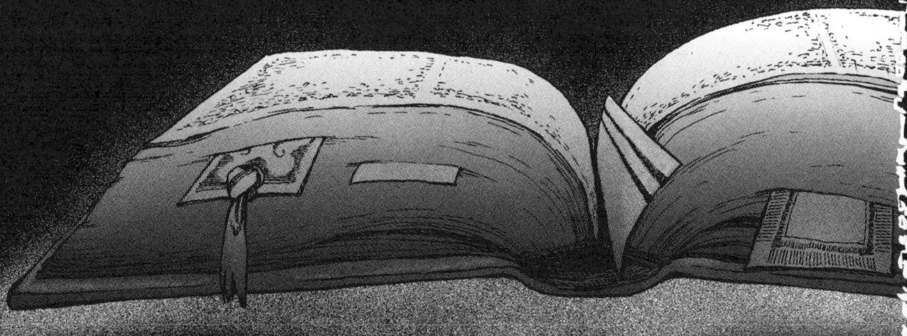

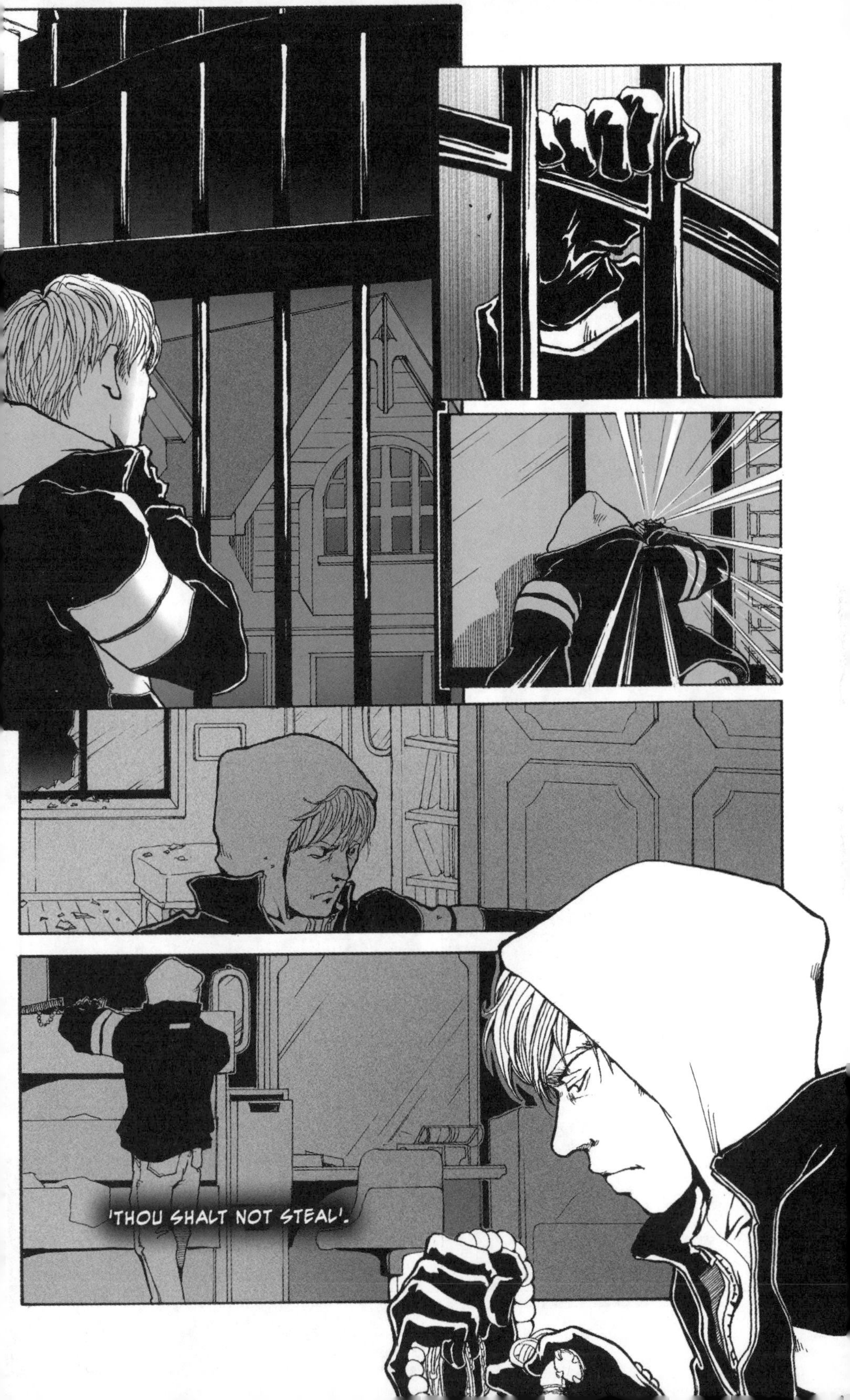
'THOU SHALT NOT STEAL'.

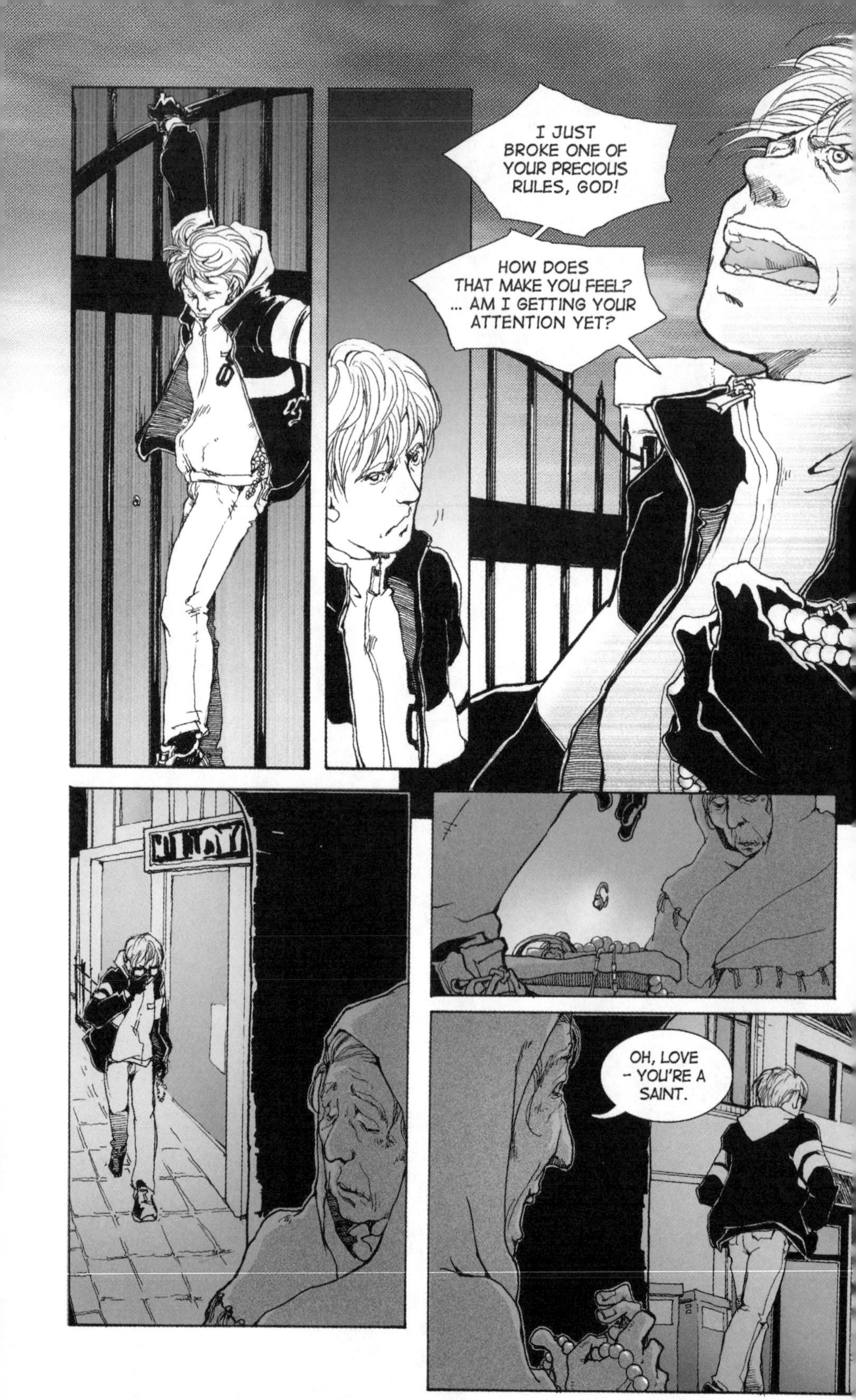
I JUST BROKE ONE OF YOUR PRECIOUS RULES, GOD!
HOW DOES THAT MAKE YOU FEEL? ... AM I GETTING YOUR ATTENTION YET?
OH, LOVE - YOU'RE A SAINT.

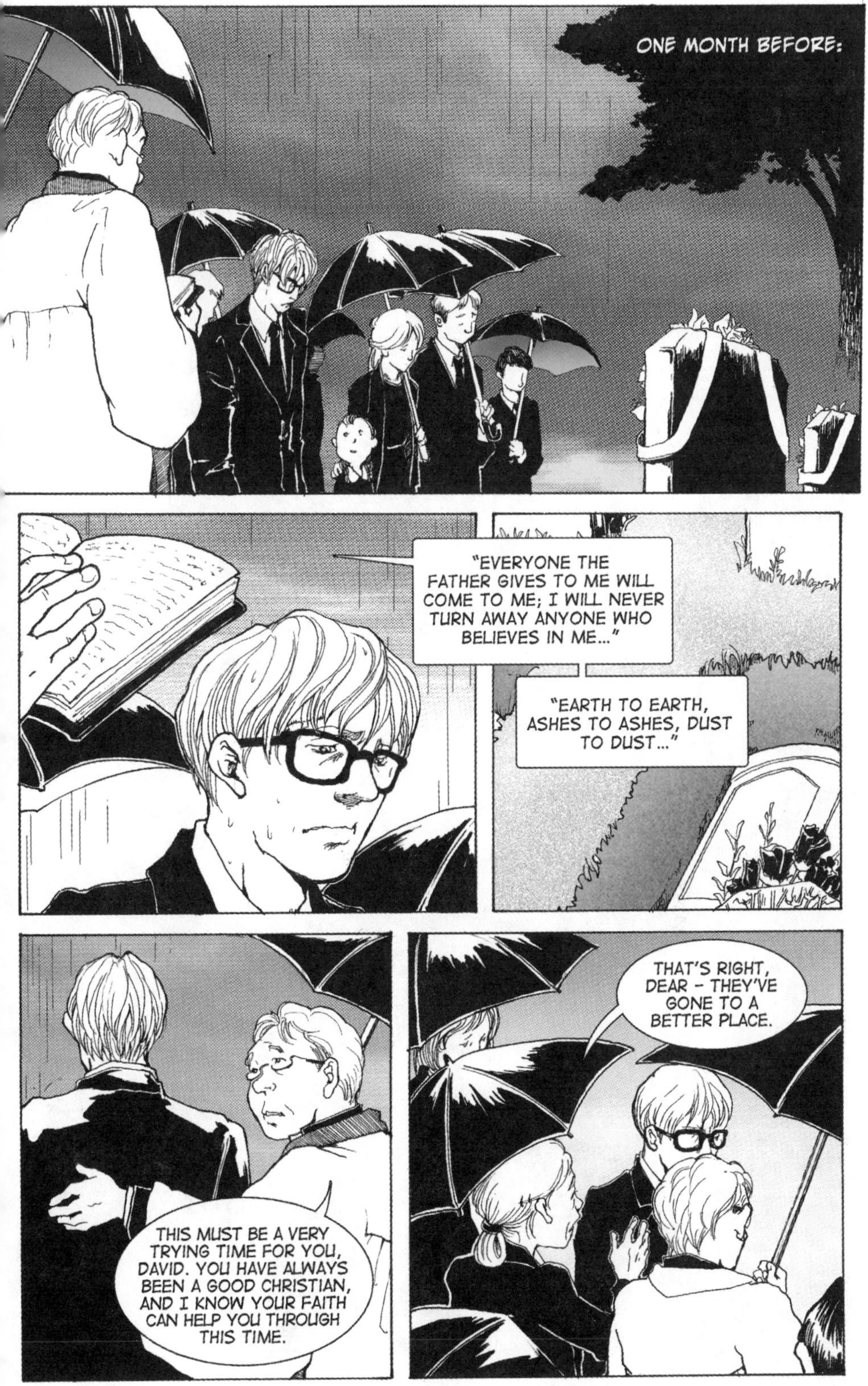
ONE MONTH BEFORE:
"EVERYONE THE FATHER GIVES TO ME WILL COME TO ME; I WILL NEVER TURN AWAY ANYONE WHO BELIEVES IN ME..."
"EARTH TO EARTH, ASHES TO ASHES, DUST TO DUST..."
THIS MUST BE A VERY TRYING TIME FOR YOU, DAVID. YOU HAVE ALWAYS BEEN A GOOD CHRISTIAN, AND I KNOW YOUR FAITH CAN HELP YOU THROUGH THIS TIME.
THAT'S RIGHT, DEAR - THEY'VE GONE TO A BETTER PLACE.

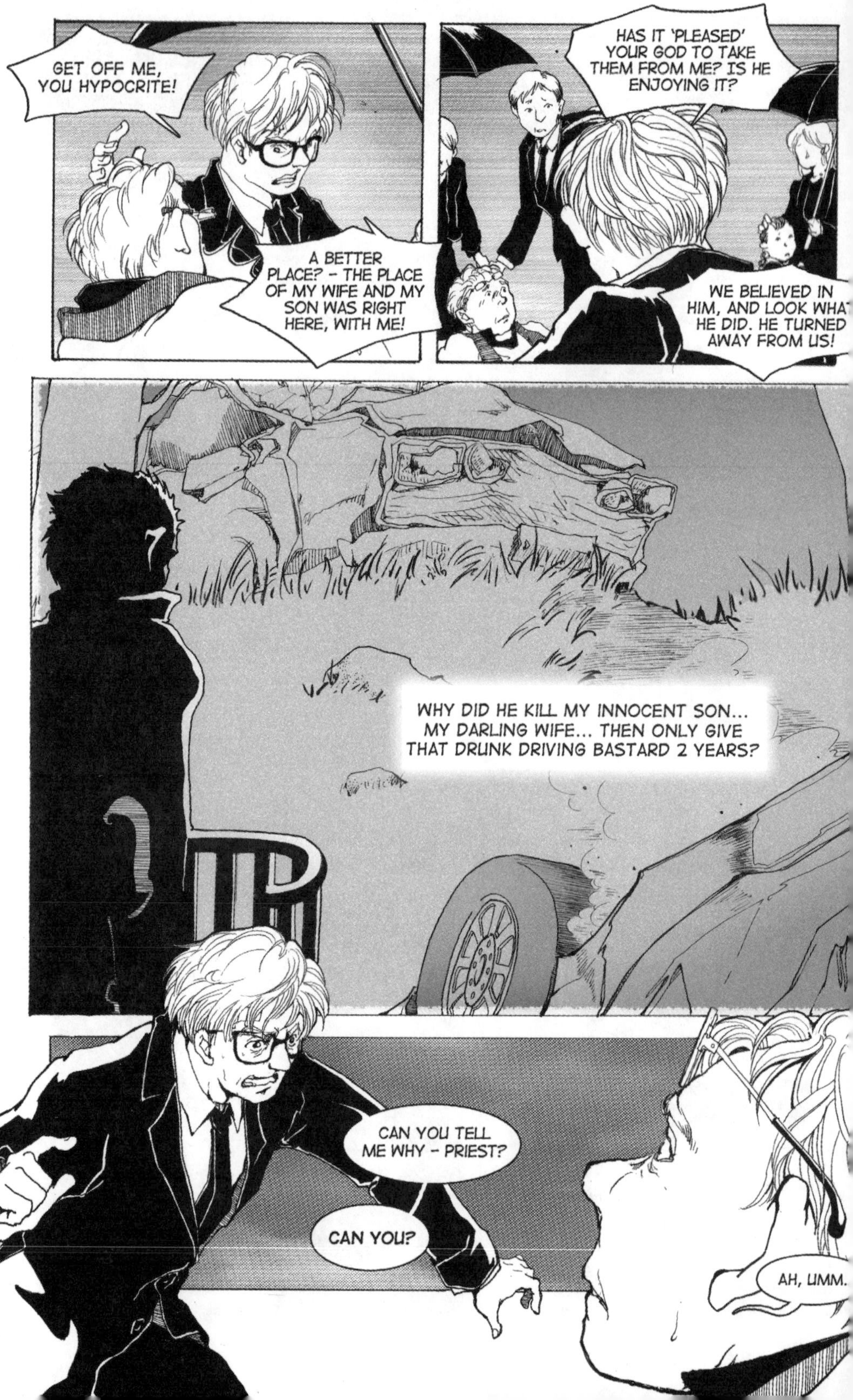
GET OFF ME, YOU HYPOCRITE!
A BETTER PLACE? - THE PLACE OF MY WIFE AND MY SON WAS RIGHT HERE, WITH ME!
HAS IT 'PLEASED' YOUR GOD TO TAKE THEM FROM ME? IS HE ENJOYING IT?
WE BELIEVED IN HIM, AND LOOK WHAT HE DID. HE TURNED AWAY FROM US!
WHY DID HE KILL MY INNOCENT SON... MY DARLING WIFE... THEN ONLY GIVE THAT DRUNK DRIVING BASTARD 2 YEARS?
CAN YOU TELL ME WHY - PRIEST?
CAN YOU?
AH, UMM.

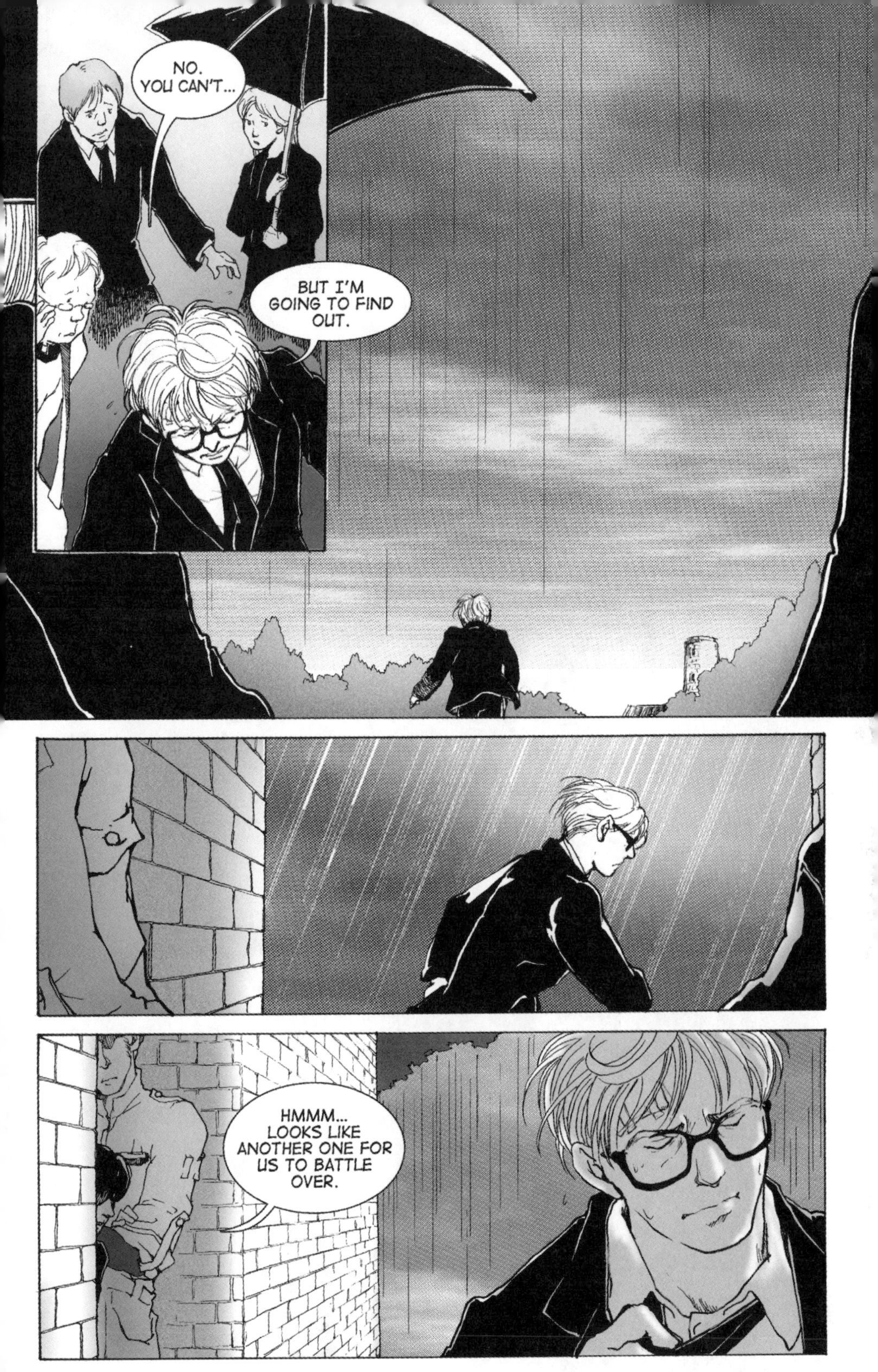
NO. YOU CAN'T...
BUT I'M GOING TO FIND OUT.
HMMM... LOOKS LIKE ANOTHER ONE FOR US TO BATTLE OVER.

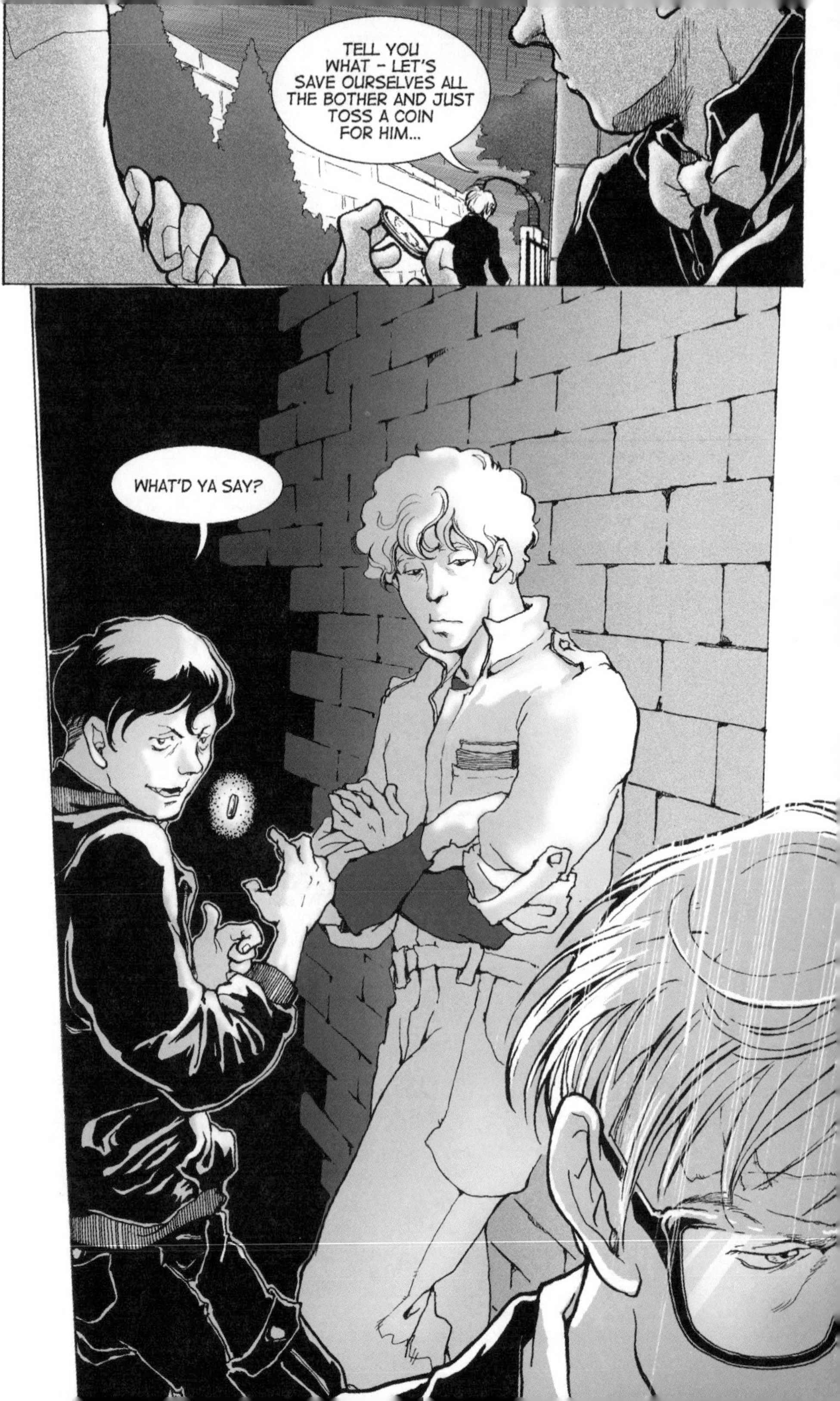
TELL YOU WHAT - LET'S SAVE OURSELVES ALL THE BOTHER AND JUST TOSS A COIN FOR HIM...
WHAT'D YA SAY?

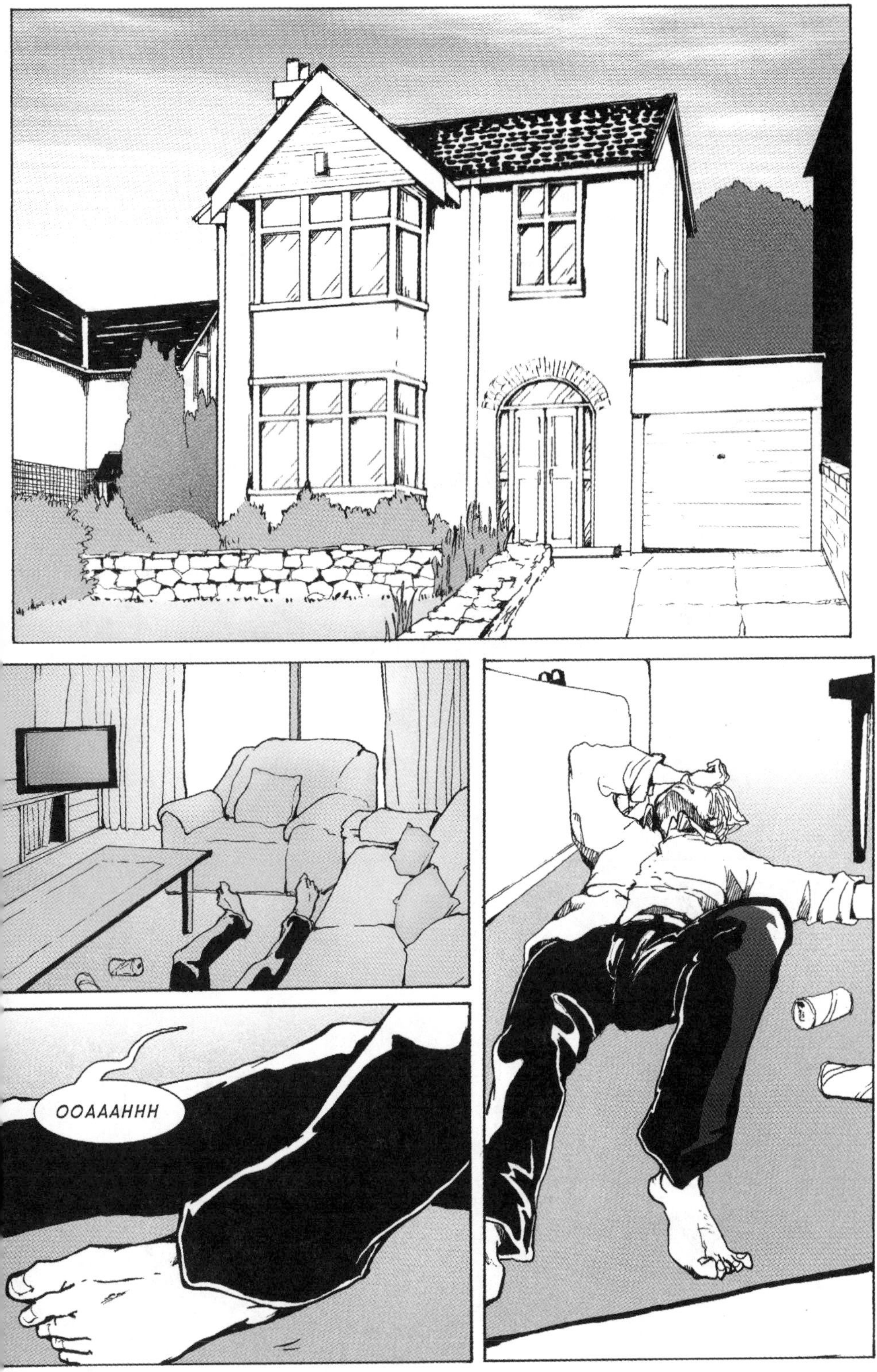
OOAAAHHH

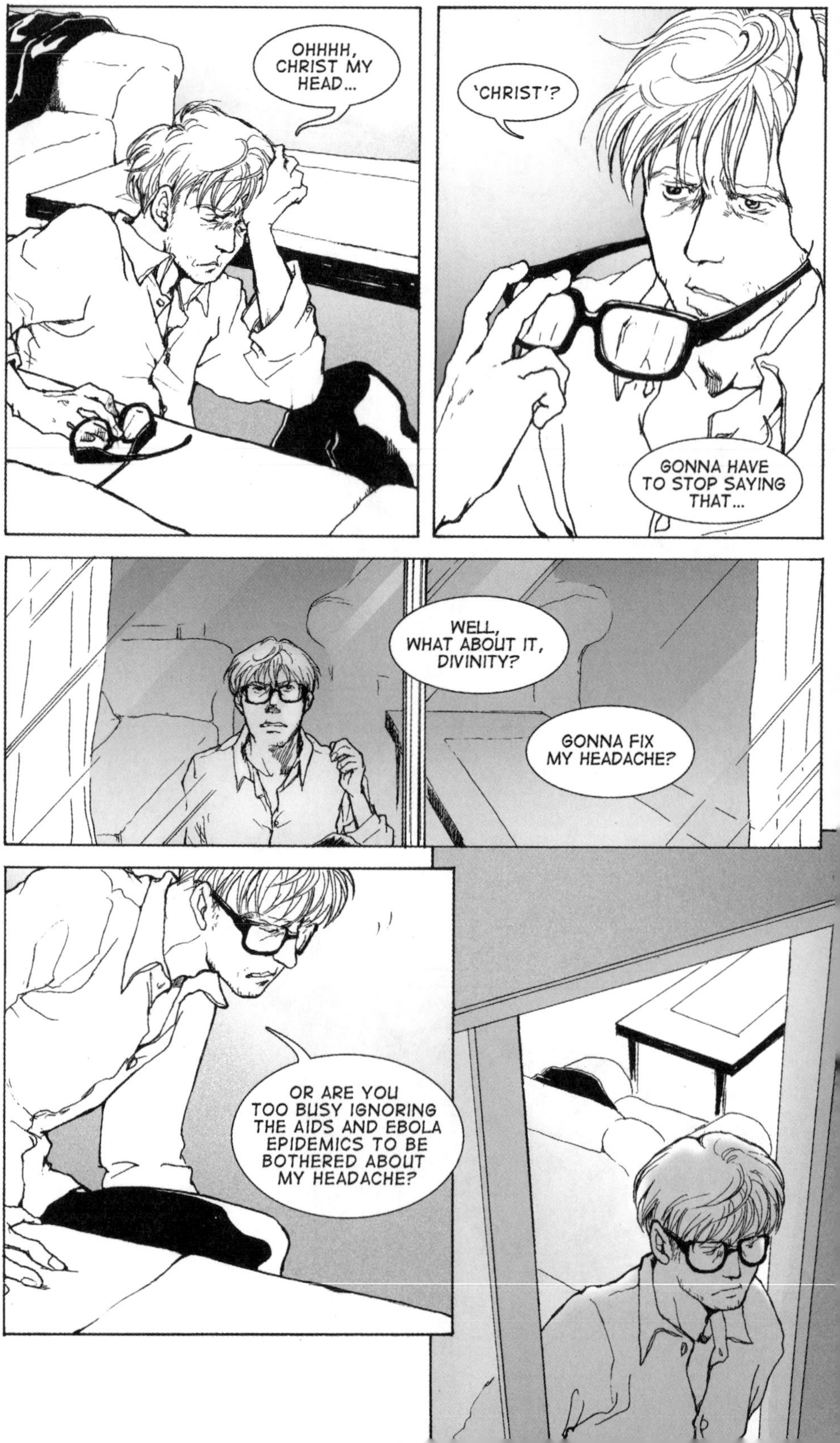
OHHHH, CHRIST MY HEAD...
'CHRIST'?
GONNA HAVE TO STOP SAYING THAT...
WELL, WHAT ABOUT IT, DIVINITY?
GONNA FIX MY HEADACHE?
OR ARE YOU TOO BUSY IGNORING THE AIDS AND EBOLA EPIDEMICS TO BE BOTHERED ABOUT MY HEADACHE?

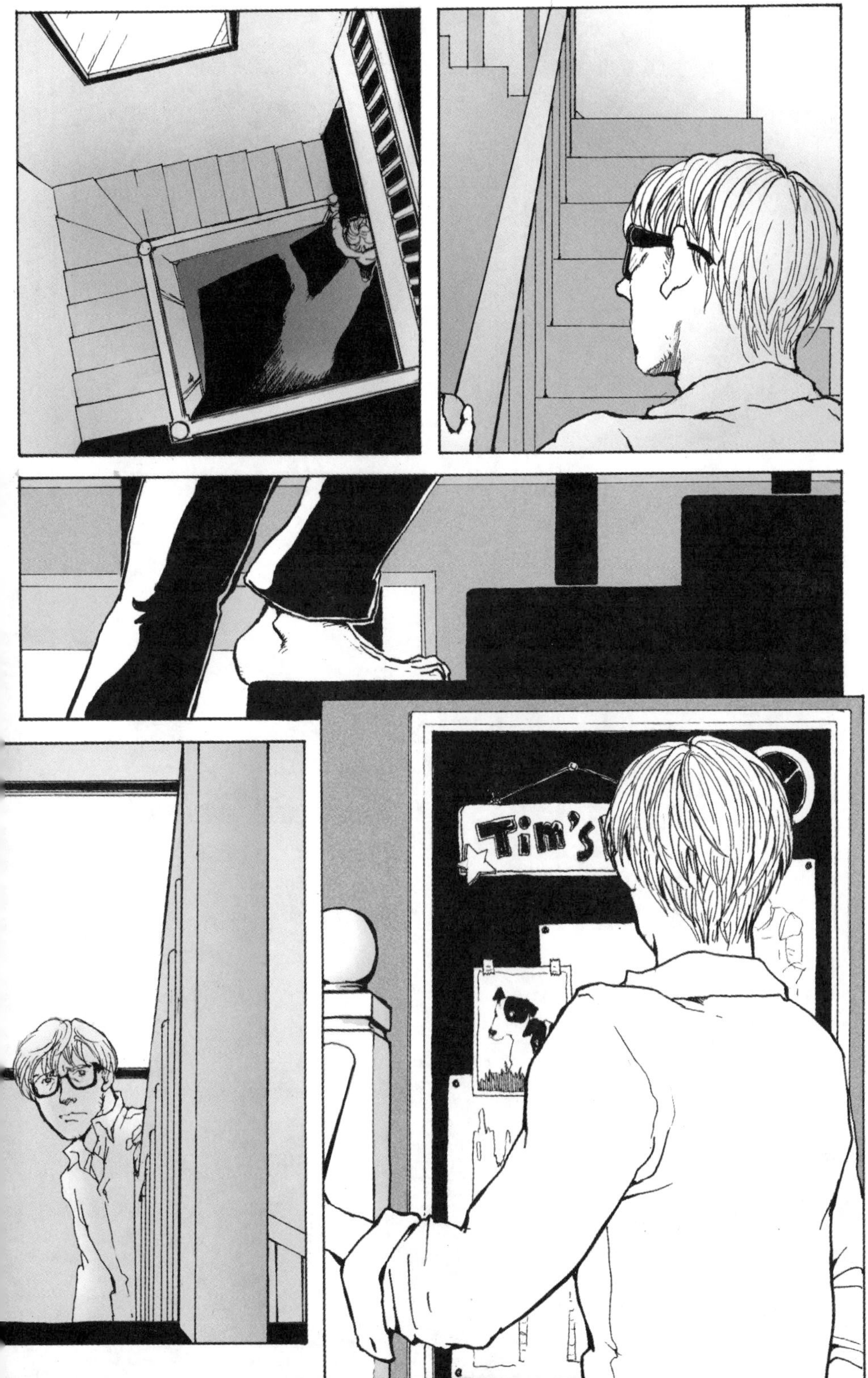
Tim's

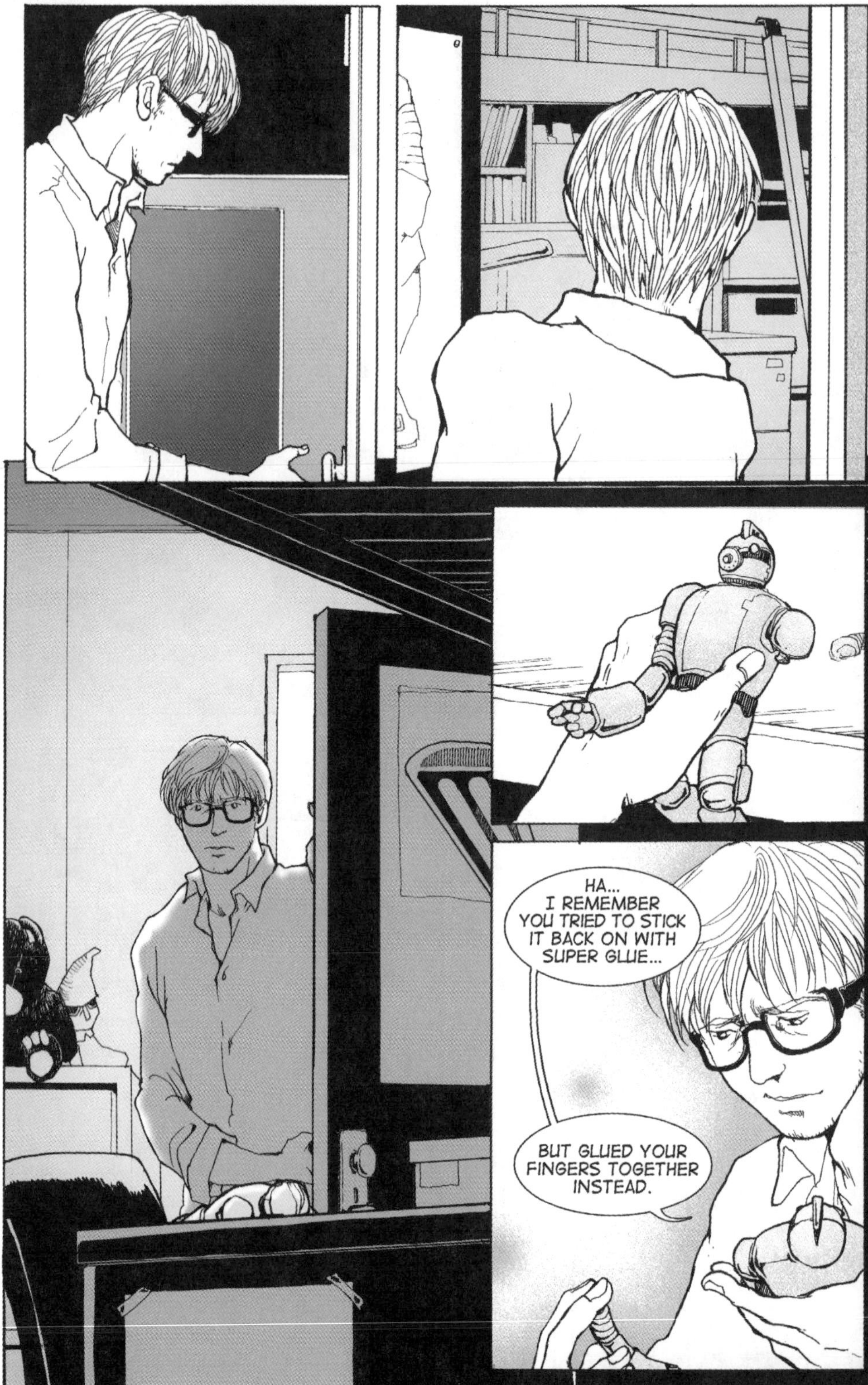
HA...
I REMEMBER
YOU TRIED TO STICK
IT BACK ON WITH
SUPER GLUE...
BUT GLUED YOUR
FINGERS TOGETHER
INSTEAD.

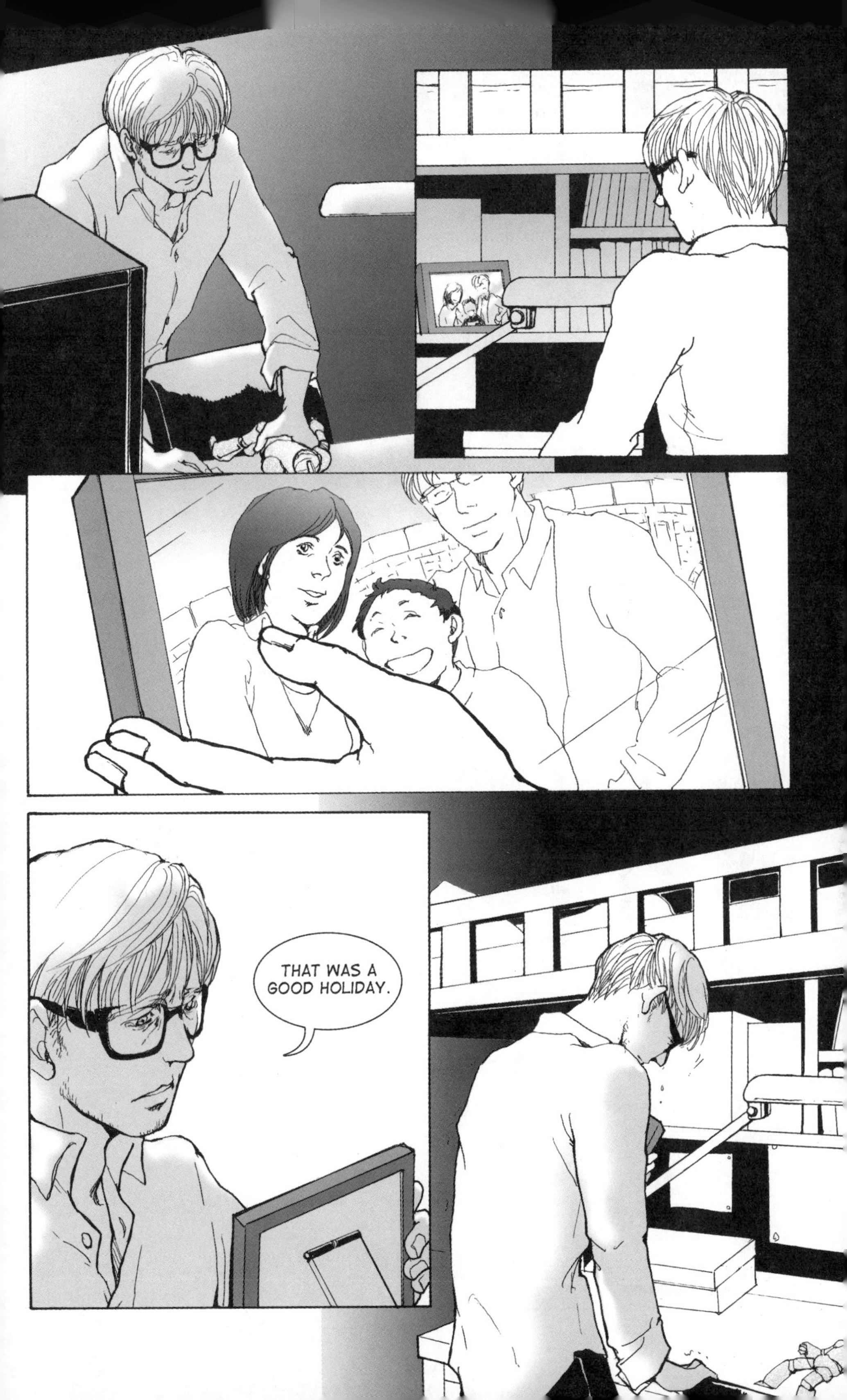
THAT WAS A GOOD HOLIDAY.

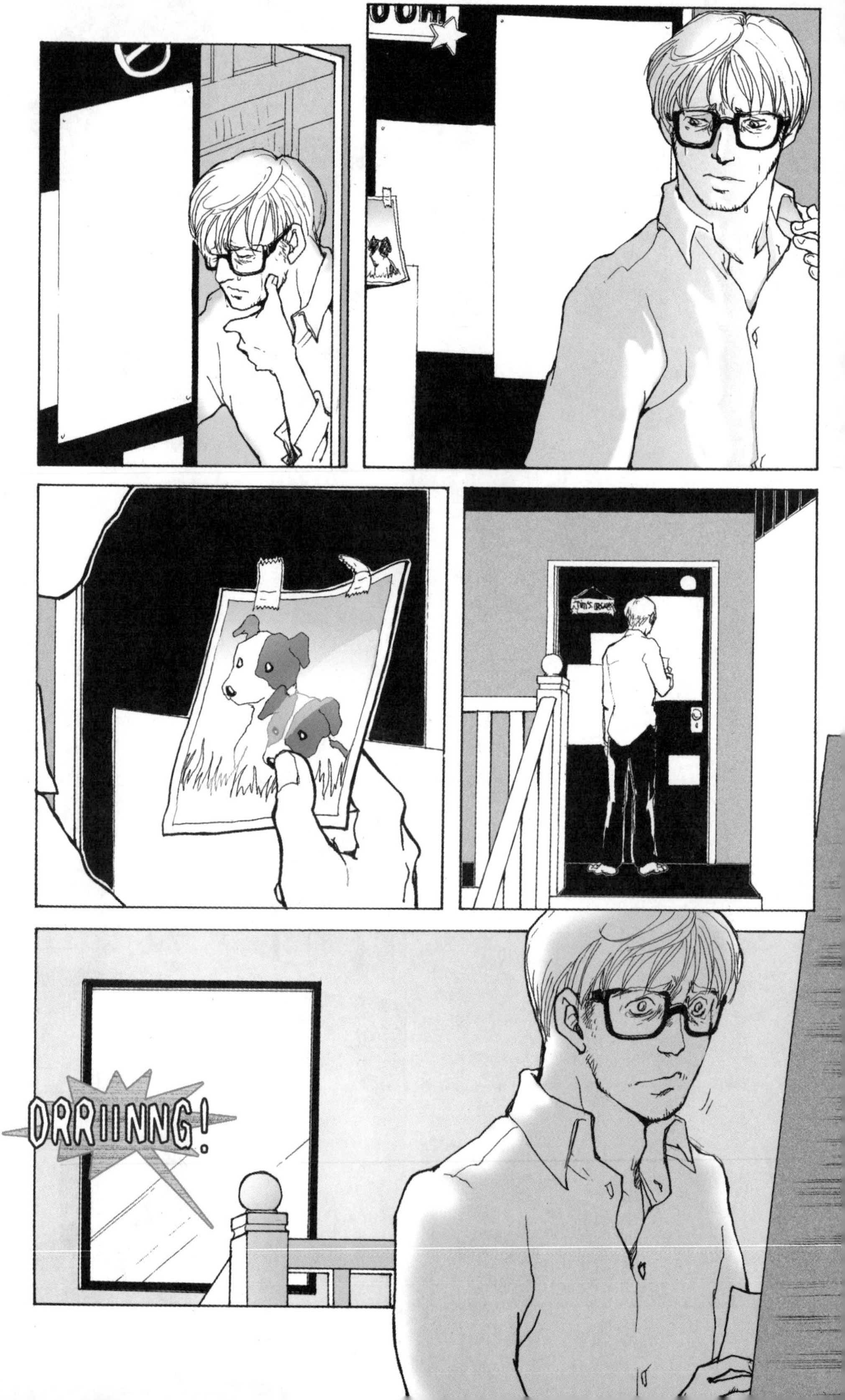
DRRIINNG!

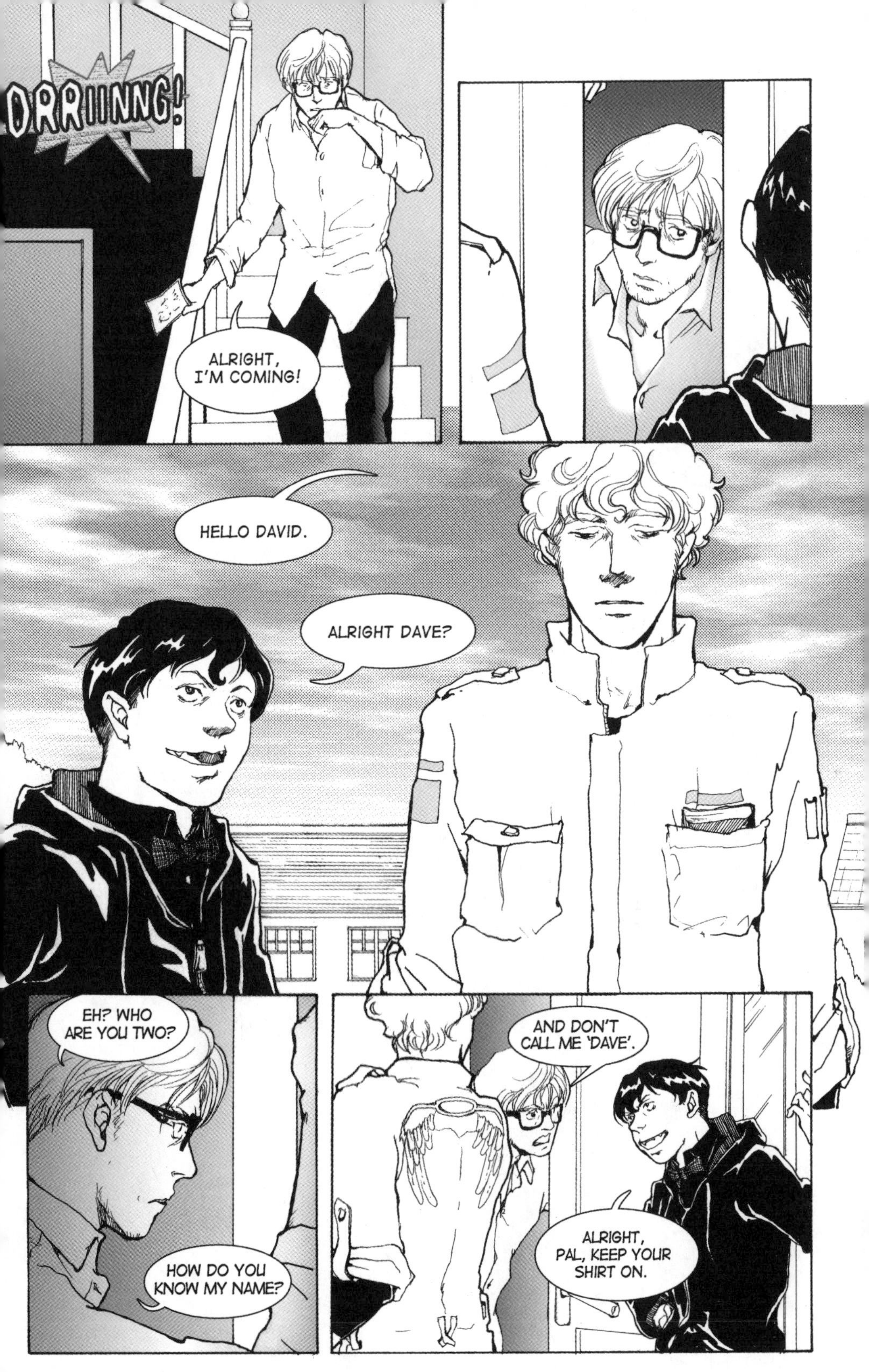
ORRIINNG!
ALRIGHT, I'M COMING!
HELLO DAVID.
ALRIGHT DAVE?
EH? WHO ARE YOU TWO?
HOW DO YOU KNOW MY NAME?
AND DON'T CALL ME 'DAVE'.
ALRIGHT, PAL, KEEP YOUR SHIRT ON.

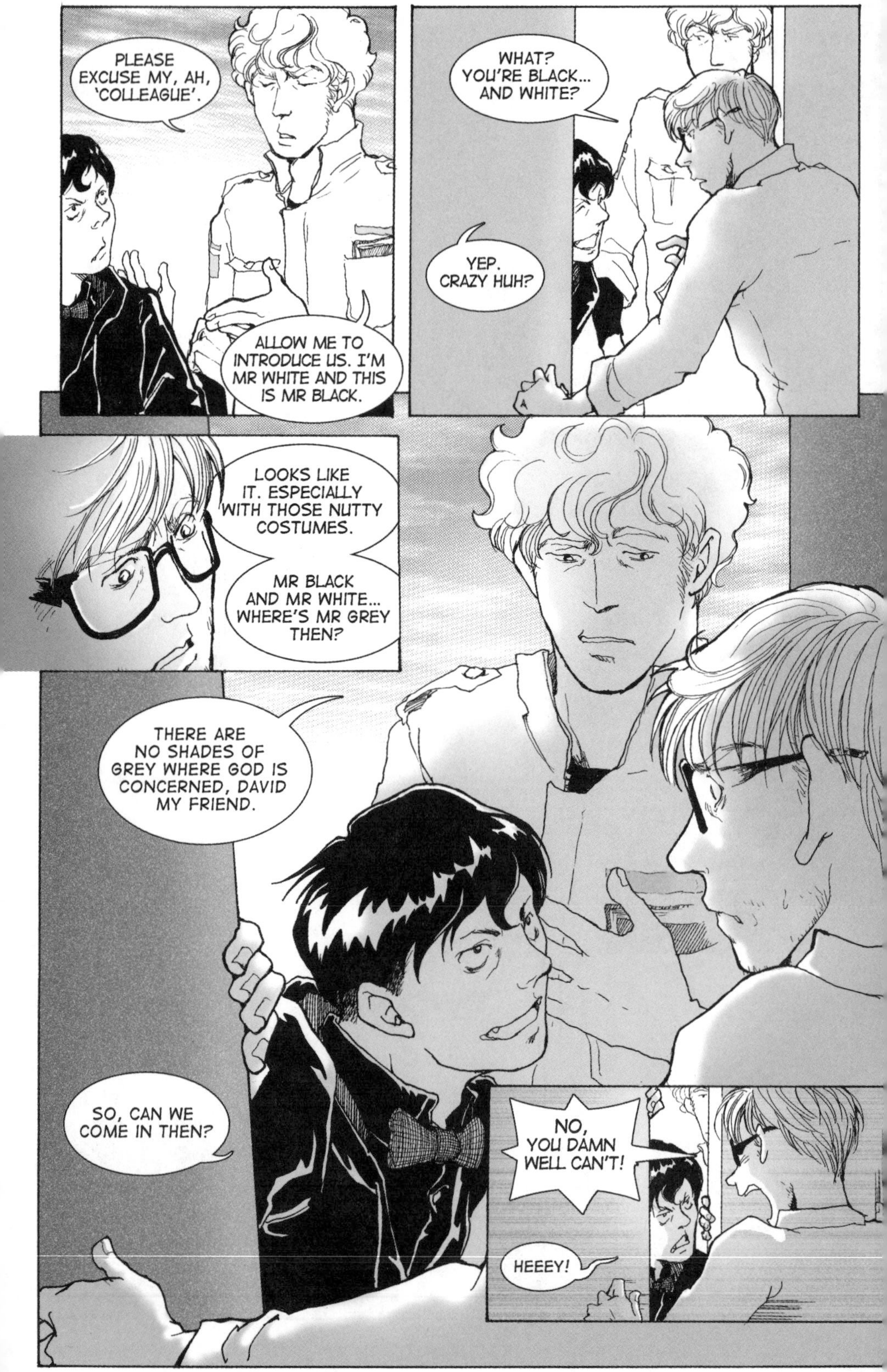
PLEASE EXCUSE MY, AH, 'COLLEAGUE'.
ALLOW ME TO INTRODUCE US. I'M MR WHITE AND THIS IS MR BLACK.
WHAT? YOU'RE BLACK... AND WHITE?
YEP. CRAZY HUH?
LOOKS LIKE IT. ESPECIALLY WITH THOSE NUTTY COSTUMES.
MR BLACK AND MR WHITE... WHERE'S MR GREY THEN?
THERE ARE NO SHADES OF GREY WHERE GOD IS CONCERNED, DAVID MY FRIEND.
SO, CAN WE COME IN THEN?
NO, YOU DAMN WELL CAN'T!
HEEEY!

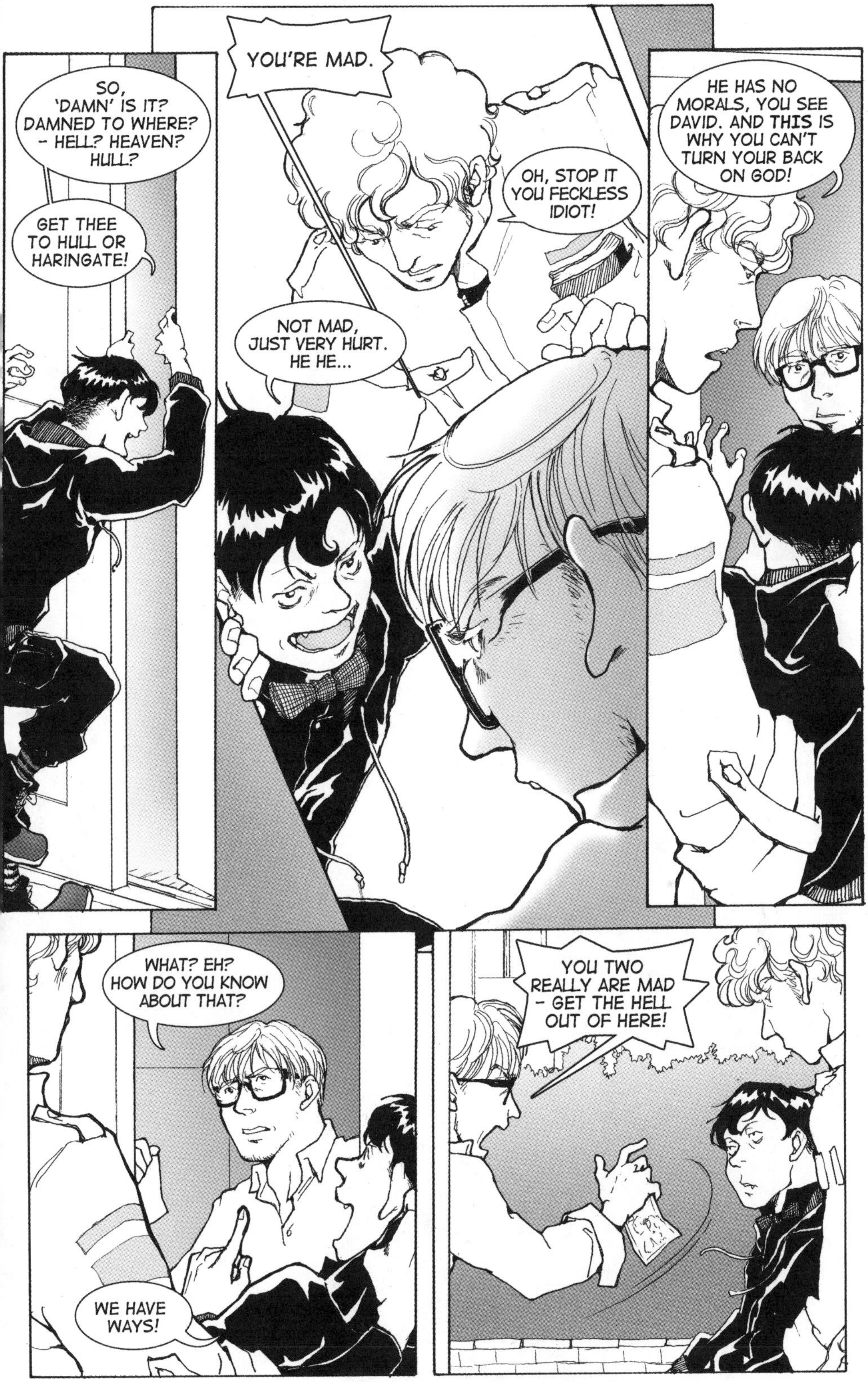
SO, 'DAMN' IS IT? DAMNED TO WHERE? - HELL? HEAVEN? HULL?
GET THEE TO HULL OR HARINGATE!
YOU'RE MAD.
OH, STOP IT YOU FECKLESS IDIOT!
NOT MAD, JUST VERY HURT. HE HE...
HE HAS NO MORALS, YOU SEE DAVID. AND THIS IS WHY YOU CAN'T TURN YOUR BACK ON GOD!
WHAT? EH? HOW DO YOU KNOW ABOUT THAT?
WE HAVE WAYS!
YOU TWO REALLY ARE MAD - GET THE HELL OUT OF HERE!

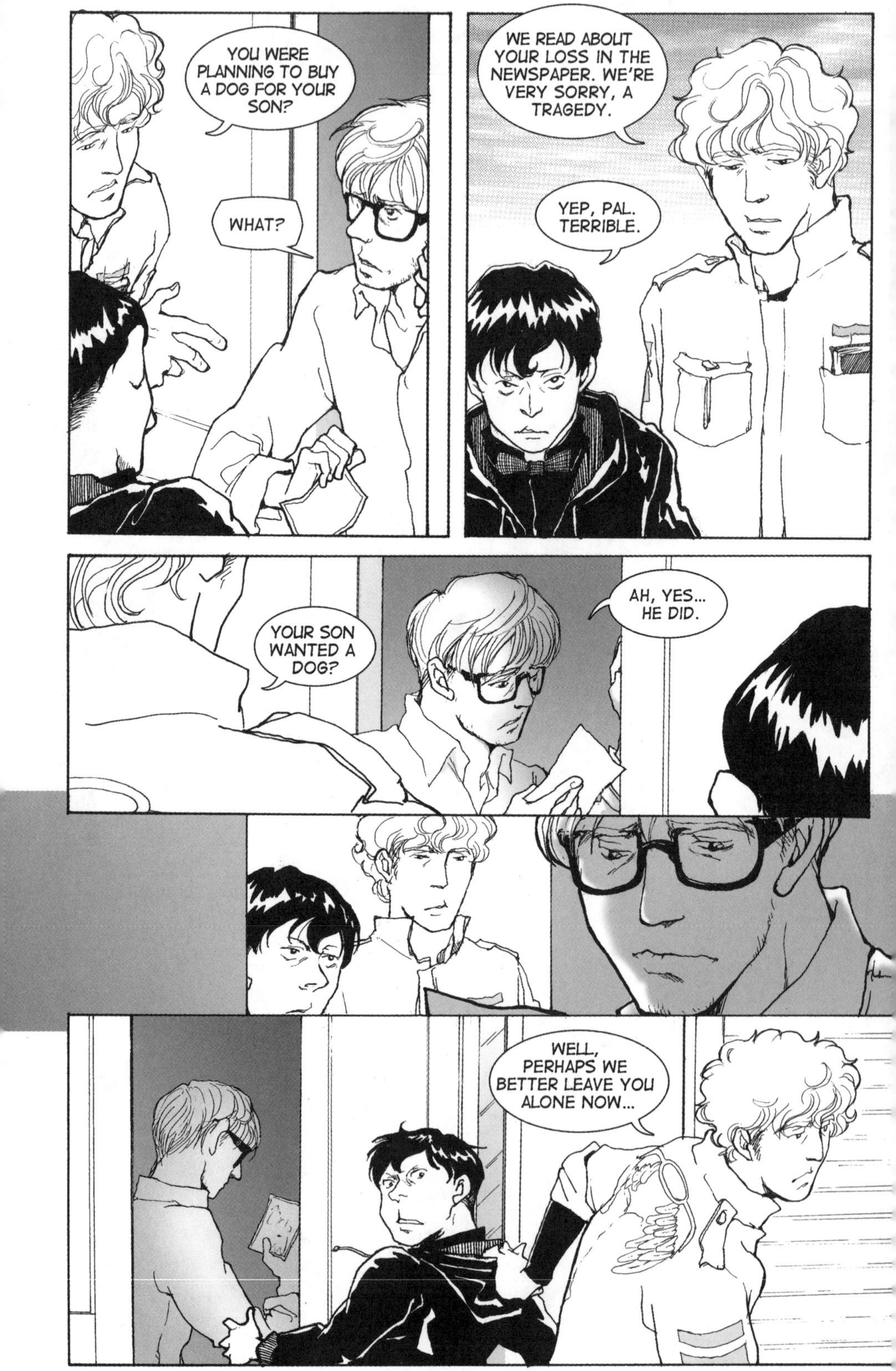
YOU WERE PLANNING TO BUY A DOG FOR YOUR SON?
WHAT?
WE READ ABOUT YOUR LOSS IN THE NEWSPAPER. WE'RE VERY SORRY, A TRAGEDY.
YEP, PAL. TERRIBLE.
YOUR SON WANTED A DOG?
AH, YES... HE DID.
WELL, PERHAPS WE BETTER LEAVE YOU ALONE NOW...

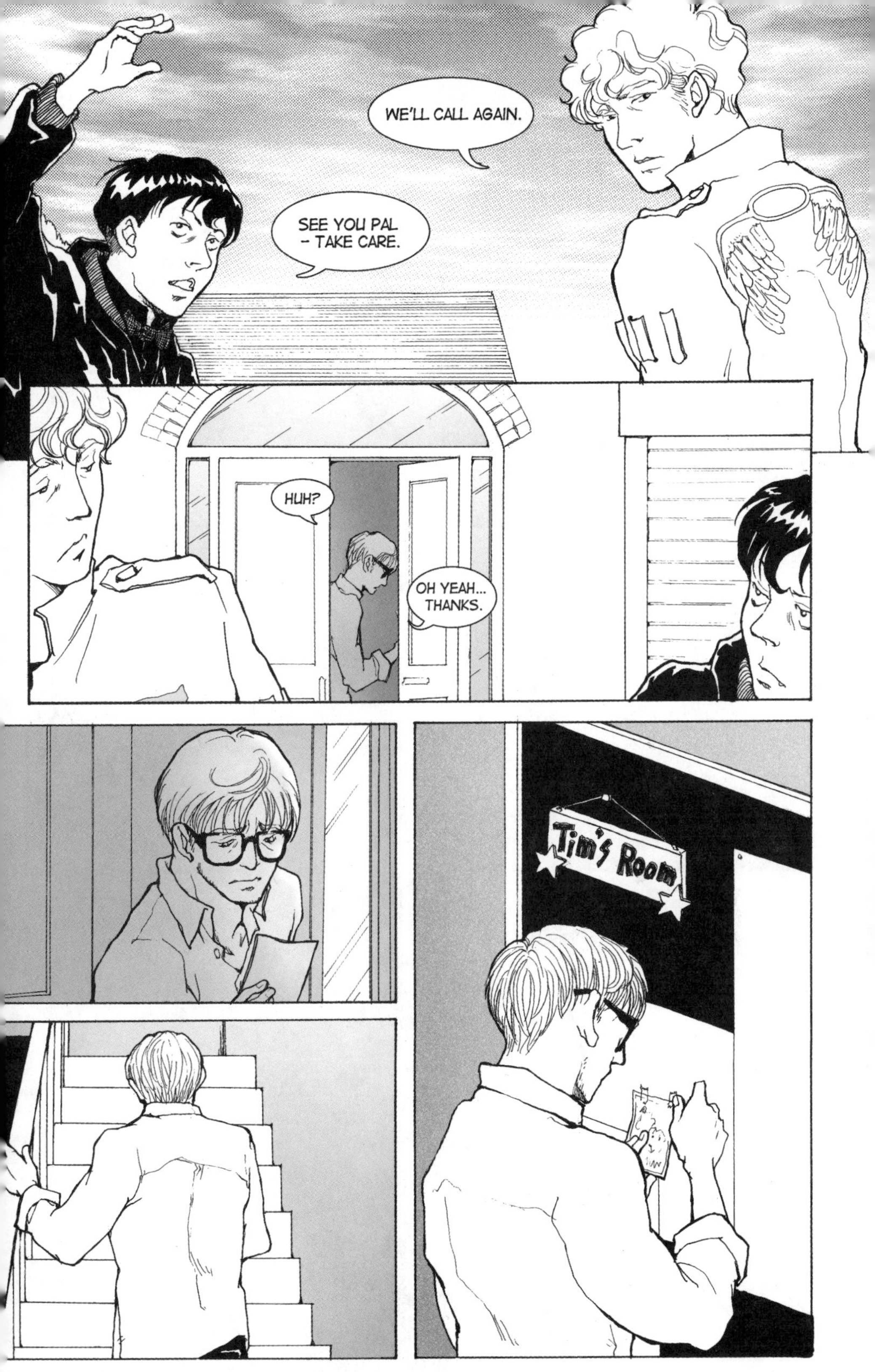
SEE YOU PAL - TAKE CARE.
WE'LL CALL AGAIN.
HUH?
OH YEAH... THANKS.
Tim's Room

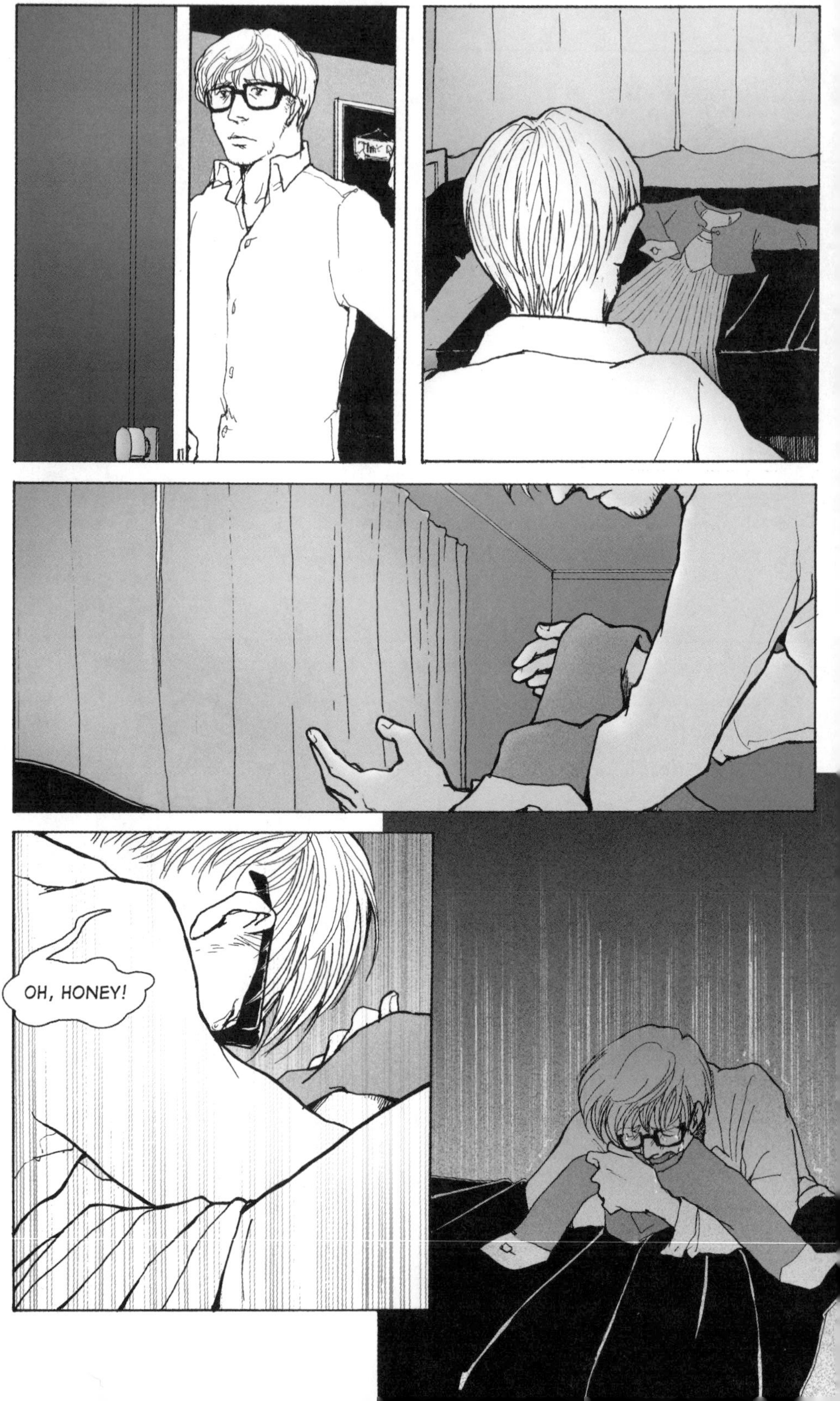
OH, HONEY!

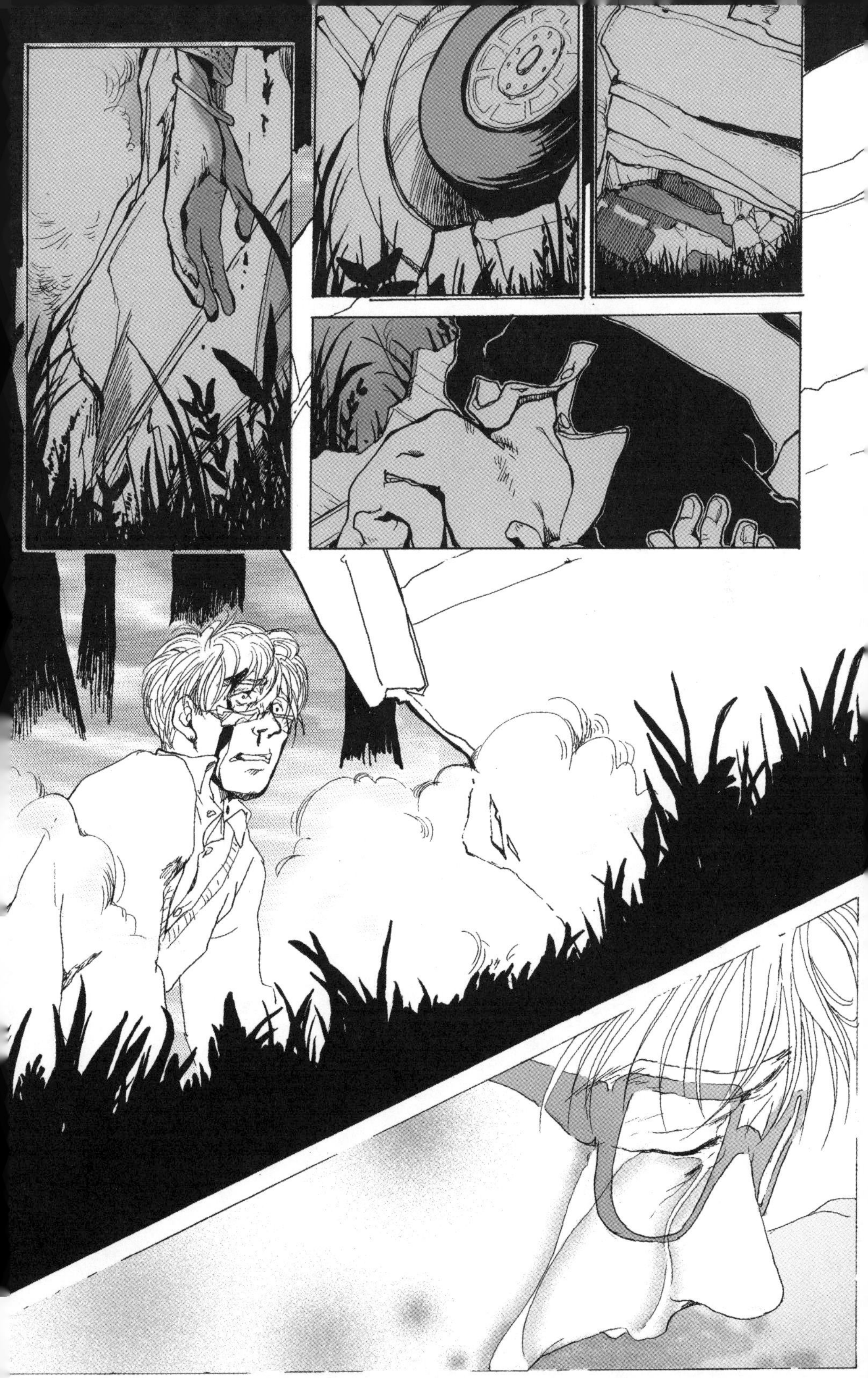

Chapter 2

'Thou shalt not covet your
neighbor's house; thou shalt not
covet your neighbor's
wife, nor his male servant,
nor his female servant,
nor his ox, nor his donkey,
nor anything that is
your neighbor's.'

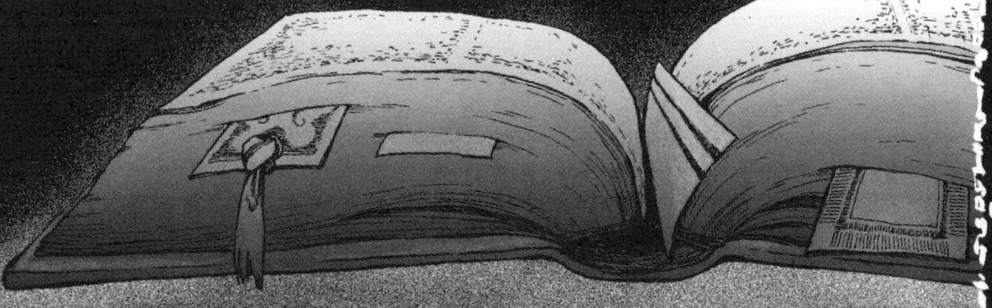

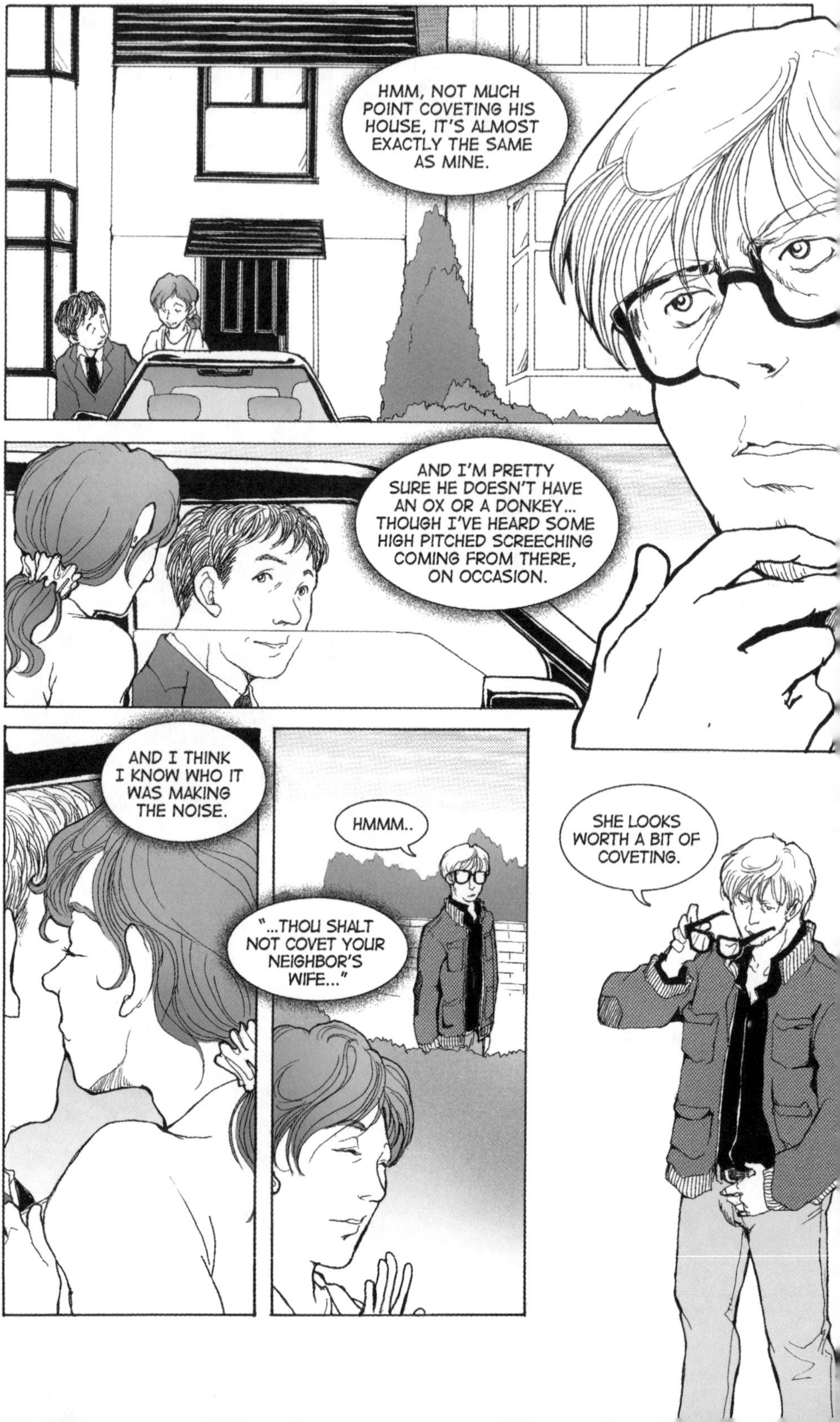
HMM, NOT MUCH POINT COVETING HIS HOUSE, IT'S ALMOST EXACTLY THE SAME AS MINE.
AND I'M PRETTY SURE HE DOESN'T HAVE AN OX OR A DONKEY... THOUGH I'VE HEARD SOME HIGH PITCHED SCREECHING COMING FROM THERE, ON OCCASION.
AND I THINK I KNOW WHO IT WAS MAKING THE NOISE.
HMMM..
"...THOU SHALT NOT COVET YOUR NEIGHBOR'S WIFE..."
SHE LOOKS WORTH A BIT OF COVETING.

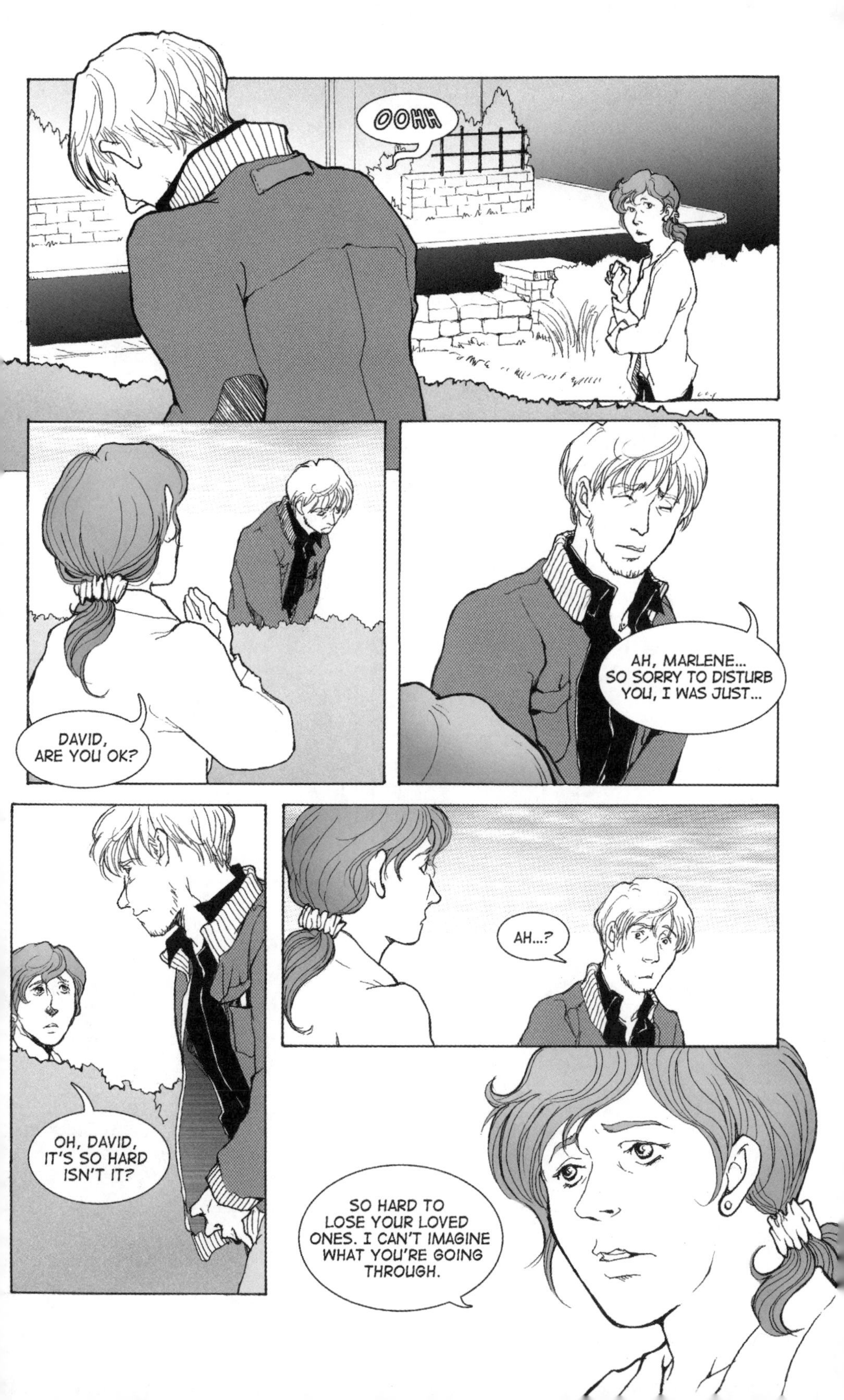
OOHH
DAVID, ARE YOU OK?
AH, MARLENE... SO SORRY TO DISTURB YOU, I WAS JUST...
OH, DAVID, IT'S SO HARD ISN'T IT?
AH...?
SO HARD TO LOSE YOUR LOVED ONES. I CAN'T IMAGINE WHAT YOU'RE GOING THROUGH.

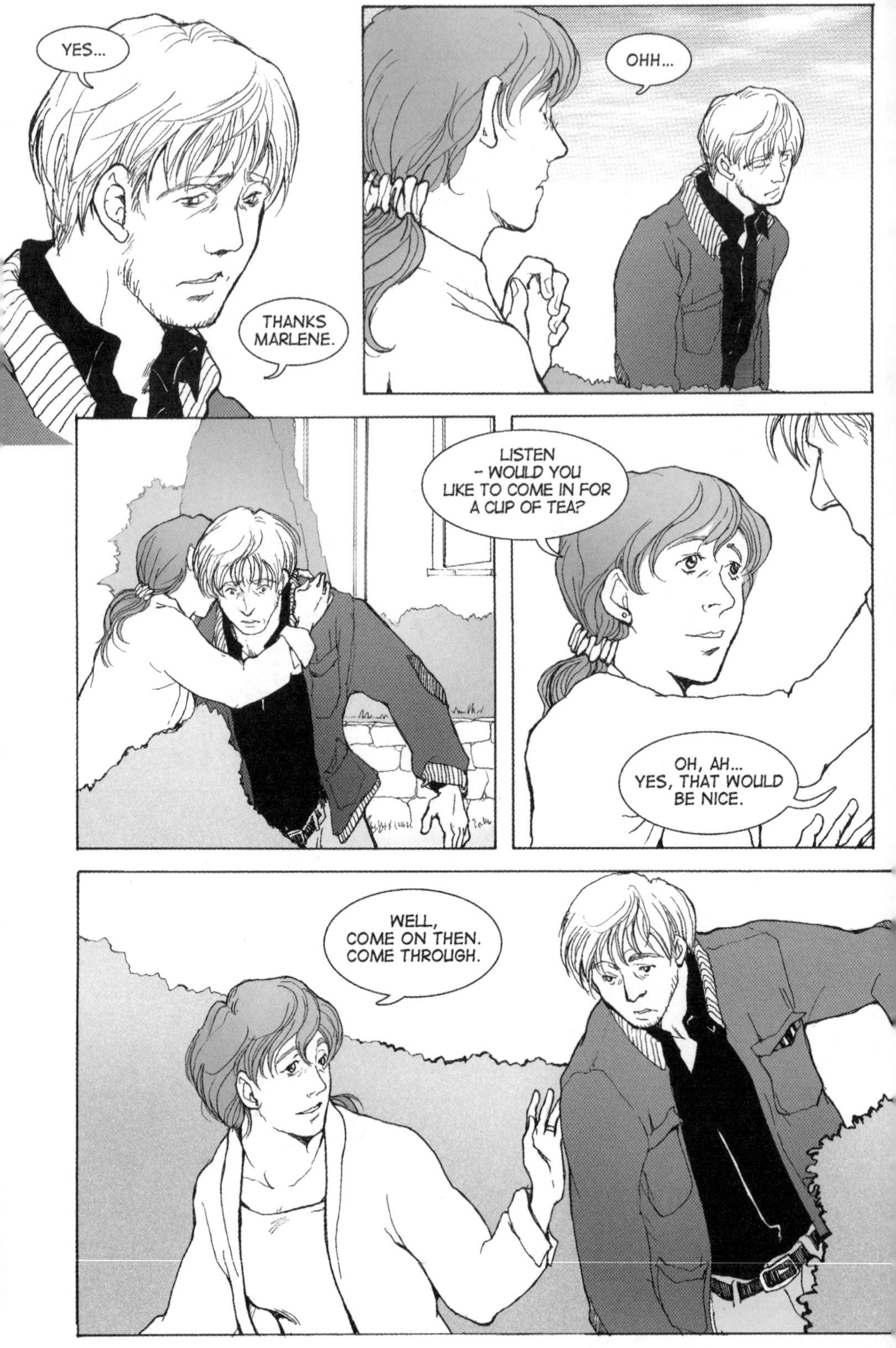
YES...
THANKS MARLENE.
OHH...
LISTEN - WOULD YOU LIKE TO COME IN FOR A CUP OF TEA?
OH, AH... YES, THAT WOULD BE NICE.
WELL, COME ON THEN. COME THROUGH.

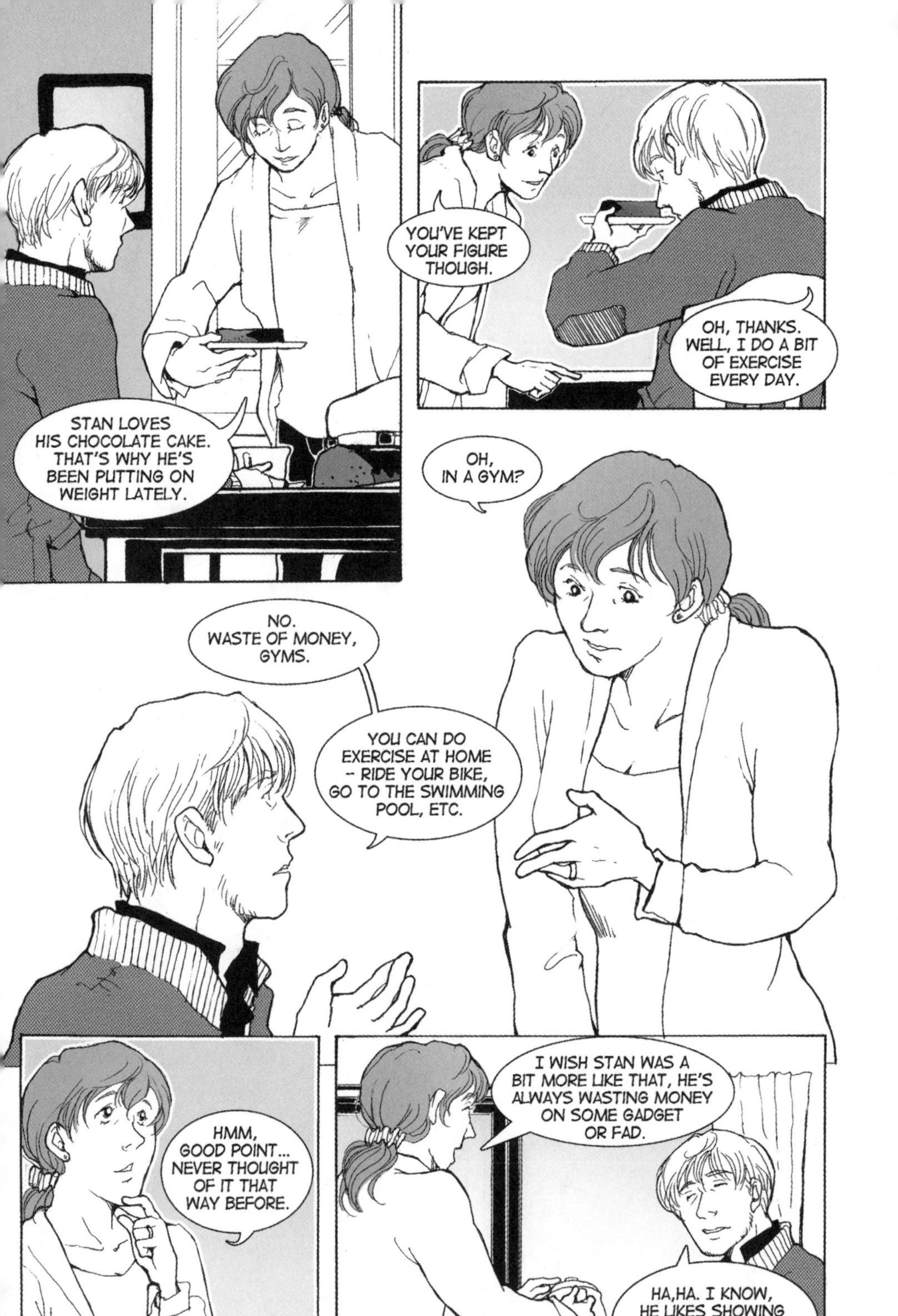
STAN LOVES HIS CHOCOLATE CAKE. THAT'S WHY HE'S BEEN PUTTING ON WEIGHT LATELY.
YOU'VE KEPT YOUR FIGURE THOUGH.
OH, THANKS. WELL, I DO A BIT OF EXERCISE EVERY DAY.
OH, IN A GYM?
NO. WASTE OF MONEY, GYMS.
YOU CAN DO EXERCISE AT HOME - RIDE YOUR BIKE, GO TO THE SWIMMING POOL, ETC.
HMM, GOOD POINT... NEVER THOUGHT OF IT THAT WAY BEFORE.
I WISH STAN WAS A BIT MORE LIKE THAT, HE'S ALWAYS WASTING MONEY ON SOME GADGET OR FAD.
HA,HA. I KNOW, HE LIKES SHOWING OFF TO ME ABOUT ALL HIS NEW STUFF.

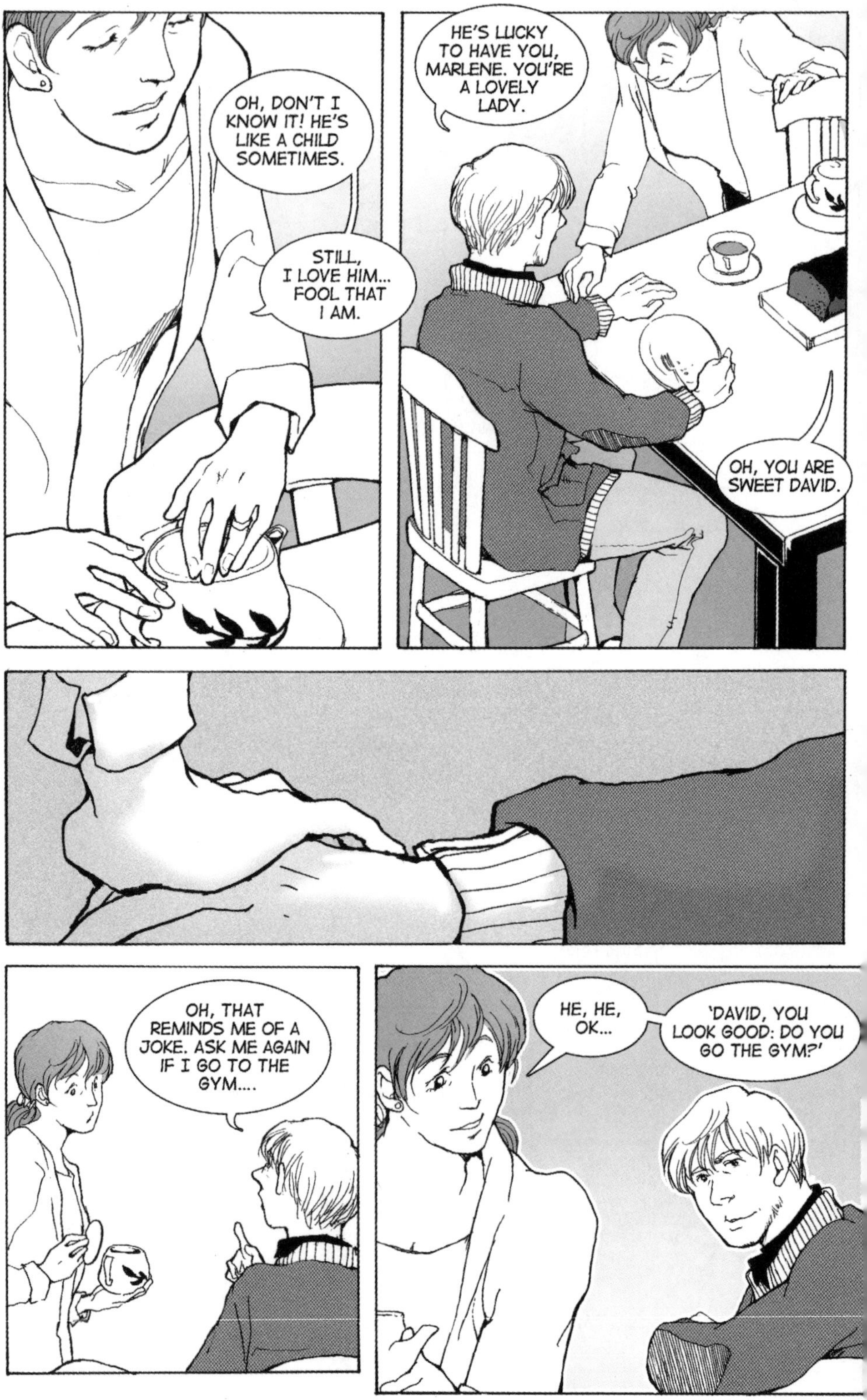
OH, DON'T I KNOW IT! HE'S LIKE A CHILD SOMETIMES.
STILL, I LOVE HIM... FOOL THAT I AM.
HE'S LUCKY TO HAVE YOU, MARLENE. YOU'RE A LOVELY LADY.
OH, YOU ARE SWEET DAVID.
OH, THAT REMINDS ME OF A JOKE. ASK ME AGAIN IF I GO TO THE GYM....
HE, HE, OK...
'DAVID, YOU LOOK GOOD: DO YOU GO THE GYM?'

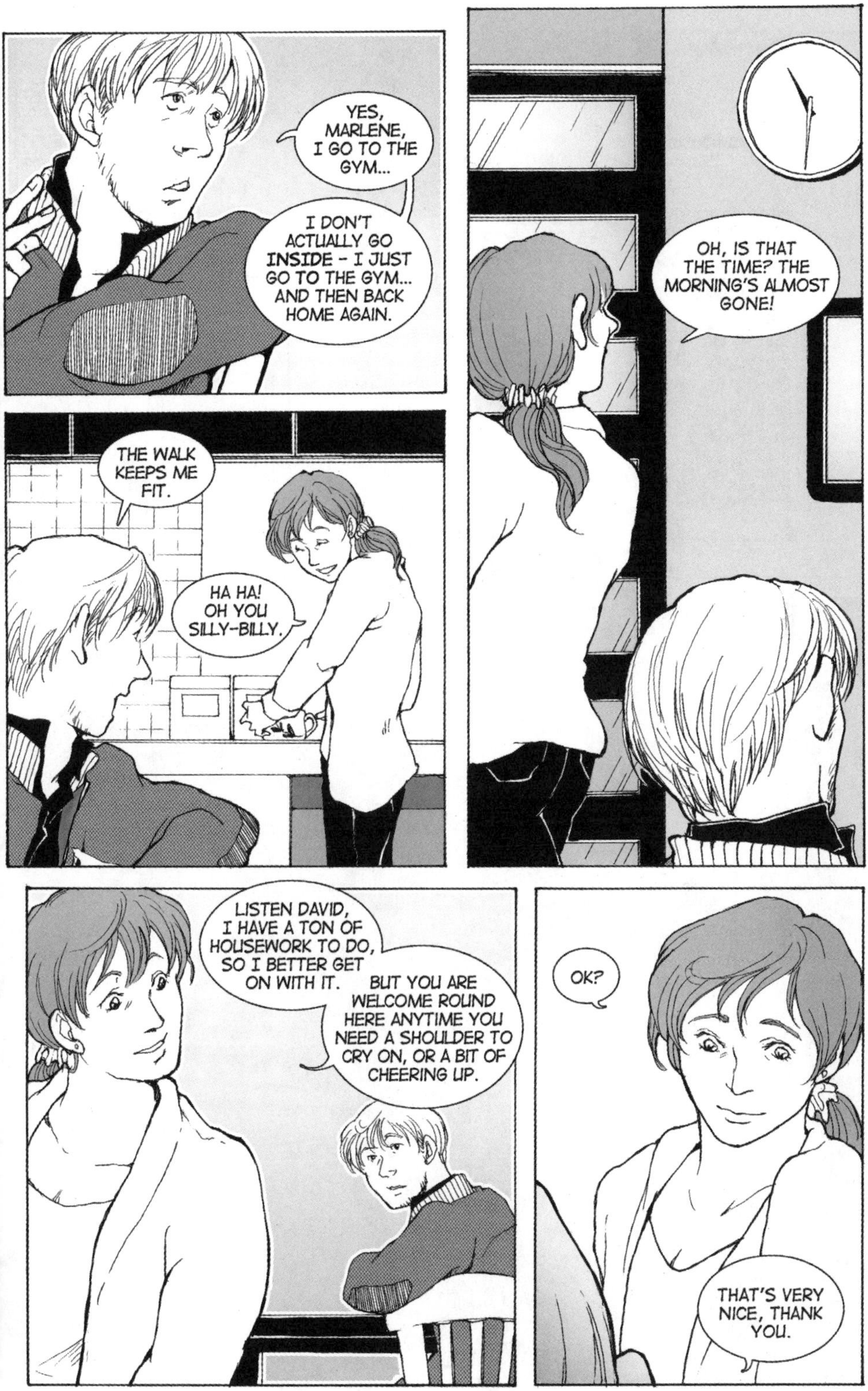
YES, MARLENE, I GO TO THE GYM...
I DON'T ACTUALLY GO **INSIDE** - I JUST GO TO THE GYM... AND THEN BACK HOME AGAIN.
OH, IS THAT THE TIME? THE MORNING'S ALMOST GONE!
THE WALK KEEPS ME FIT.
HA HA! OH YOU SILLY-BILLY.
LISTEN DAVID, I HAVE A TON OF HOUSEWORK TO DO, SO I BETTER GET ON WITH IT.
BUT YOU ARE WELCOME ROUND HERE ANYTIME YOU NEED A SHOULDER TO CRY ON, OR A BIT OF CHEERING UP.
OK?
THAT'S VERY NICE, THANK YOU.

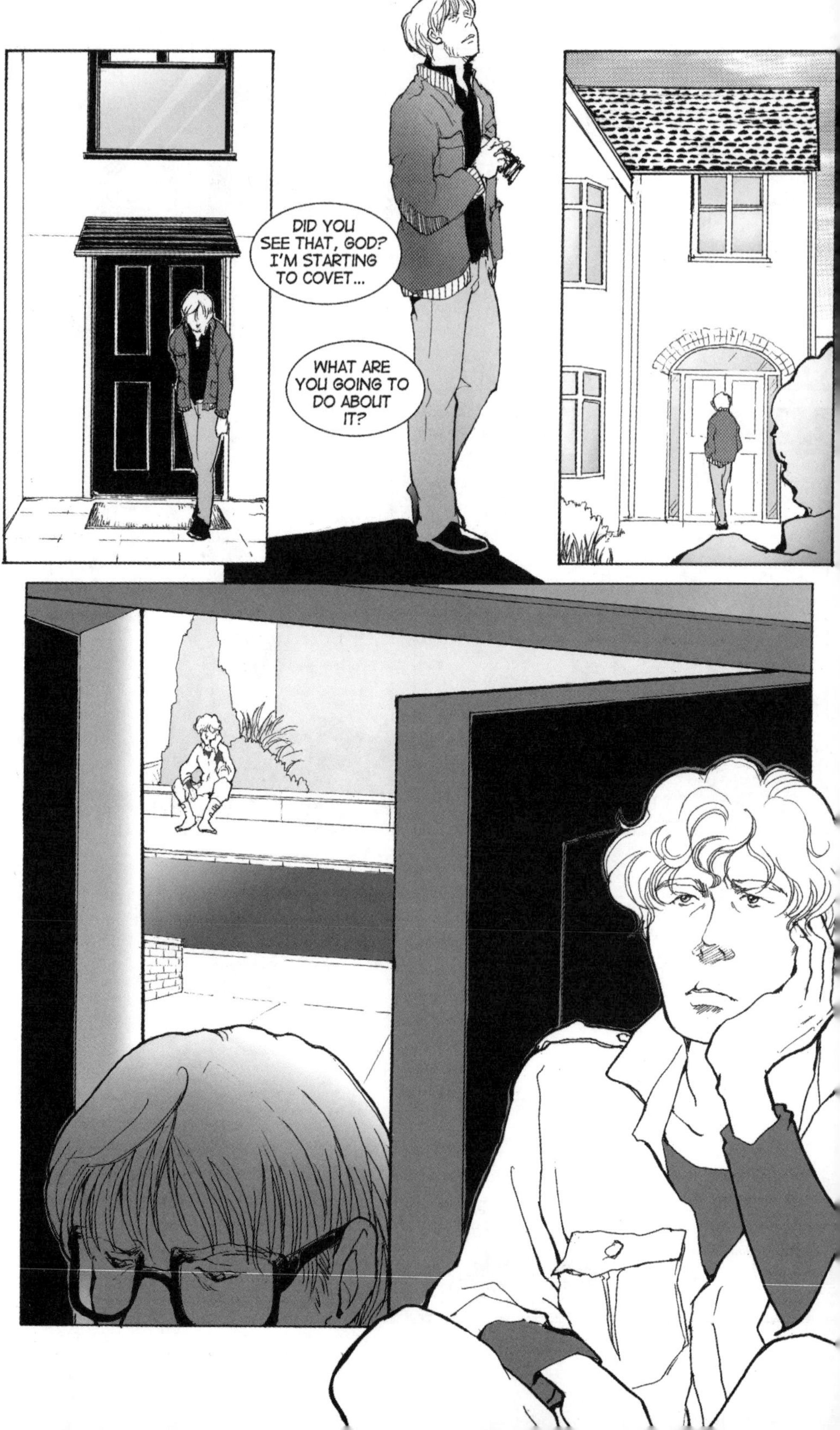
DID YOU SEE THAT, GOD? I'M STARTING TO COVET...
WHAT ARE YOU GOING TO DO ABOUT IT?

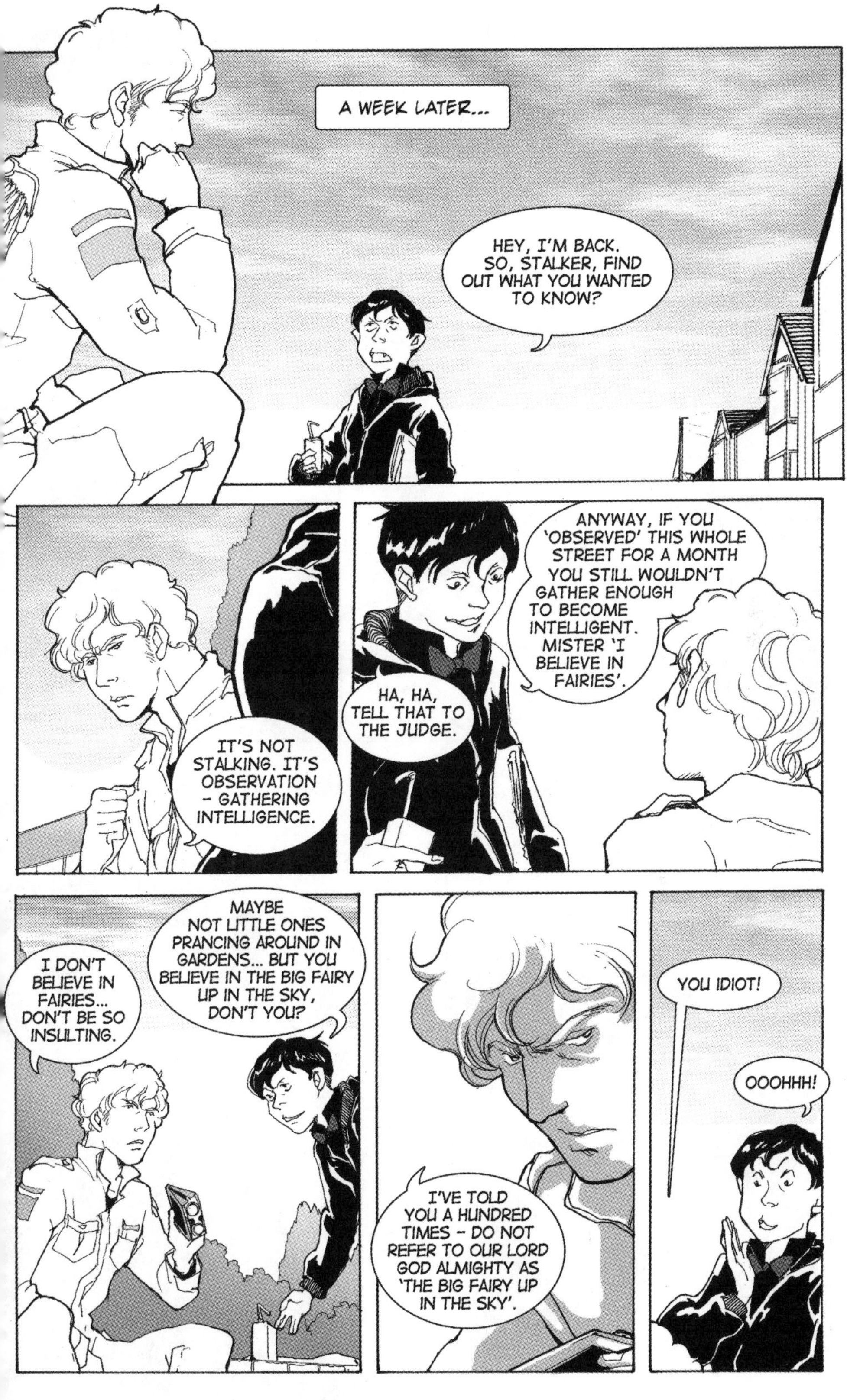
A WEEK LATER...
HEY, I'M BACK. SO, STALKER, FIND OUT WHAT YOU WANTED TO KNOW?
IT'S NOT STALKING. IT'S OBSERVATION – GATHERING INTELLIGENCE.
HA, HA, TELL THAT TO THE JUDGE.
ANYWAY, IF YOU 'OBSERVED' THIS WHOLE STREET FOR A MONTH YOU STILL WOULDN'T GATHER ENOUGH TO BECOME INTELLIGENT. MISTER 'I BELIEVE IN FAIRIES'.
I DON'T BELIEVE IN FAIRIES... DON'T BE SO INSULTING.
MAYBE NOT LITTLE ONES PRANCING AROUND IN GARDENS... BUT YOU BELIEVE IN THE BIG FAIRY UP IN THE SKY, DON'T YOU?
I'VE TOLD YOU A HUNDRED TIMES – DO NOT REFER TO OUR LORD GOD ALMIGHTY AS 'THE BIG FAIRY UP IN THE SKY'.
YOU IDIOT!
OOOHHH!

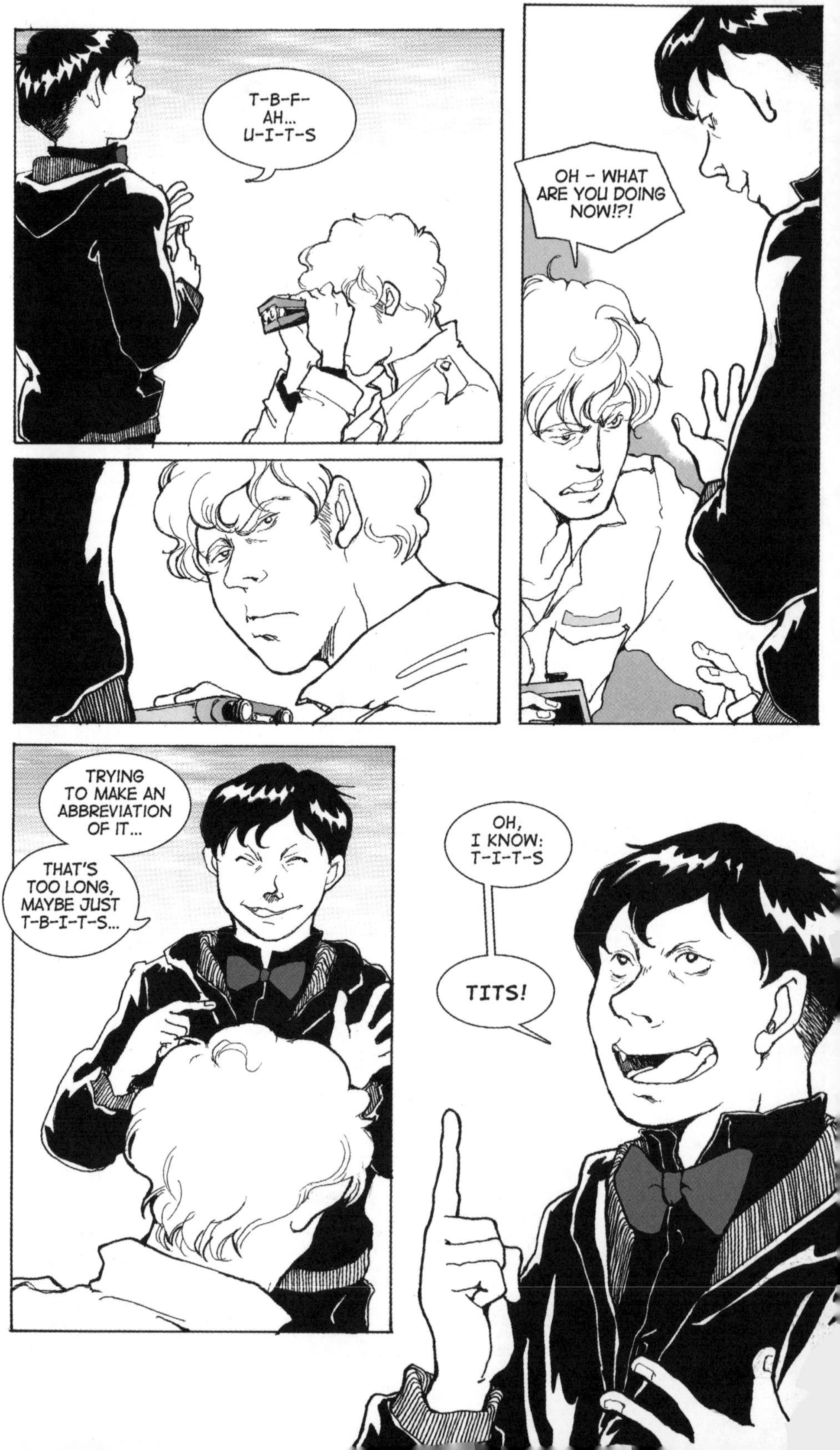
T-B-F- AH... U-I-T-S
OH - WHAT ARE YOU DOING NOW!?!
TRYING TO MAKE AN ABBREVIATION OF IT...
THAT'S TOO LONG, MAYBE JUST T-B-I-T-S...
OH, I KNOW: T-I-T-S
TITS!

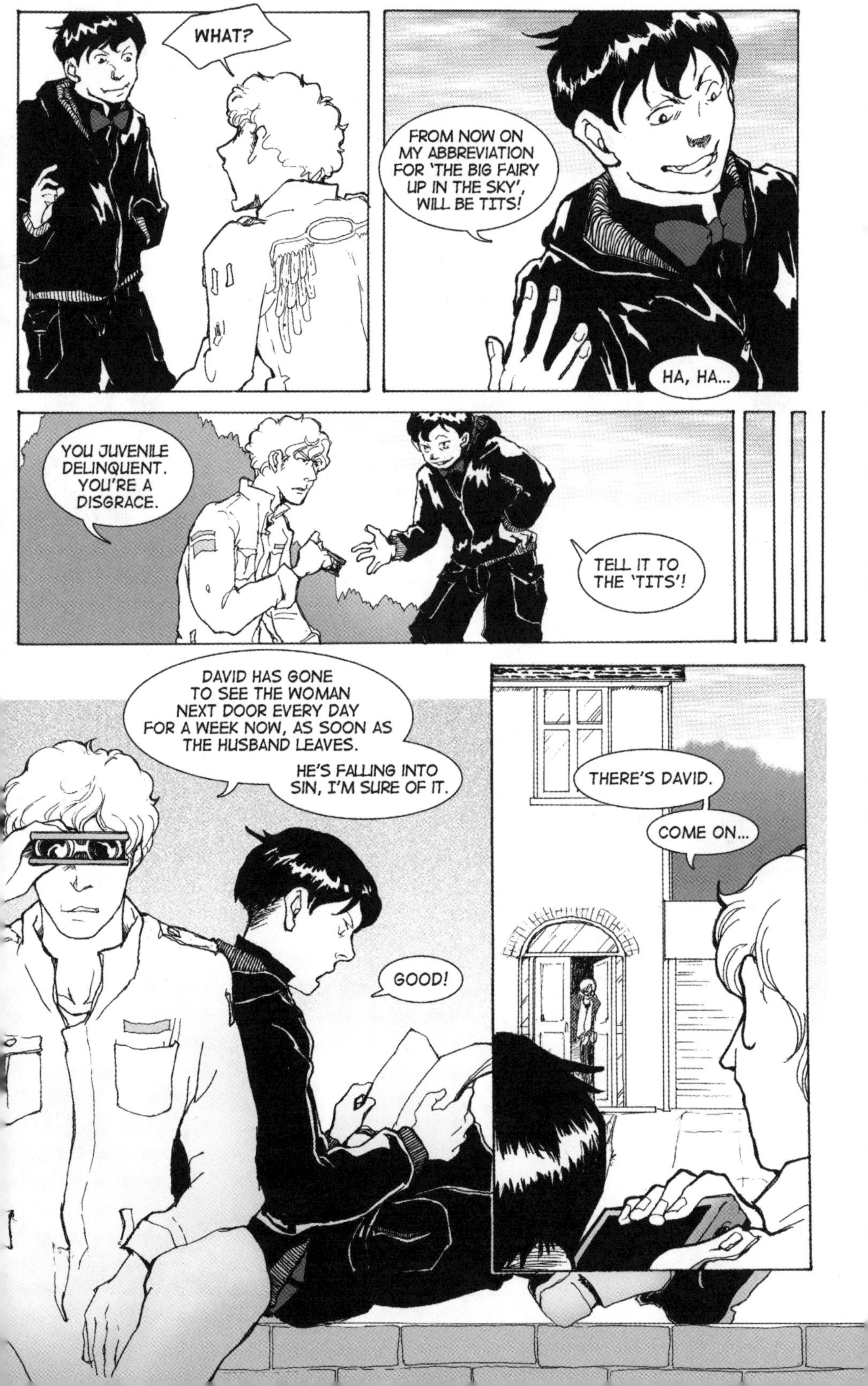
WHAT?
FROM NOW ON MY ABBREVIATION FOR 'THE BIG FAIRY UP IN THE SKY', WILL BE TITS!
HA, HA...
YOU JUVENILE DELINQUENT. YOU'RE A DISGRACE.
TELL IT TO THE 'TITS'!
DAVID HAS GONE TO SEE THE WOMAN NEXT DOOR EVERY DAY FOR A WEEK NOW, AS SOON AS THE HUSBAND LEAVES.
HE'S FALLING INTO SIN, I'M SURE OF IT.
GOOD!
THERE'S DAVID.
COME ON...

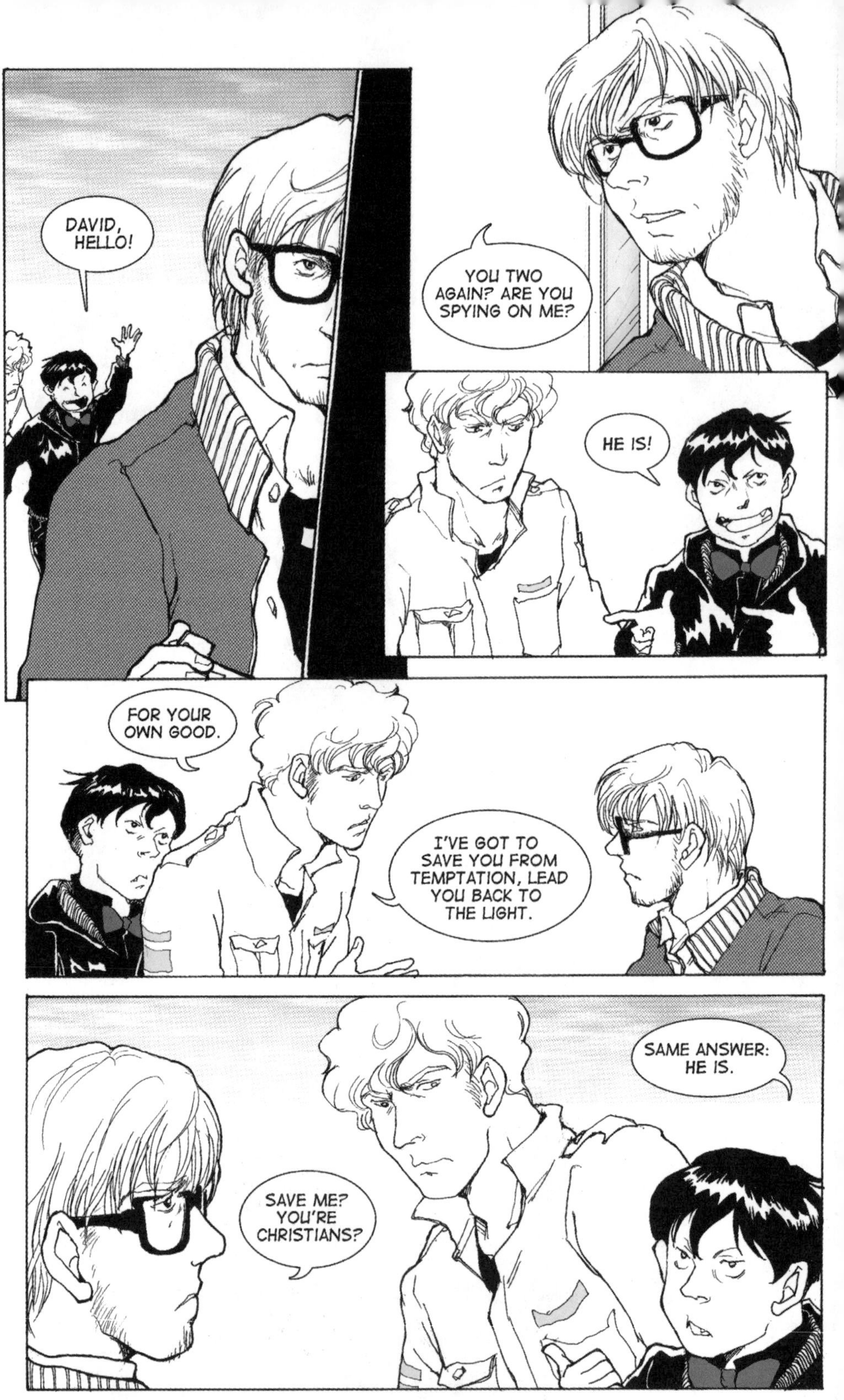
DAVID, HELLO!
YOU TWO AGAIN? ARE YOU SPYING ON ME?
HE IS!
FOR YOUR OWN GOOD.
I'VE GOT TO SAVE YOU FROM TEMPTATION, LEAD YOU BACK TO THE LIGHT.
SAME ANSWER: HE IS.
SAVE ME? YOU'RE CHRISTIANS?

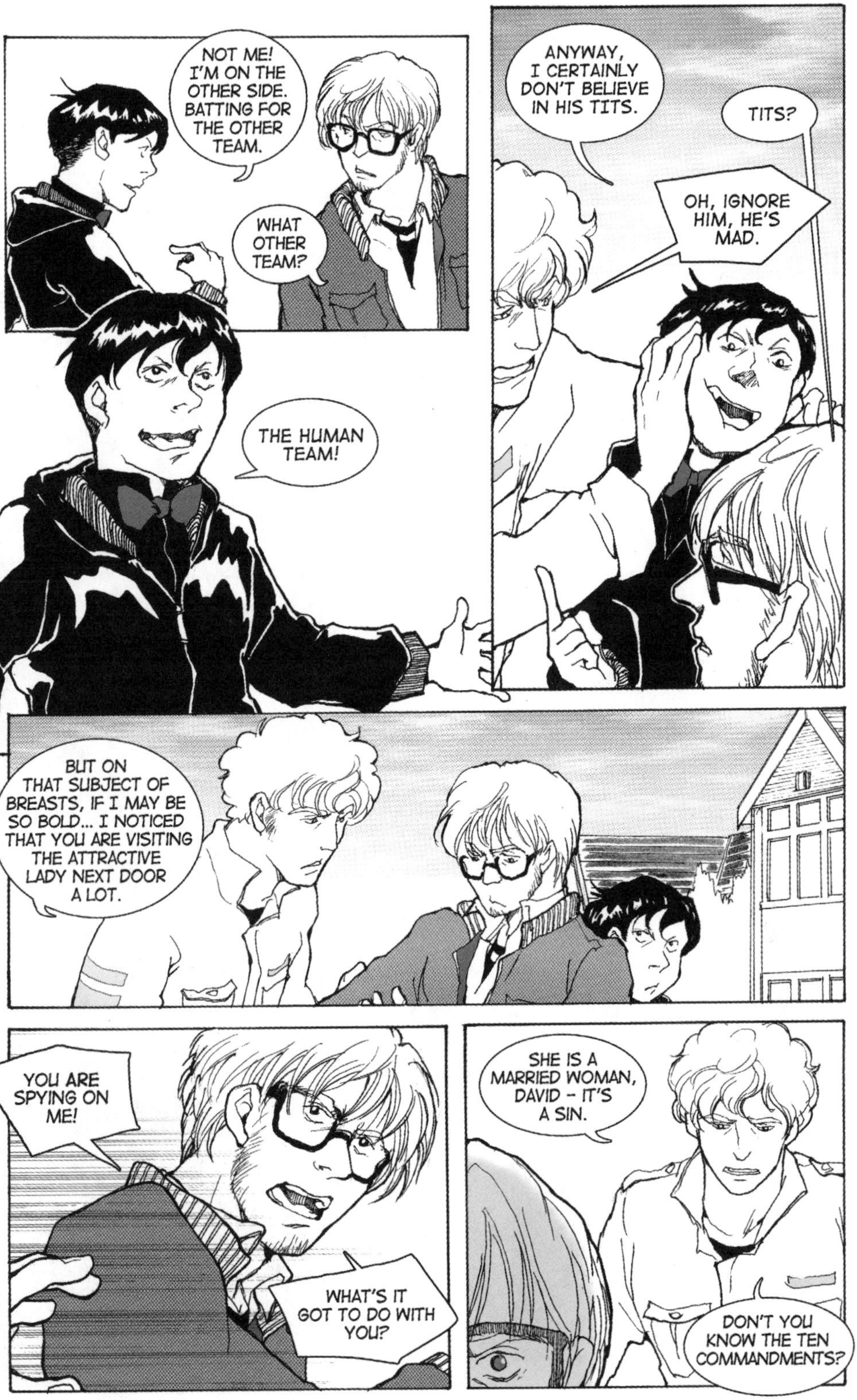
NOT ME! I'M ON THE OTHER SIDE. BATTING FOR THE OTHER TEAM.
WHAT OTHER TEAM?
THE HUMAN TEAM!
ANYWAY, I CERTAINLY DON'T BELIEVE IN HIS TITS.
TITS?
OH, IGNORE HIM, HE'S MAD.
BUT ON THAT SUBJECT OF BREASTS, IF I MAY BE SO BOLD... I NOTICED THAT YOU ARE VISITING THE ATTRACTIVE LADY NEXT DOOR A LOT.
YOU ARE SPYING ON ME!
WHAT'S IT GOT TO DO WITH YOU?
SHE IS A MARRIED WOMAN, DAVID - IT'S A SIN.
DON'T YOU KNOW THE TEN COMMANDMENTS?

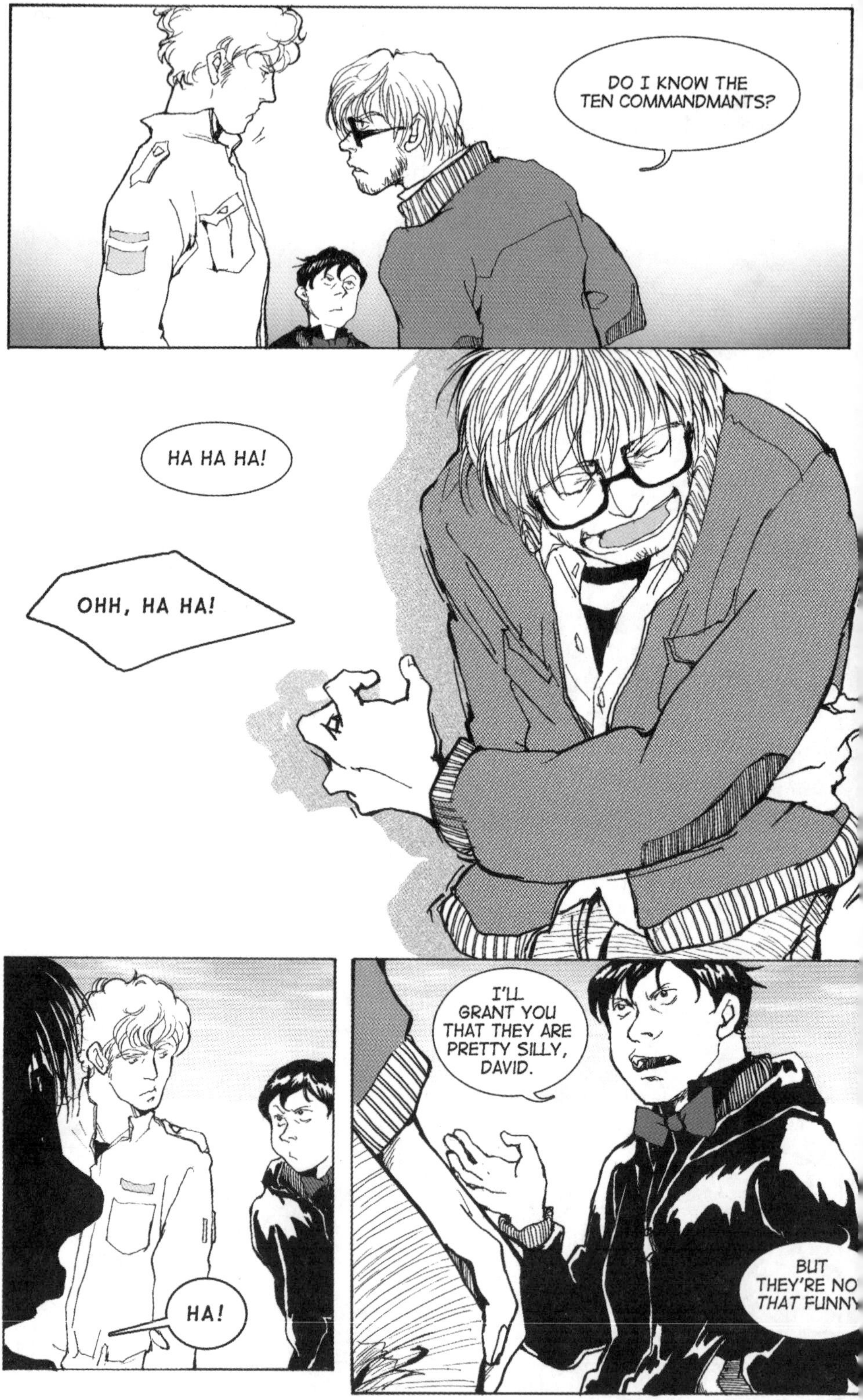
DO I KNOW THE TEN COMMANDMANTS?
HA HA HA!
OHH, HA HA!
HA!
I'LL GRANT YOU THAT THEY ARE PRETTY SILLY, DAVID.
BUT THEY'RE NO *THAT* FUNNY

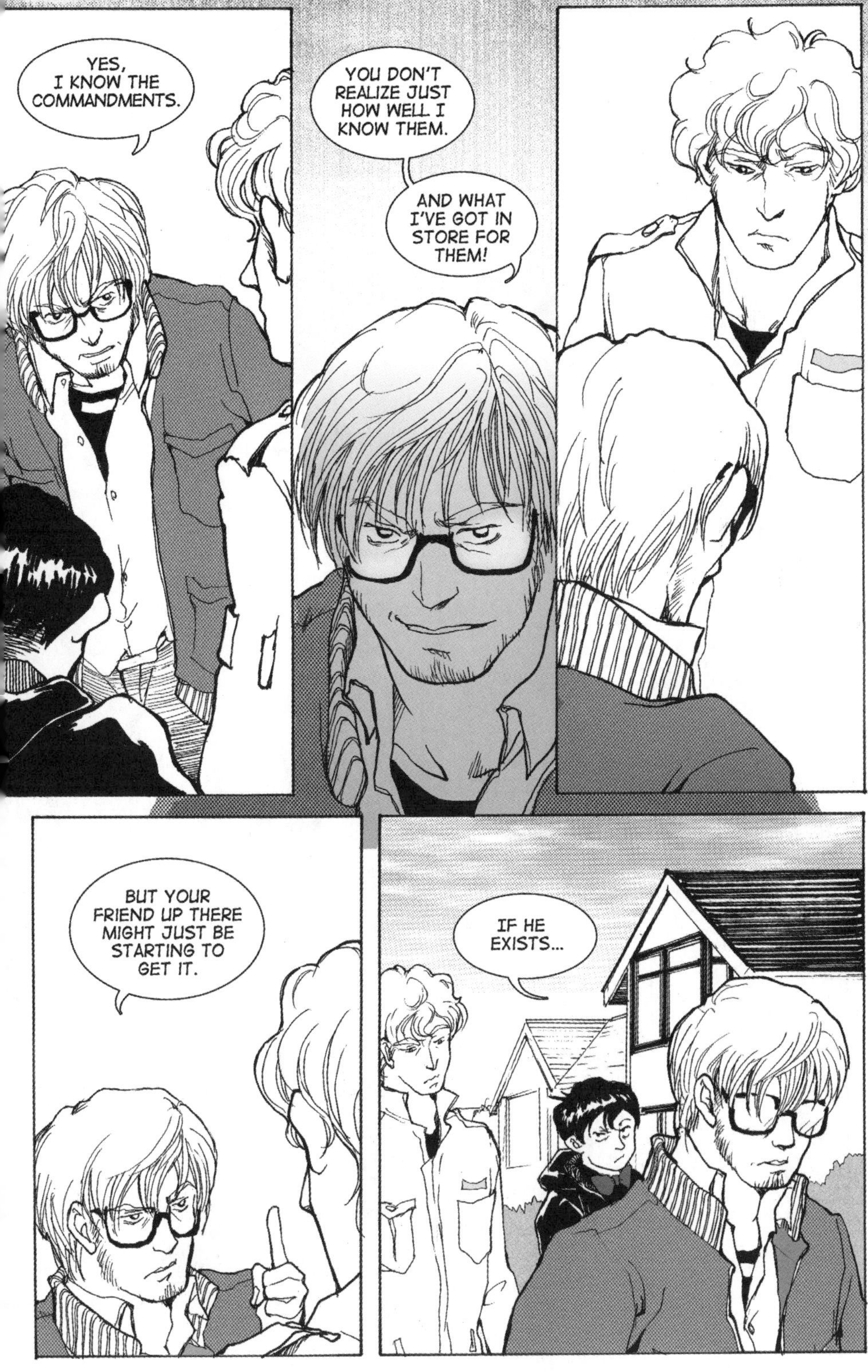
YES, I KNOW THE COMMANDMENTS.
YOU DON'T REALIZE JUST HOW WELL I KNOW THEM.
AND WHAT I'VE GOT IN STORE FOR THEM!
BUT YOUR FRIEND UP THERE MIGHT JUST BE STARTING TO GET IT.
IF HE EXISTS...

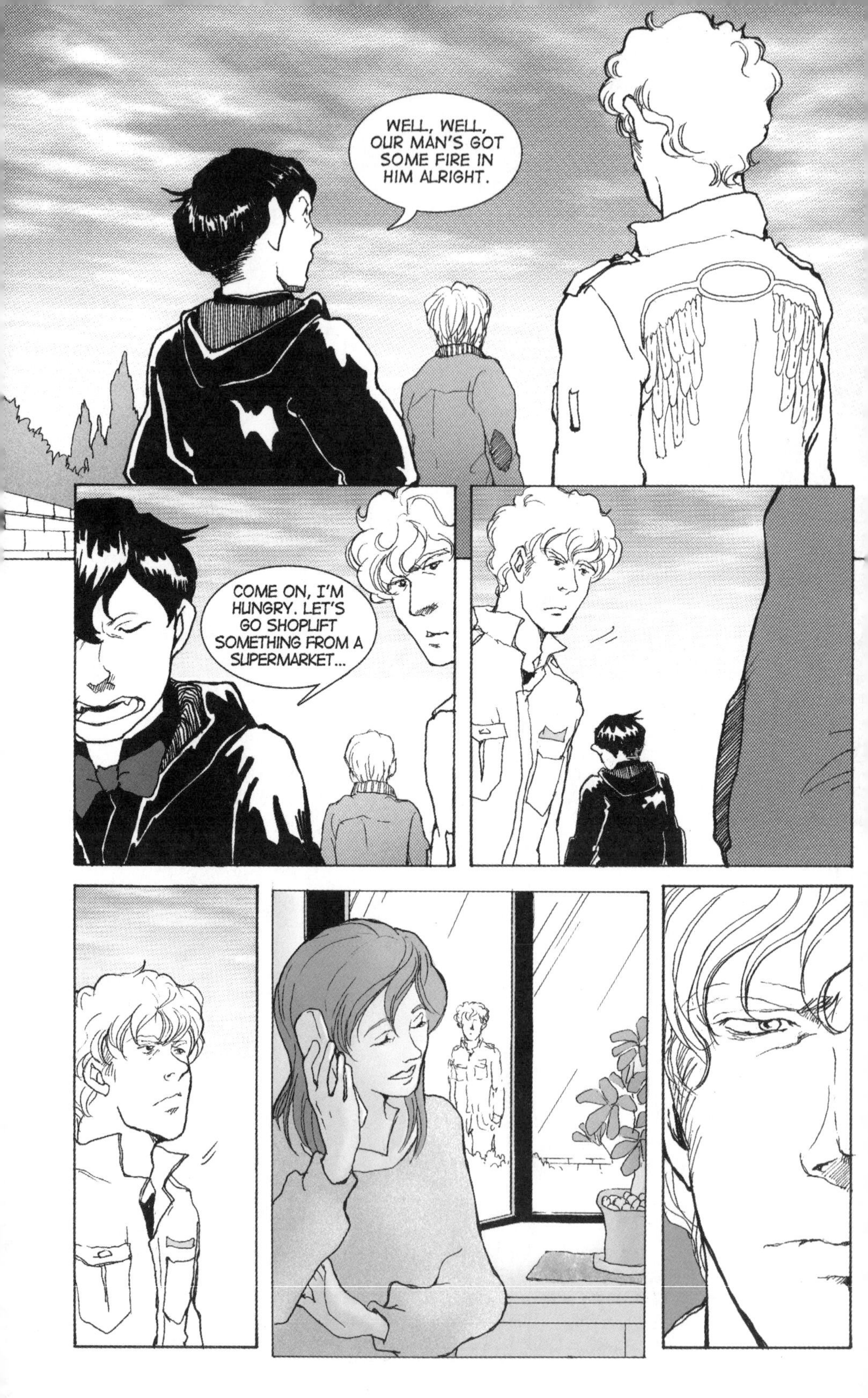
WELL, WELL, OUR MAN'S GOT SOME FIRE IN HIM ALRIGHT.
COME ON, I'M HUNGRY. LET'S GO SHOPLIFT SOMETHING FROM A SUPERMARKET...

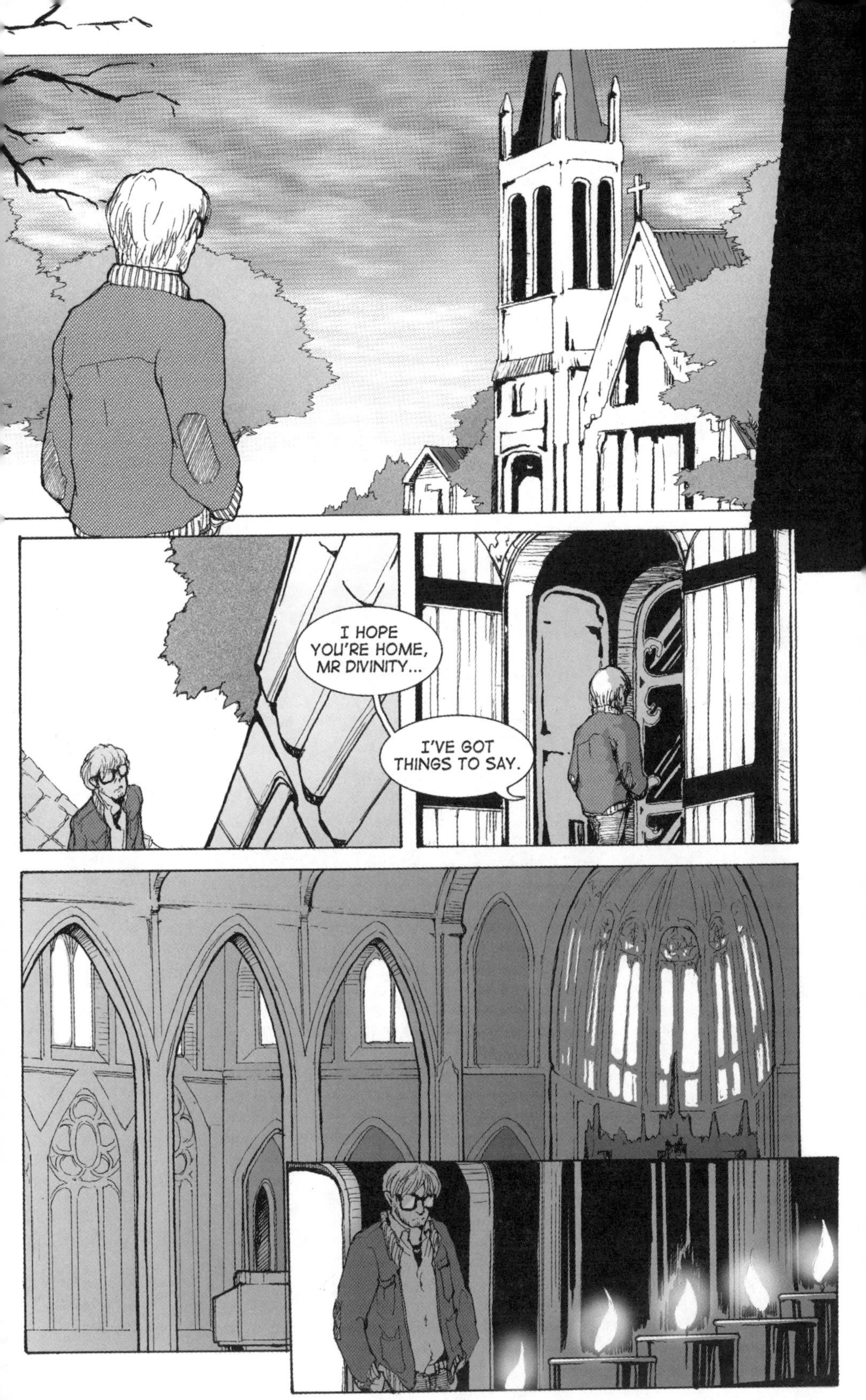
I HOPE YOU'RE HOME, MR DIVINITY...
I'VE GOT THINGS TO SAY.

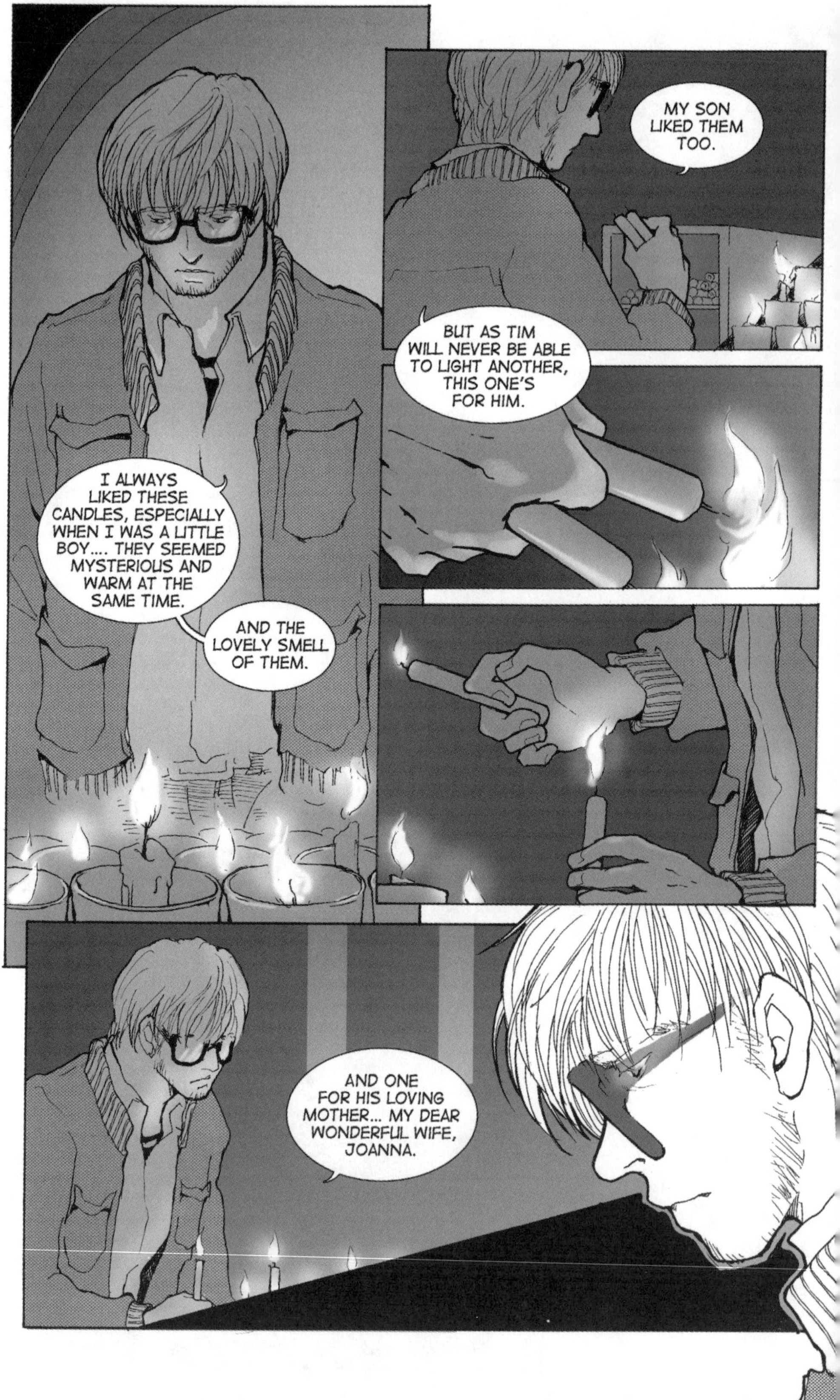
I ALWAYS LIKED THESE CANDLES, ESPECIALLY WHEN I WAS A LITTLE BOY.... THEY SEEMED MYSTERIOUS AND WARM AT THE SAME TIME.
AND THE LOVELY SMELL OF THEM.
MY SON LIKED THEM TOO.
BUT AS TIM WILL NEVER BE ABLE TO LIGHT ANOTHER, THIS ONE'S FOR HIM.
AND ONE FOR HIS LOVING MOTHER... MY DEAR WONDERFUL WIFE, JOANNA.

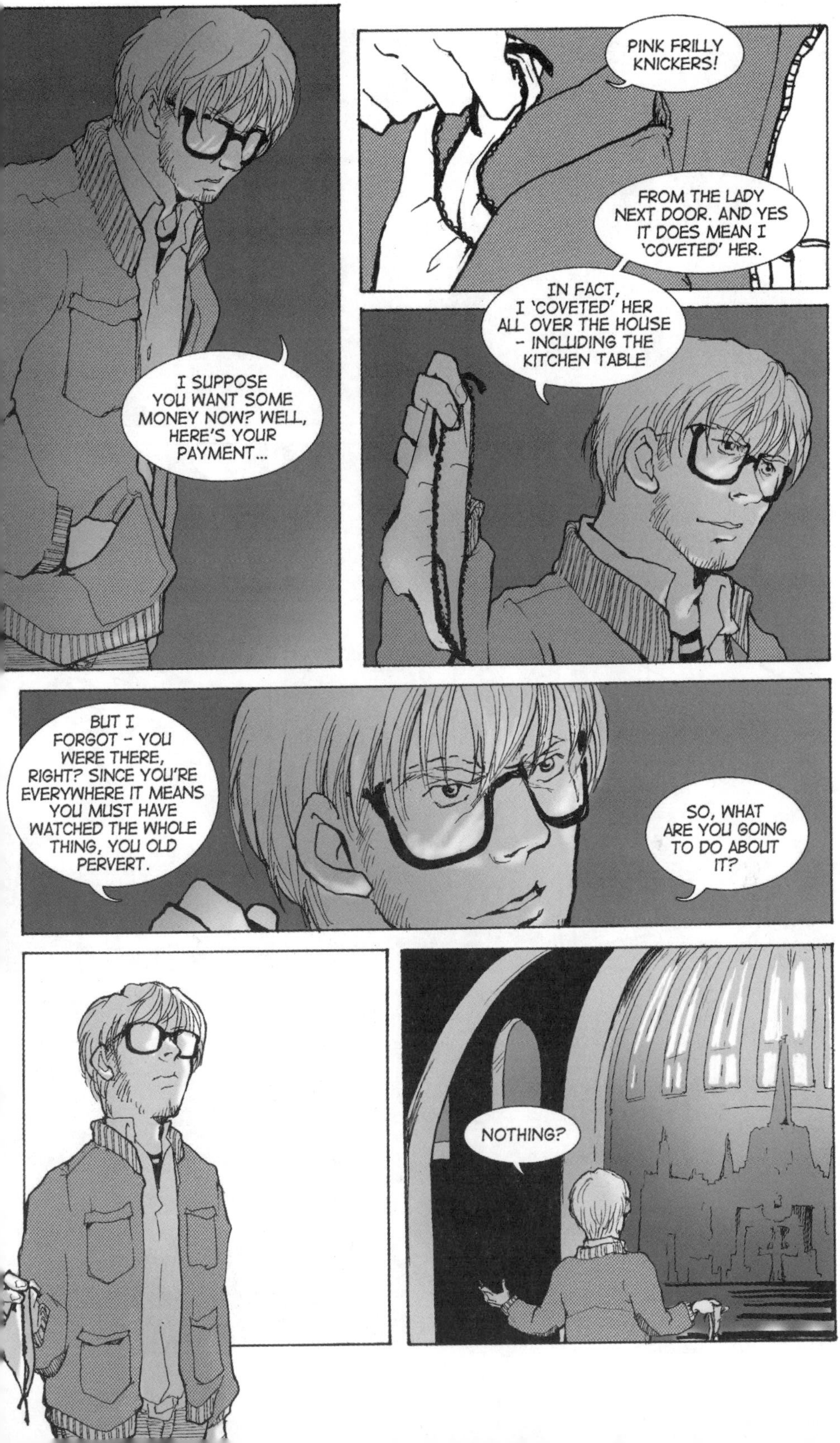
I SUPPOSE YOU WANT SOME MONEY NOW? WELL, HERE'S YOUR PAYMENT...
PINK FRILLY KNICKERS!
FROM THE LADY NEXT DOOR. AND YES IT DOES MEAN I 'COVETED' HER.
IN FACT, I 'COVETED' HER ALL OVER THE HOUSE - INCLUDING THE KITCHEN TABLE
BUT I FORGOT - YOU WERE THERE, RIGHT? SINCE YOU'RE EVERYWHERE IT MEANS YOU MUST HAVE WATCHED THE WHOLE THING, YOU OLD PERVERT.
SO, WHAT ARE YOU GOING TO DO ABOUT IT?
NOTHING?

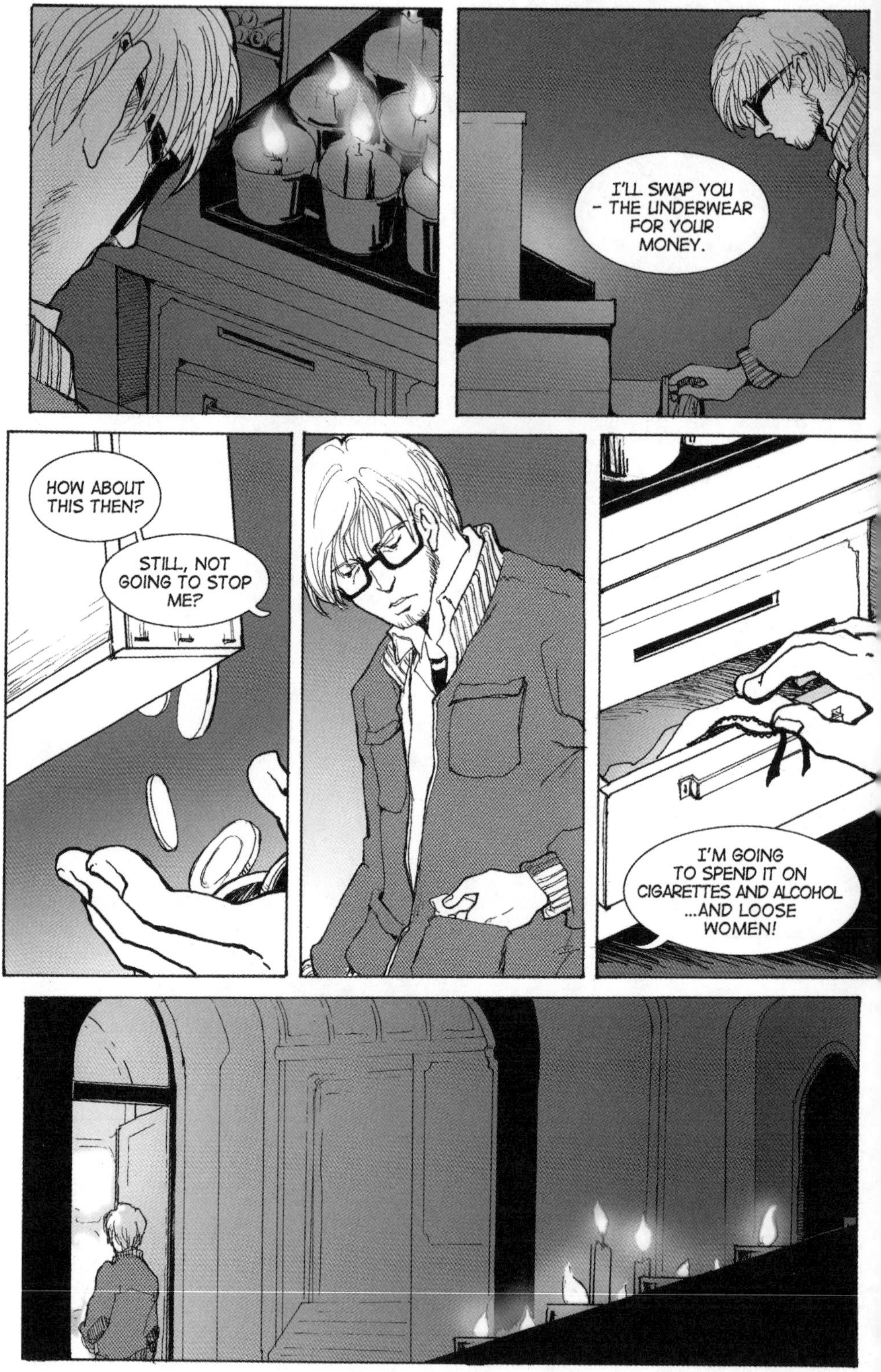
I'LL SWAP YOU - THE UNDERWEAR FOR YOUR MONEY.
HOW ABOUT THIS THEN?
STILL, NOT GOING TO STOP ME?
I'M GOING TO SPEND IT ON CIGARETTES AND ALCOHOL ...AND LOOSE WOMEN!

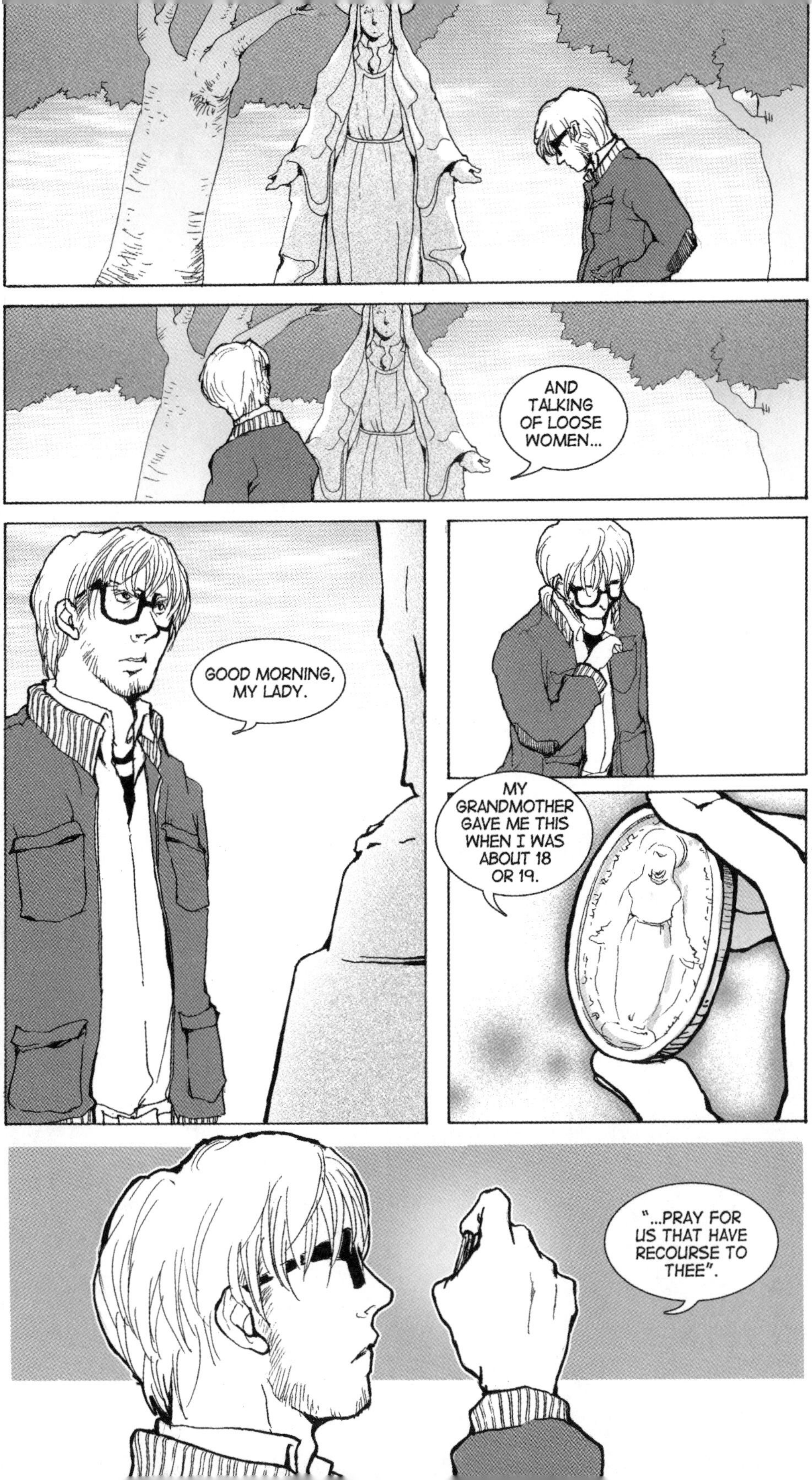
AND TALKING OF LOOSE WOMEN...
GOOD MORNING, MY LADY.
MY GRANDMOTHER GAVE ME THIS WHEN I WAS ABOUT 18 OR 19.
"...PRAY FOR US THAT HAVE RECOURSE TO THEE".

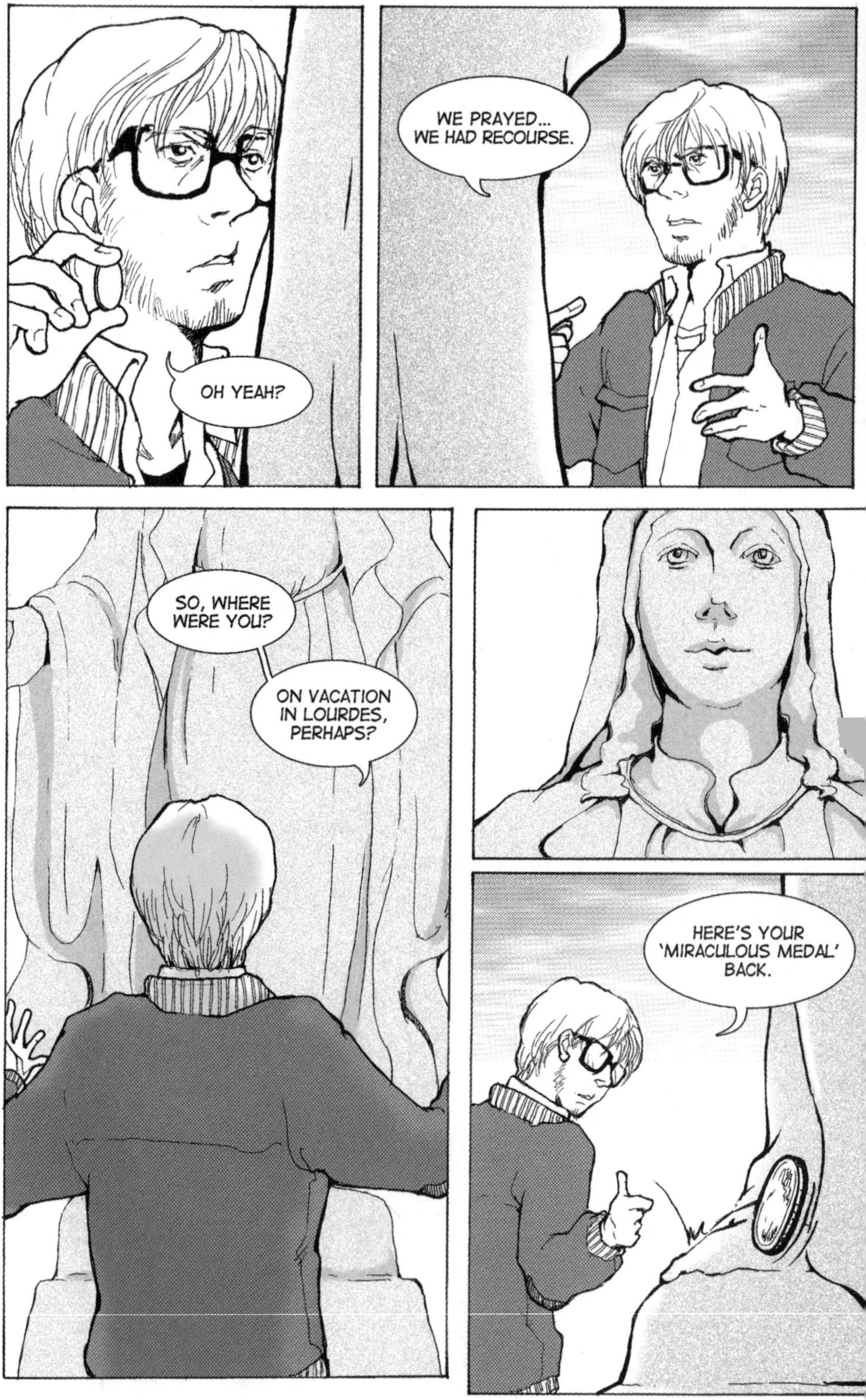
OH YEAH?
WE PRAYED... WE HAD RECOURSE.
SO, WHERE WERE YOU?
ON VACATION IN LOURDES, PERHAPS?
HERE'S YOUR 'MIRACULOUS MEDAL' BACK.

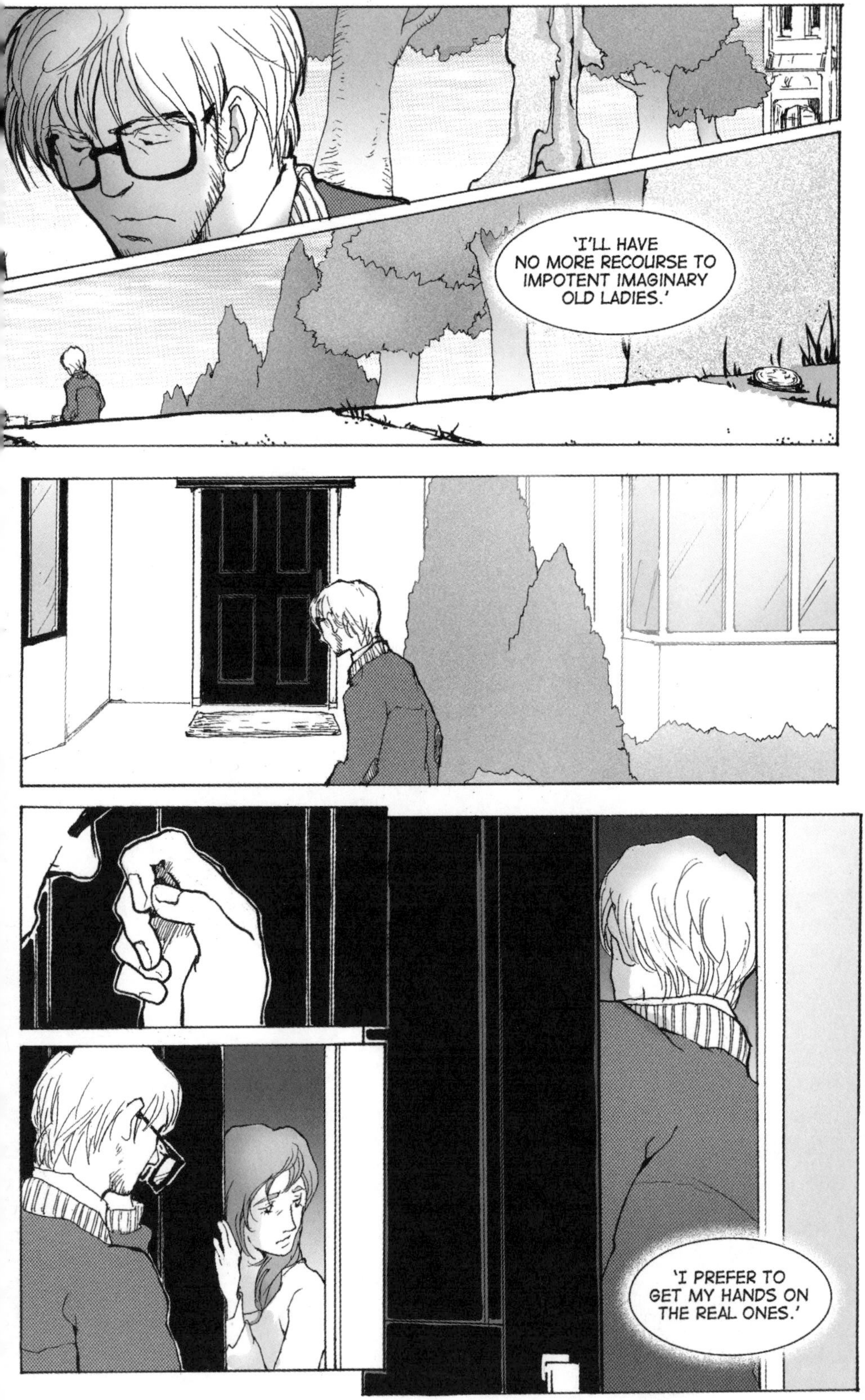
'I'LL HAVE NO MORE RECOURSE TO IMPOTENT IMAGINARY OLD LADIES.'
'I PREFER TO GET MY HANDS ON THE REAL ONES.'

Chapter 3

*'Remember the Sabbath day,
to keep it holy.'*

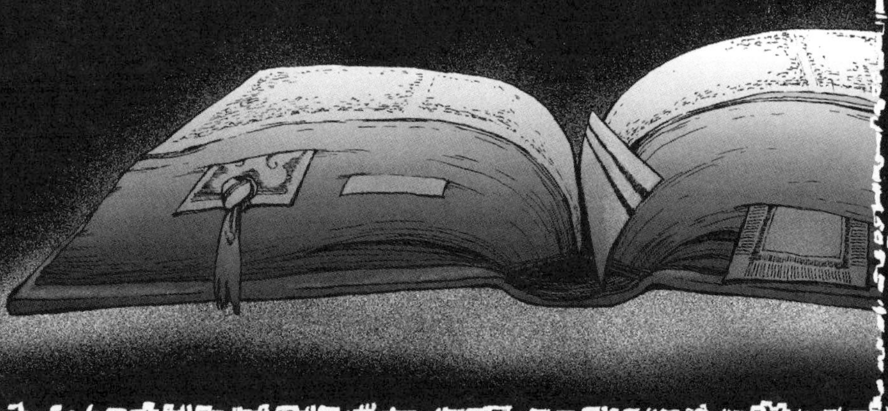

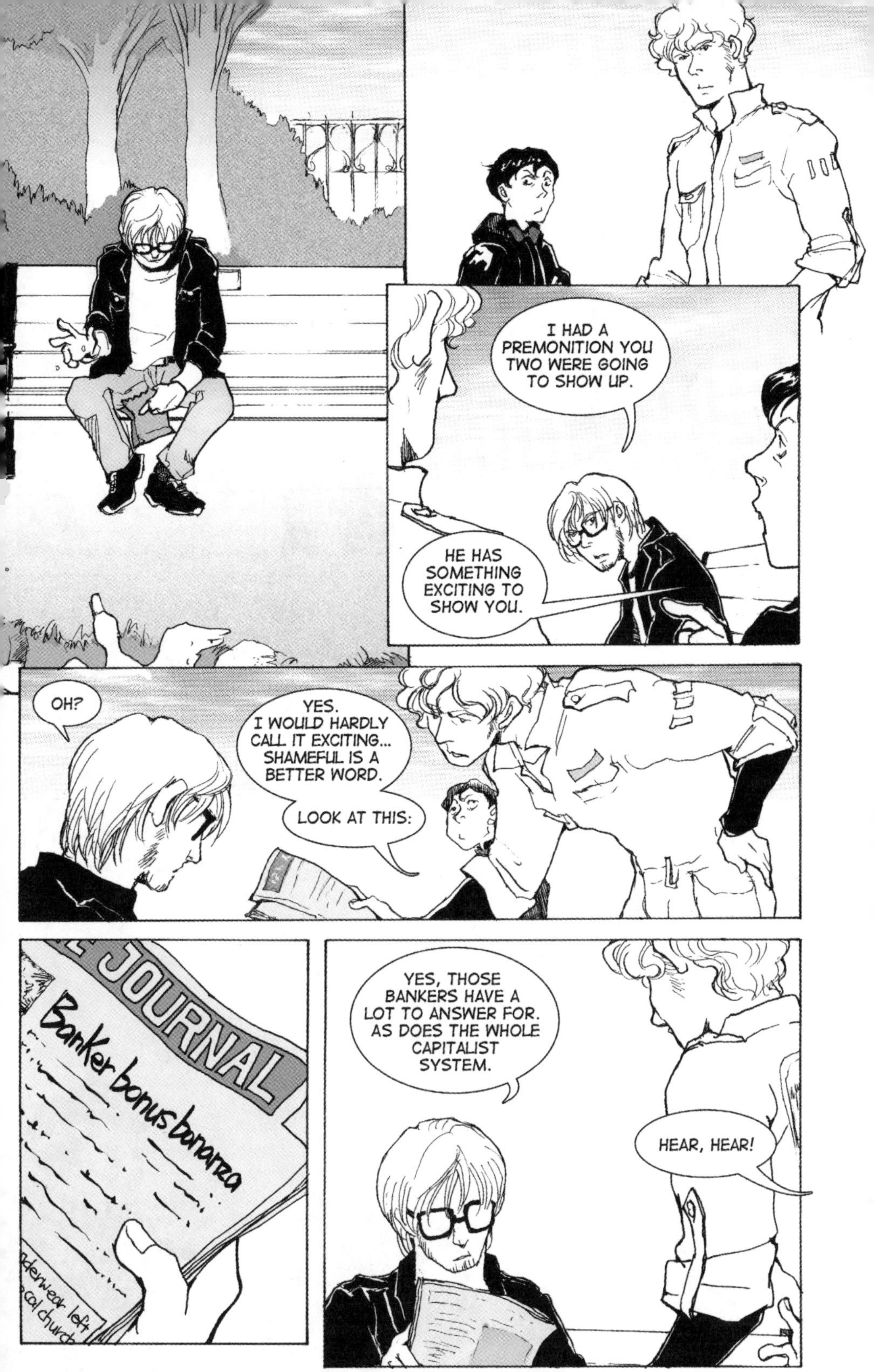
I HAD A PREMONITION YOU TWO WERE GOING TO SHOW UP.
HE HAS SOMETHING EXCITING TO SHOW YOU.
OH?
YES. I WOULD HARDLY CALL IT EXCITING... SHAMEFUL IS A BETTER WORD.
LOOK AT THIS:
JOURNAL
Banker bonus bonanza
YES, THOSE BANKERS HAVE A LOT TO ANSWER FOR. AS DOES THE WHOLE CAPITALIST SYSTEM.
HEAR, HEAR!

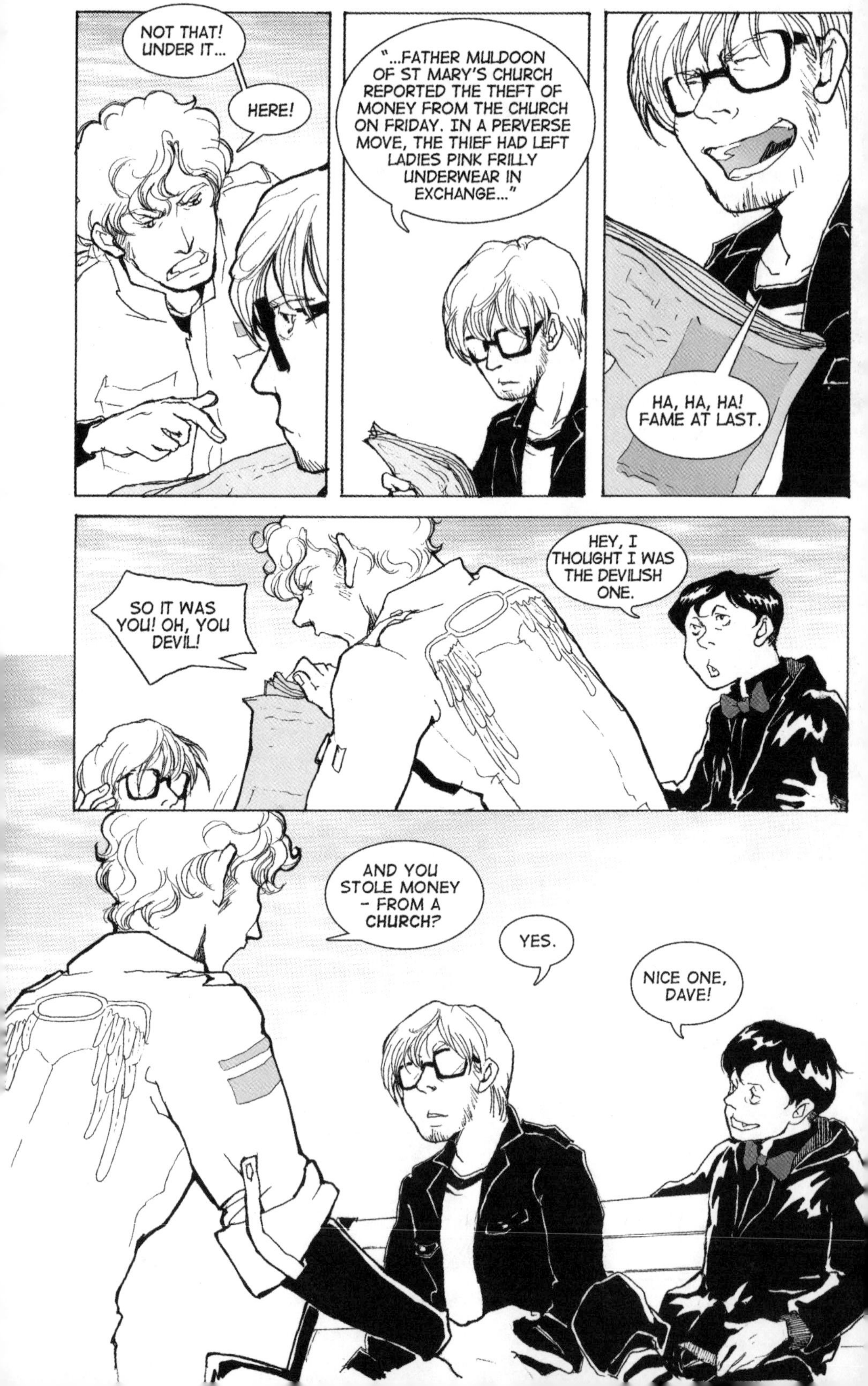
NOT THAT! UNDER IT...
HERE!
"...FATHER MULDOON OF ST MARY'S CHURCH REPORTED THE THEFT OF MONEY FROM THE CHURCH ON FRIDAY. IN A PERVERSE MOVE, THE THIEF HAD LEFT LADIES PINK FRILLY UNDERWEAR IN EXCHANGE..."
HA, HA, HA! FAME AT LAST.
SO IT WAS YOU! OH, YOU DEVIL!
HEY, I THOUGHT I WAS THE DEVILISH ONE.
AND YOU STOLE MONEY - FROM A CHURCH?
YES.
NICE ONE, DAVE!

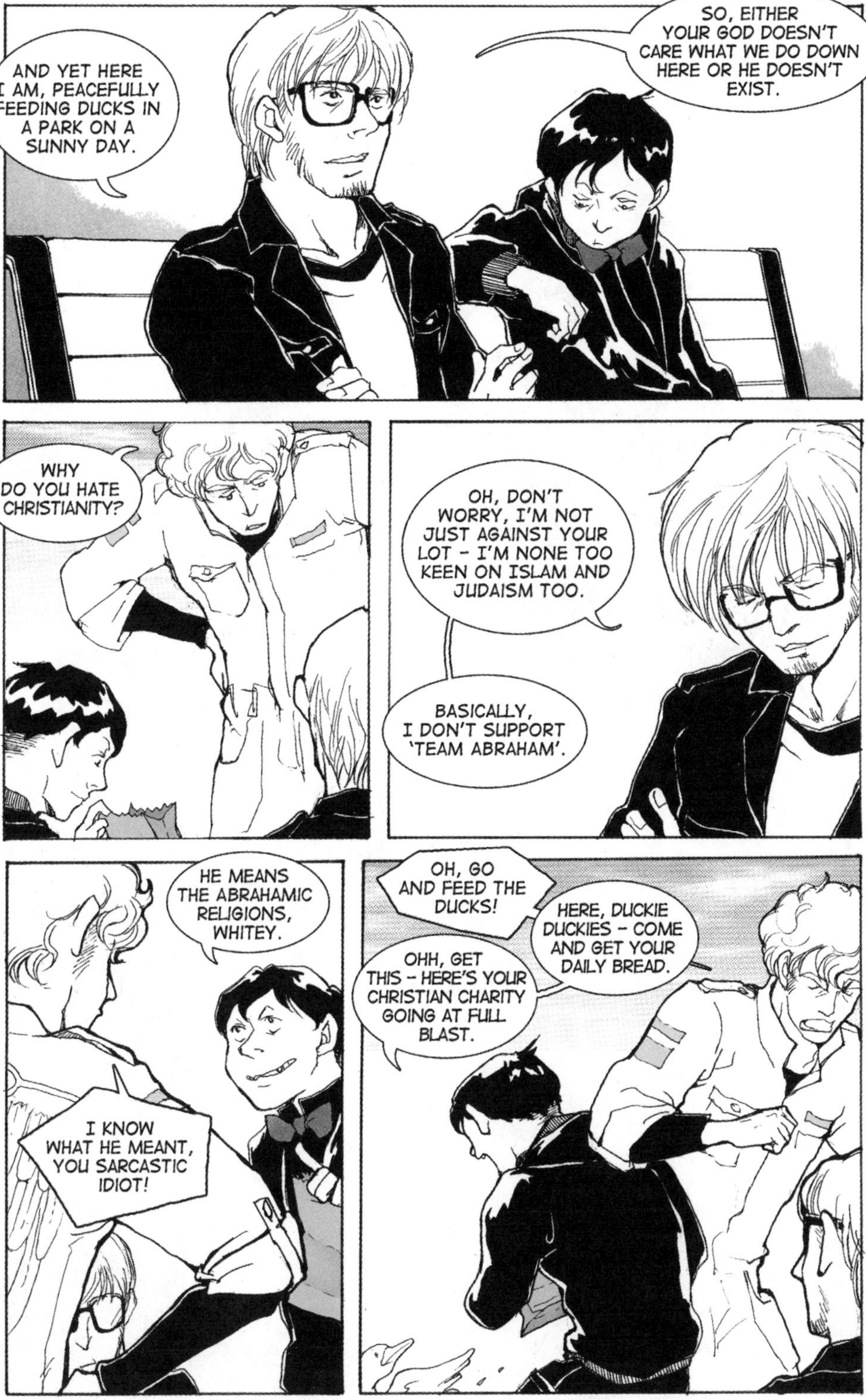
AND YET HERE I AM, PEACEFULLY FEEDING DUCKS IN A PARK ON A SUNNY DAY.
SO, EITHER YOUR GOD DOESN'T CARE WHAT WE DO DOWN HERE OR HE DOESN'T EXIST.
WHY DO YOU HATE CHRISTIANITY?
OH, DON'T WORRY, I'M NOT JUST AGAINST YOUR LOT - I'M NONE TOO KEEN ON ISLAM AND JUDAISM TOO.
BASICALLY, I DON'T SUPPORT 'TEAM ABRAHAM'.
HE MEANS THE ABRAHAMIC RELIGIONS, WHITEY.
I KNOW WHAT HE MEANT, YOU SARCASTIC IDIOT!
OH, GO AND FEED THE DUCKS!
HERE, DUCKIE DUCKIES - COME AND GET YOUR DAILY BREAD.
OHH, GET THIS - HERE'S YOUR CHRISTIAN CHARITY GOING AT FULL BLAST.

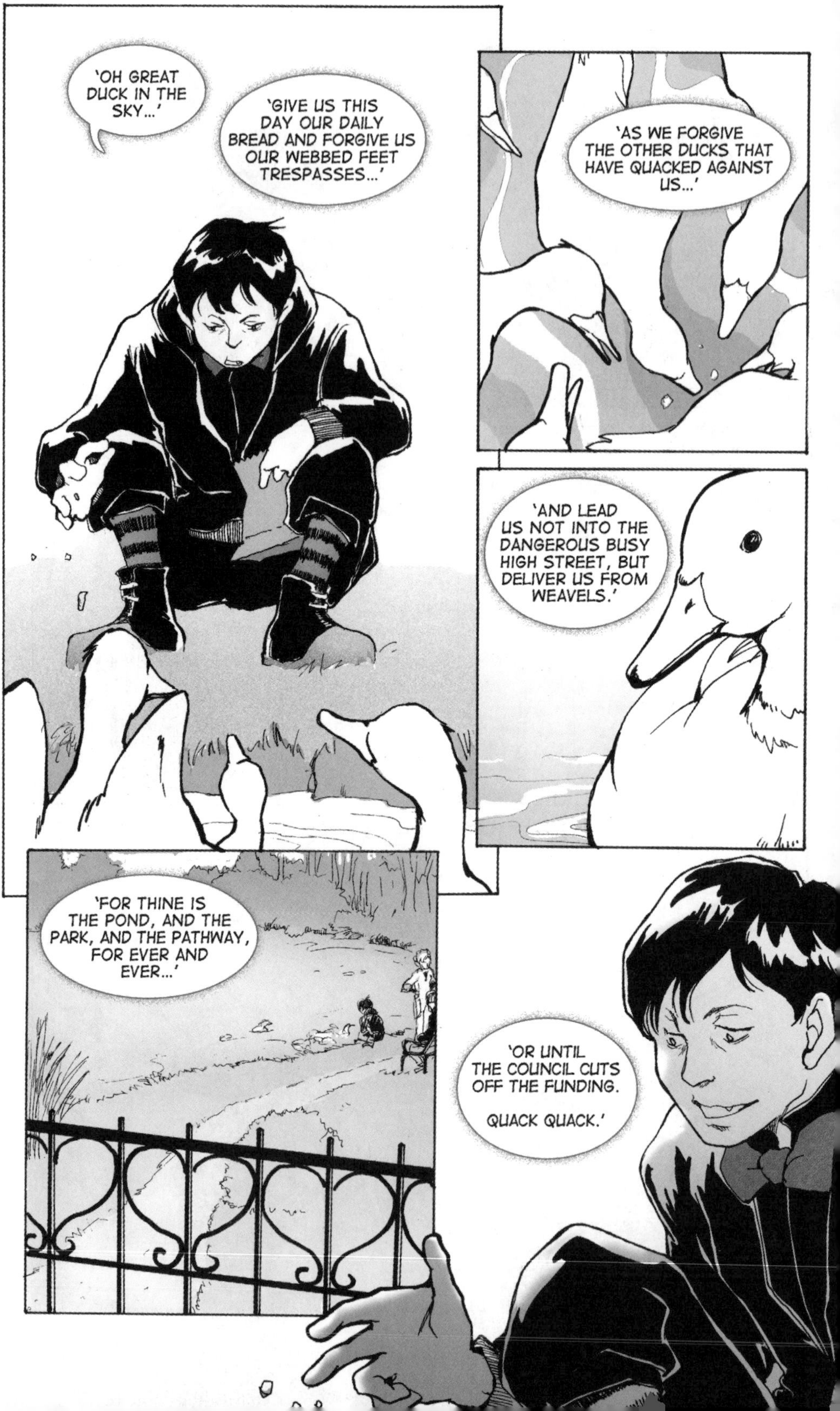
'OH GREAT DUCK IN THE SKY...'
'GIVE US THIS DAY OUR DAILY BREAD AND FORGIVE US OUR WEBBED FEET TRESPASSES...'
'AS WE FORGIVE THE OTHER DUCKS THAT HAVE QUACKED AGAINST US...'
'AND LEAD US NOT INTO THE DANGEROUS BUSY HIGH STREET, BUT DELIVER US FROM WEAVELS.'
'FOR THINE IS THE POND, AND THE PARK, AND THE PATHWAY, FOR EVER AND EVER...'
'OR UNTIL THE COUNCIL CUTS OFF THE FUNDING.
QUACK QUACK.'

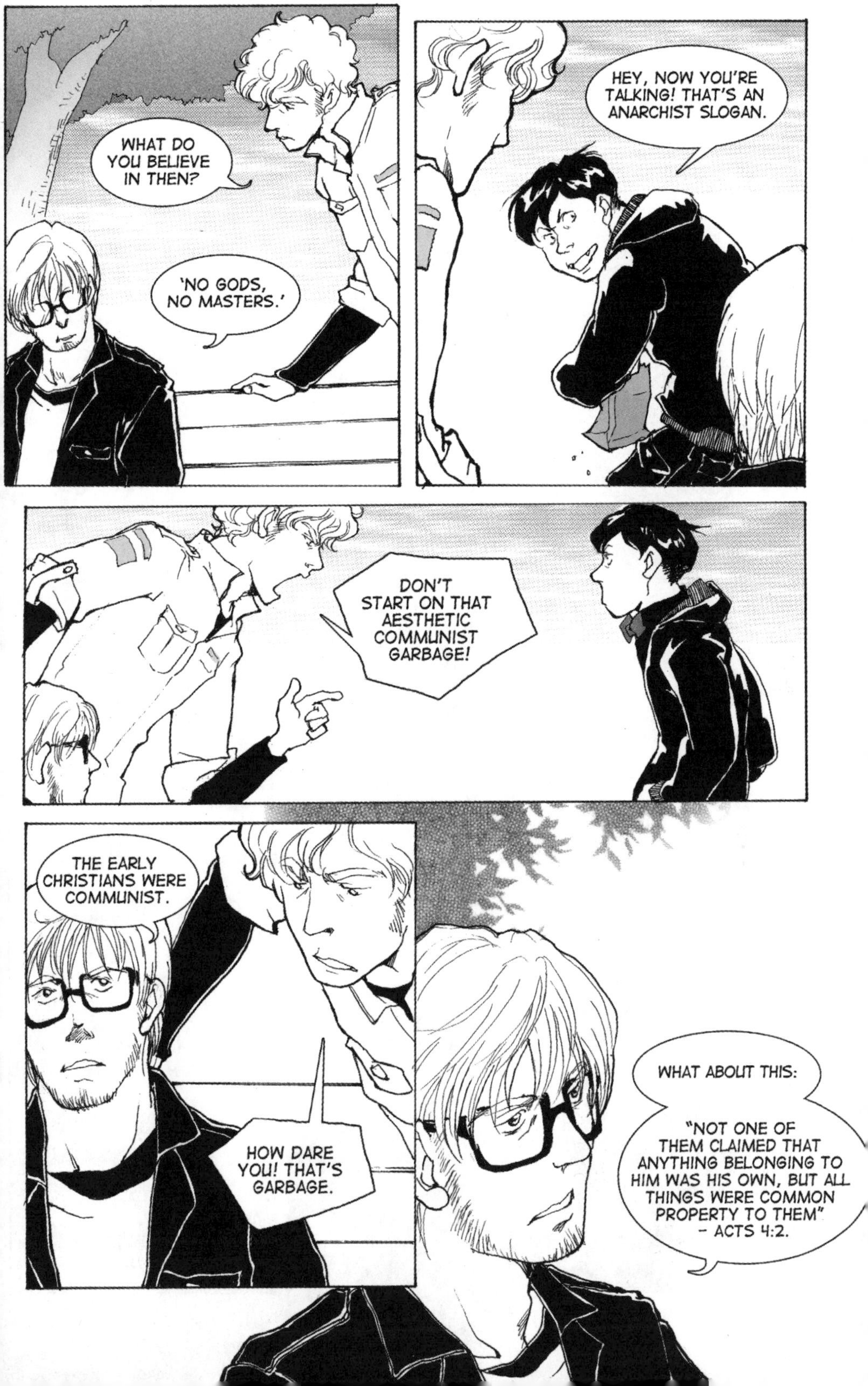
WHAT DO YOU BELIEVE IN THEN?
'NO GODS, NO MASTERS.'
HEY, NOW YOU'RE TALKING! THAT'S AN ANARCHIST SLOGAN.
DON'T START ON THAT AESTHETIC COMMUNIST GARBAGE!
THE EARLY CHRISTIANS WERE COMMUNIST.
HOW DARE YOU! THAT'S GARBAGE.
WHAT ABOUT THIS:
"NOT ONE OF THEM CLAIMED THAT ANYTHING BELONGING TO HIM WAS HIS OWN, BUT ALL THINGS WERE COMMON PROPERTY TO THEM" – ACTS 4:2.

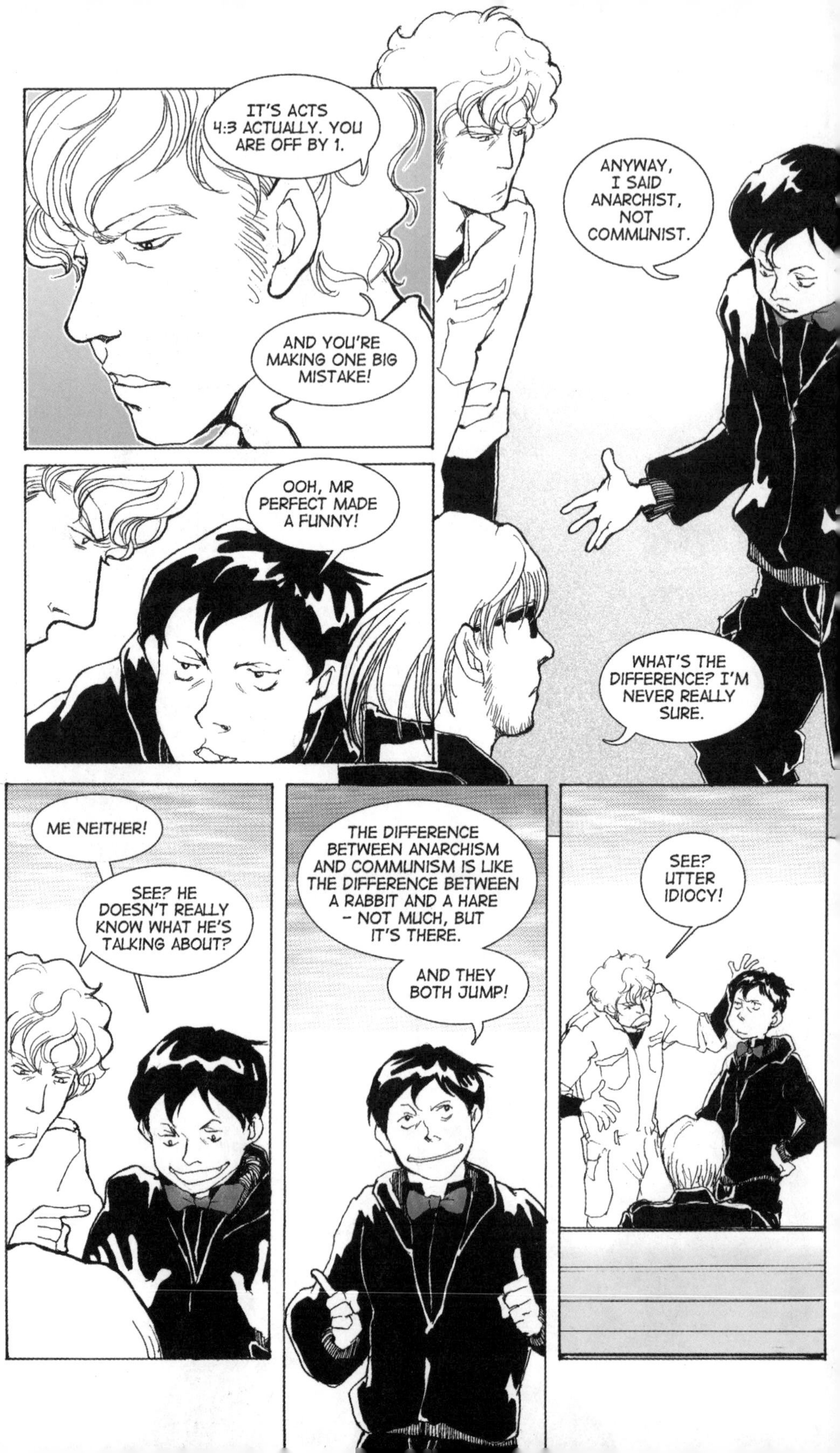
IT'S ACTS 4:3 ACTUALLY. YOU ARE OFF BY 1.
AND YOU'RE MAKING ONE BIG MISTAKE!
ANYWAY, I SAID ANARCHIST, NOT COMMUNIST.
OOH, MR PERFECT MADE A FUNNY!
WHAT'S THE DIFFERENCE? I'M NEVER REALLY SURE.
ME NEITHER!
SEE? HE DOESN'T REALLY KNOW WHAT HE'S TALKING ABOUT?
THE DIFFERENCE BETWEEN ANARCHISM AND COMMUNISM IS LIKE THE DIFFERENCE BETWEEN A RABBIT AND A HARE - NOT MUCH, BUT IT'S THERE.
AND THEY BOTH JUMP!
SEE? UTTER IDIOCY!

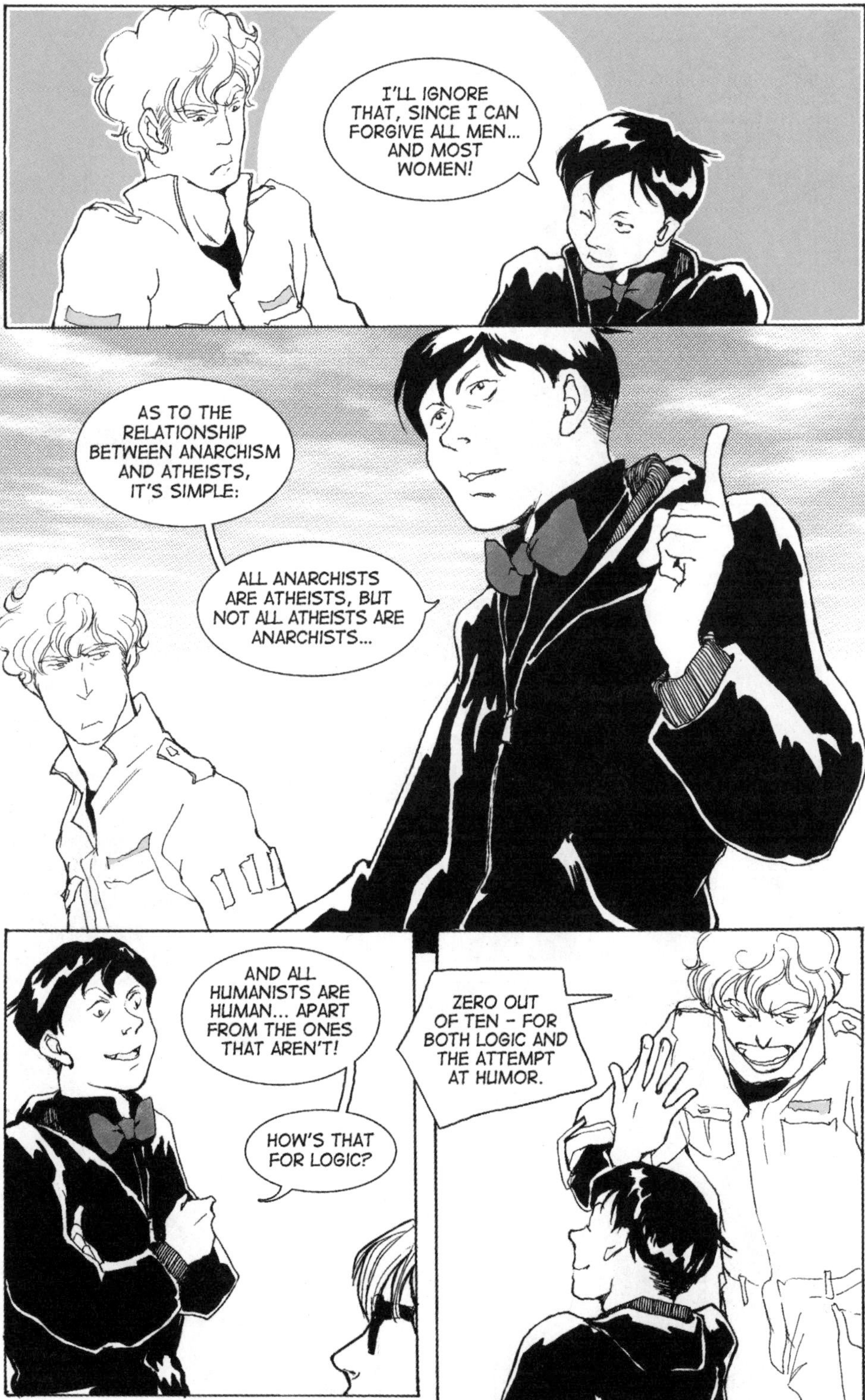
I'LL IGNORE THAT, SINCE I CAN FORGIVE ALL MEN... AND MOST WOMEN!
AS TO THE RELATIONSHIP BETWEEN ANARCHISM AND ATHEISTS, IT'S SIMPLE:
ALL ANARCHISTS ARE ATHEISTS, BUT NOT ALL ATHEISTS ARE ANARCHISTS...
AND ALL HUMANISTS ARE HUMAN... APART FROM THE ONES THAT AREN'T!
HOW'S THAT FOR LOGIC?
ZERO OUT OF TEN - FOR BOTH LOGIC AND THE ATTEMPT AT HUMOR.

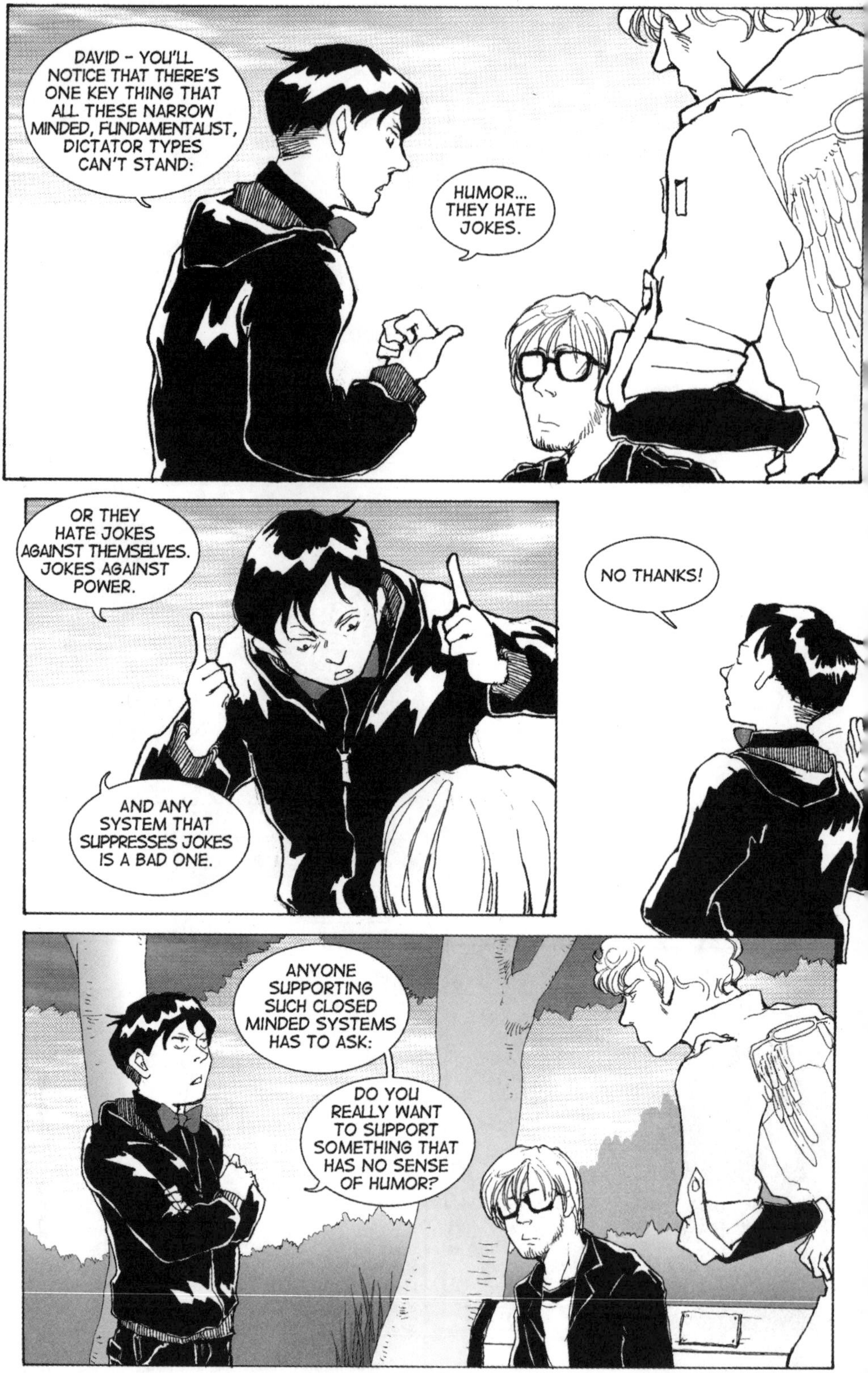
DAVID - YOU'LL NOTICE THAT THERE'S ONE KEY THING THAT ALL THESE NARROW MINDED, FUNDAMENTALIST, DICTATOR TYPES CAN'T STAND:
HUMOR... THEY HATE JOKES.
OR THEY HATE JOKES AGAINST THEMSELVES. JOKES AGAINST POWER.
AND ANY SYSTEM THAT SUPPRESSES JOKES IS A BAD ONE.
NO THANKS!
ANYONE SUPPORTING SUCH CLOSED MINDED SYSTEMS HAS TO ASK:
DO YOU REALLY WANT TO SUPPORT SOMETHING THAT HAS NO SENSE OF HUMOR?

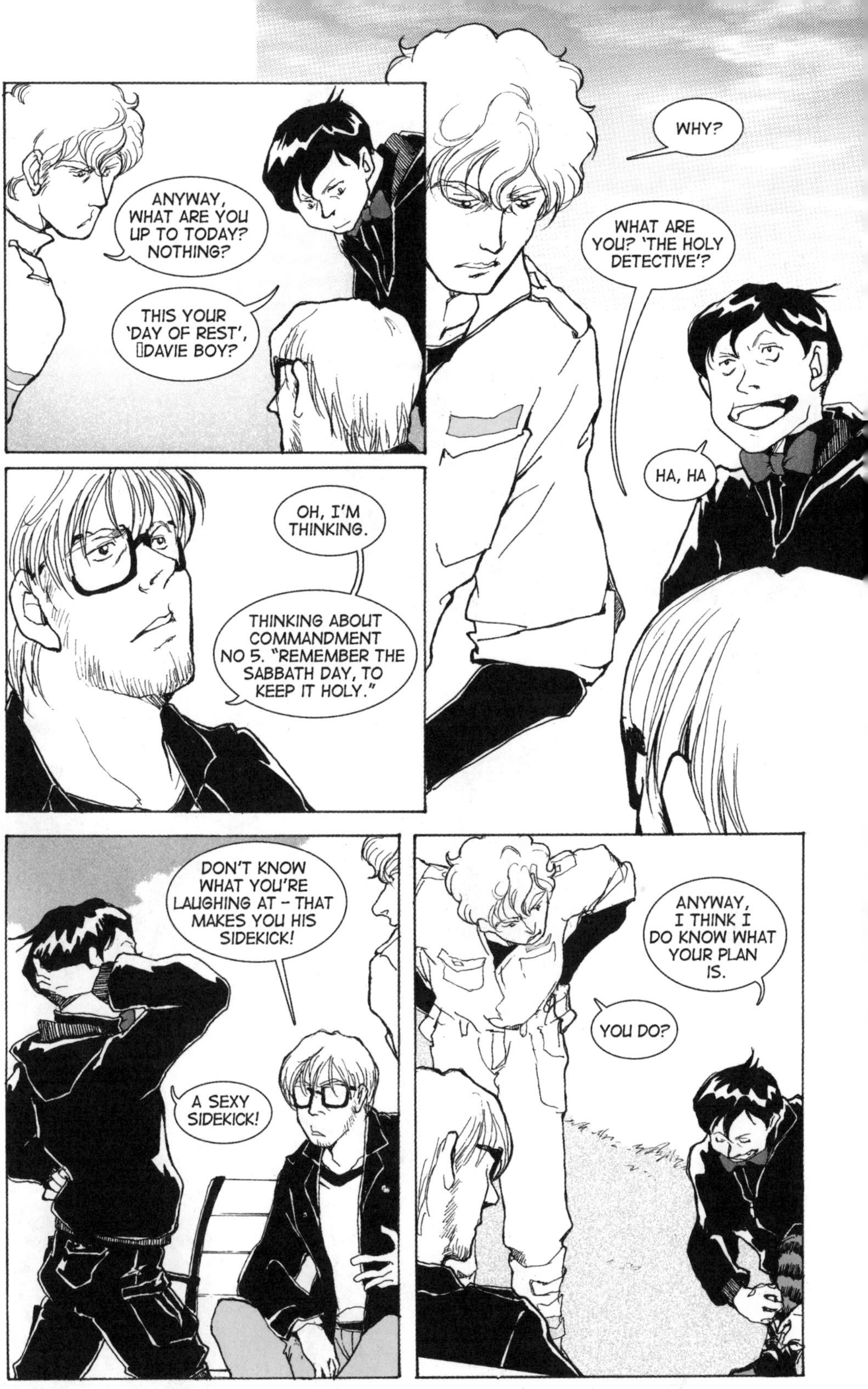
ANYWAY, WHAT ARE YOU UP TO TODAY? NOTHING?
THIS YOUR 'DAY OF REST', DAVIE BOY?
OH, I'M THINKING.
THINKING ABOUT COMMANDMENT NO 5. "REMEMBER THE SABBATH DAY, TO KEEP IT HOLY."
WHY?
WHAT ARE YOU? 'THE HOLY DETECTIVE'?
HA, HA
DON'T KNOW WHAT YOU'RE LAUGHING AT – THAT MAKES YOU HIS SIDEKICK!
A SEXY SIDEKICK!
ANYWAY, I THINK I DO KNOW WHAT YOUR PLAN IS.
YOU DO?

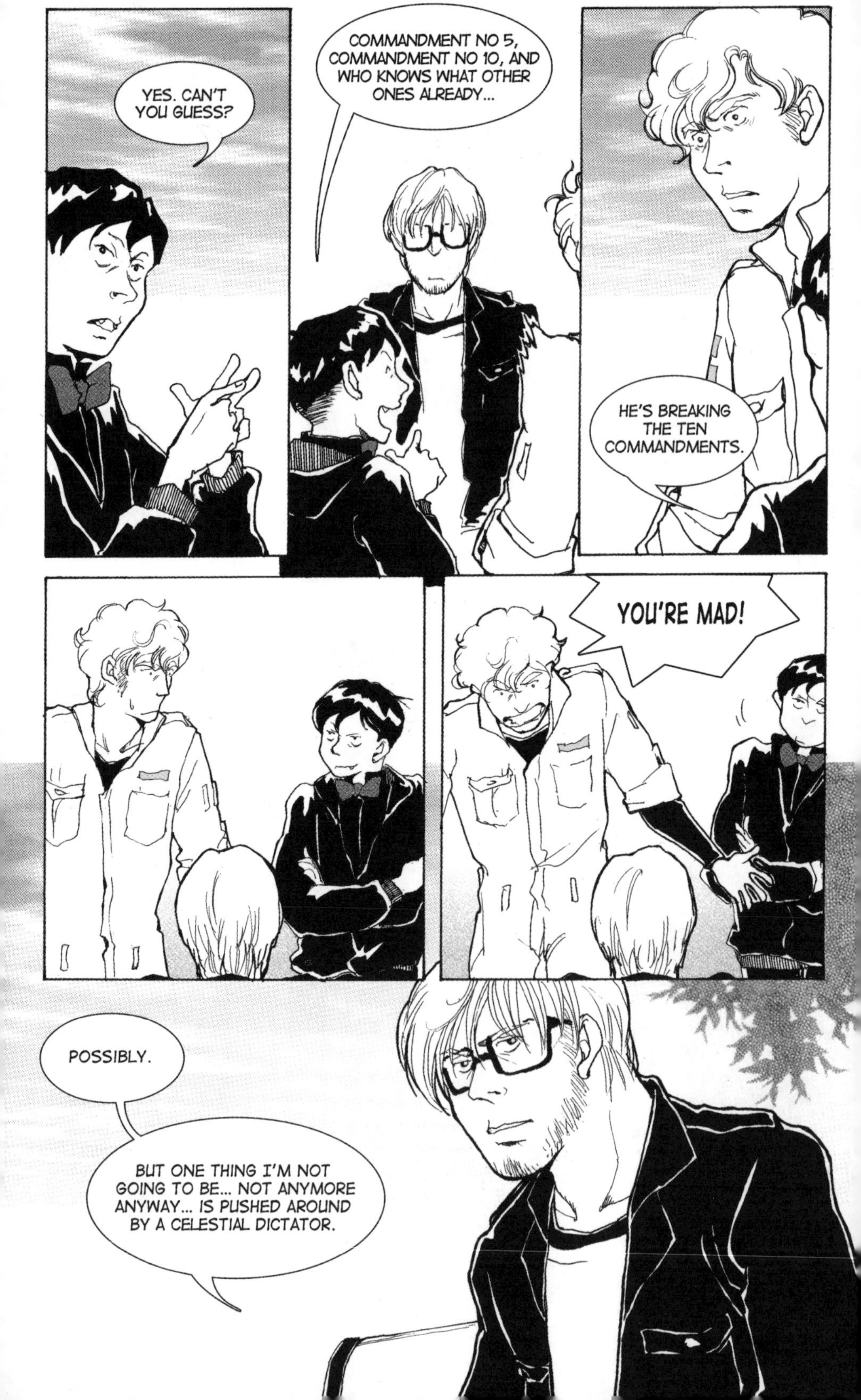
YES. CAN'T YOU GUESS?
COMMANDMENT NO 5, COMMANDMENT NO 10, AND WHO KNOWS WHAT OTHER ONES ALREADY...
HE'S BREAKING THE TEN COMMANDMENTS.
YOU'RE MAD!
POSSIBLY.
BUT ONE THING I'M NOT GOING TO BE... NOT ANYMORE ANYWAY... IS PUSHED AROUND BY A CELESTIAL DICTATOR.

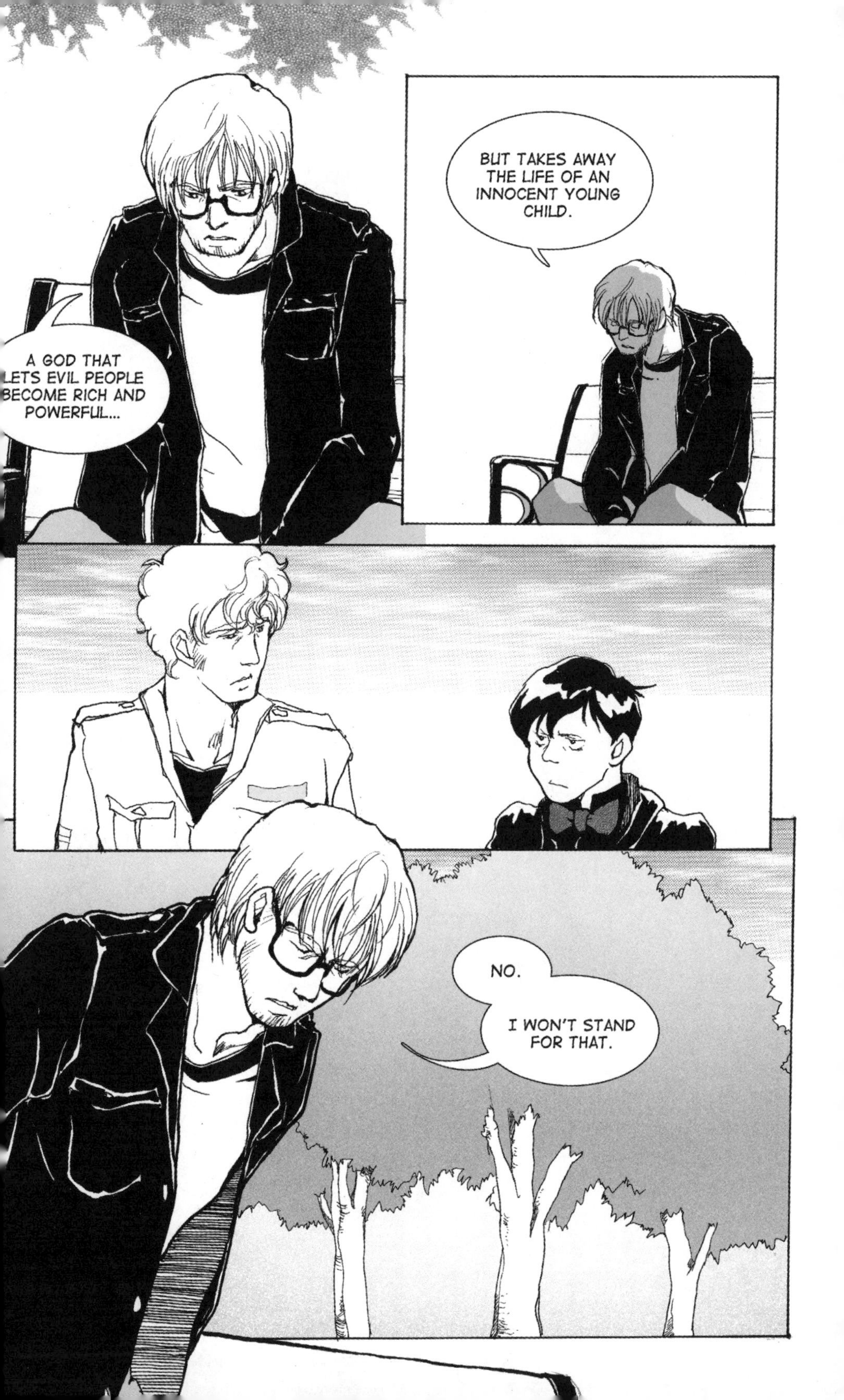
A GOD THAT LETS EVIL PEOPLE BECOME RICH AND POWERFUL...
BUT TAKES AWAY THE LIFE OF AN INNOCENT YOUNG CHILD.
NO.
I WON'T STAND FOR THAT.

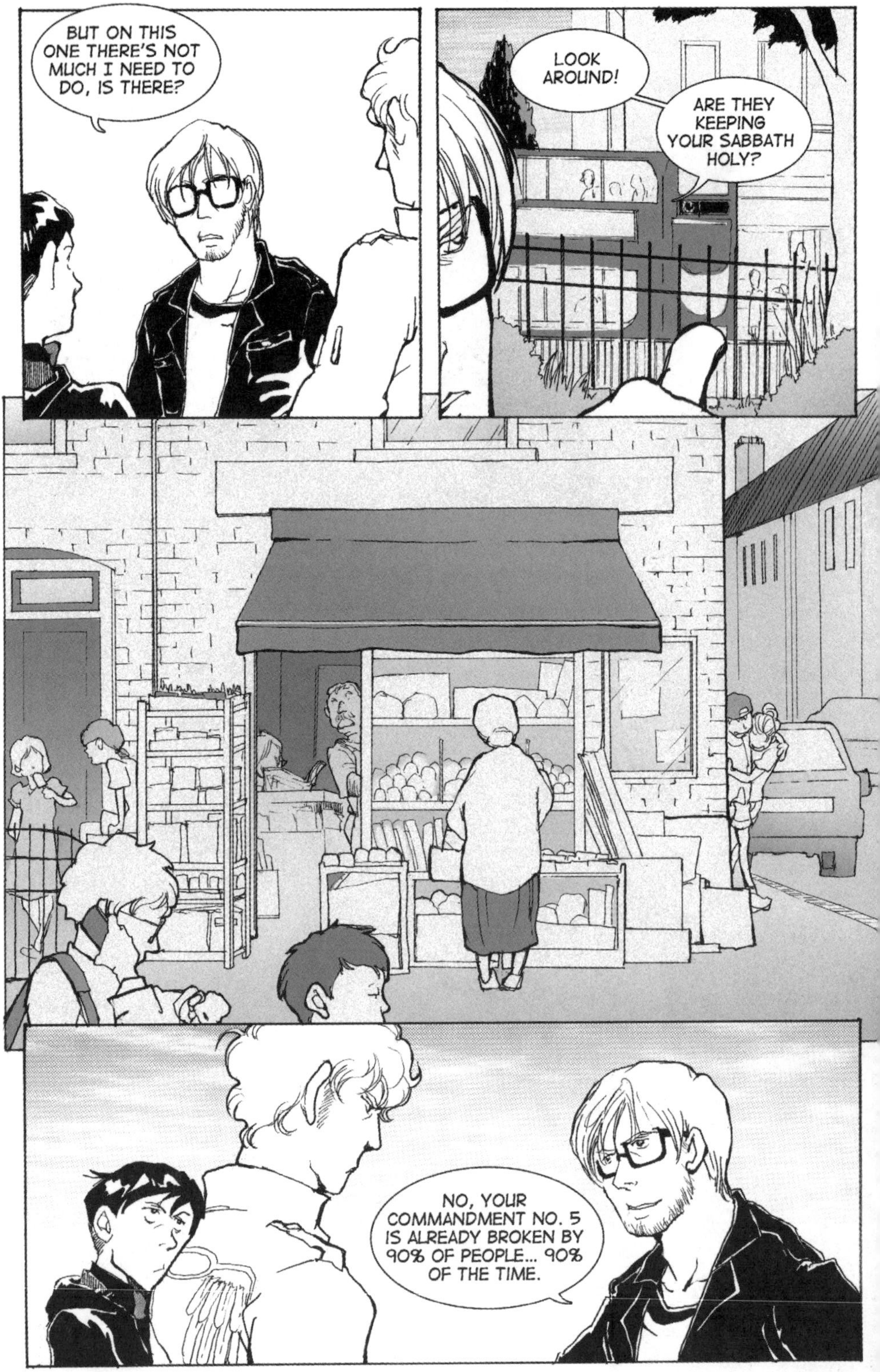
BUT ON THIS ONE THERE'S NOT MUCH I NEED TO DO, IS THERE?
LOOK AROUND!
ARE THEY KEEPING YOUR SABBATH HOLY?
NO, YOUR COMMANDMENT NO. 5 IS ALREADY BROKEN BY 90% OF PEOPLE... 90% OF THE TIME.

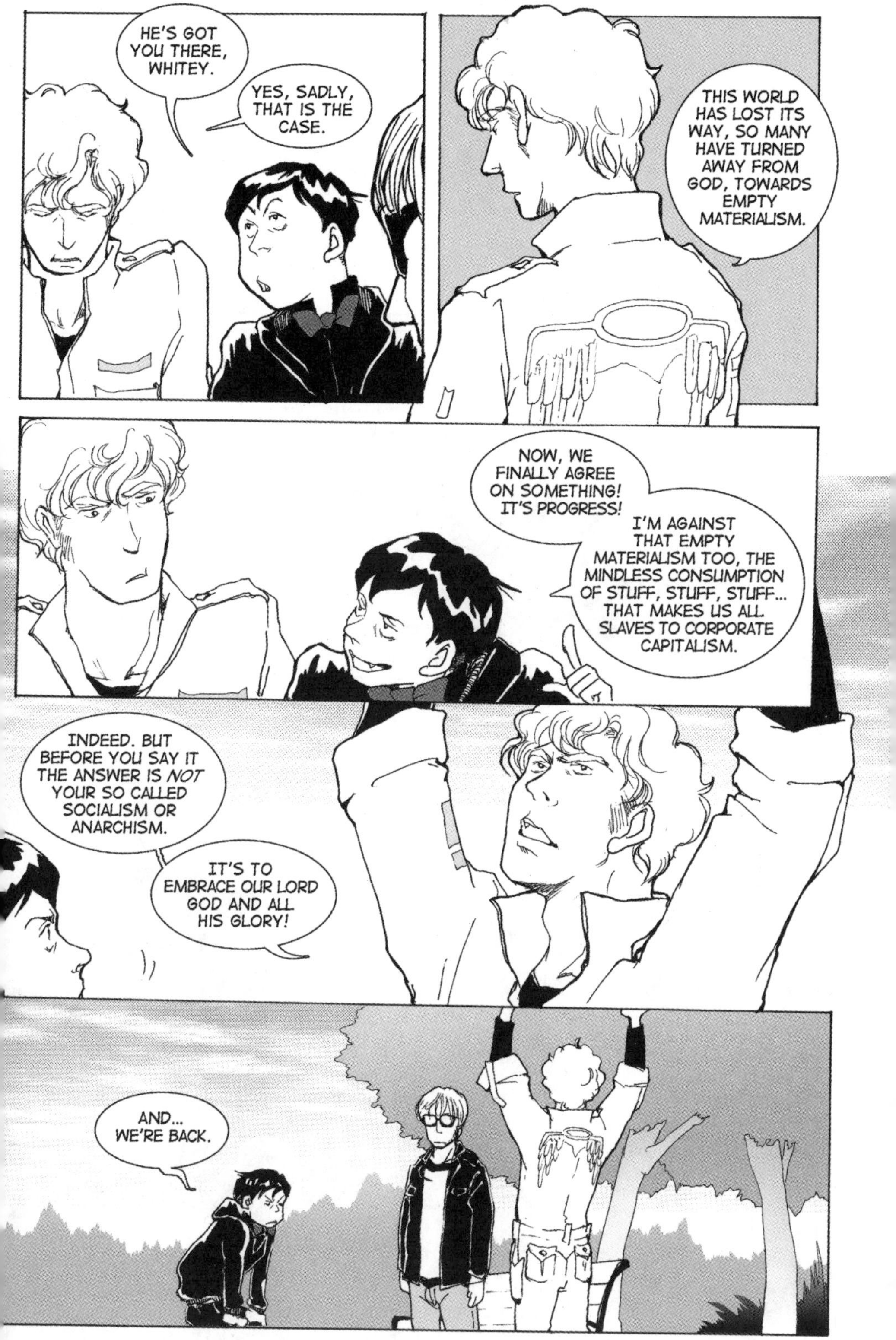

HE'S GOT YOU THERE, WHITEY.
YES, SADLY, THAT IS THE CASE.
THIS WORLD HAS LOST ITS WAY, SO MANY HAVE TURNED AWAY FROM GOD, TOWARDS EMPTY MATERIALISM.
NOW, WE FINALLY AGREE ON SOMETHING! IT'S PROGRESS!
I'M AGAINST THAT EMPTY MATERIALISM TOO, THE MINDLESS CONSUMPTION OF STUFF, STUFF, STUFF... THAT MAKES US ALL SLAVES TO CORPORATE CAPITALISM.
INDEED. BUT BEFORE YOU SAY IT THE ANSWER IS NOT YOUR SO CALLED SOCIALISM OR ANARCHISM.
IT'S TO EMBRACE OUR LORD GOD AND ALL HIS GLORY!
AND... WE'RE BACK.

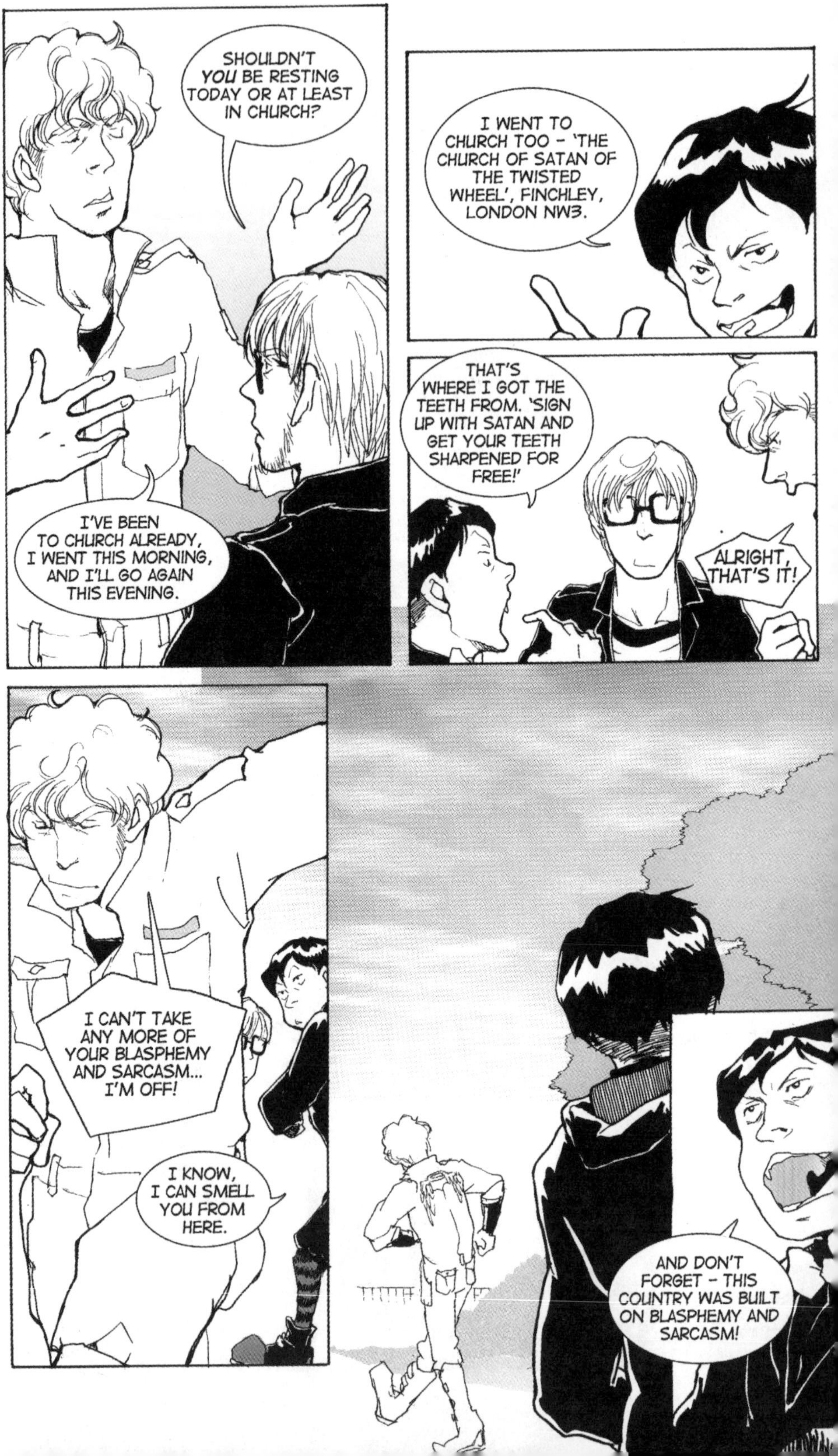

SHOULDN'T *YOU* BE RESTING TODAY OR AT LEAST IN CHURCH?
I'VE BEEN TO CHURCH ALREADY, I WENT THIS MORNING, AND I'LL GO AGAIN THIS EVENING.
I WENT TO CHURCH TOO - 'THE CHURCH OF SATAN OF THE TWISTED WHEEL', FINCHLEY, LONDON NW3.
THAT'S WHERE I GOT THE TEETH FROM. 'SIGN UP WITH SATAN AND GET YOUR TEETH SHARPENED FOR FREE!'
ALRIGHT, THAT'S IT!
I CAN'T TAKE ANY MORE OF YOUR BLASPHEMY AND SARCASM... I'M OFF!
I KNOW, I CAN SMELL YOU FROM HERE.
AND DON'T FORGET - THIS COUNTRY WAS BUILT ON BLASPHEMY AND SARCASM!

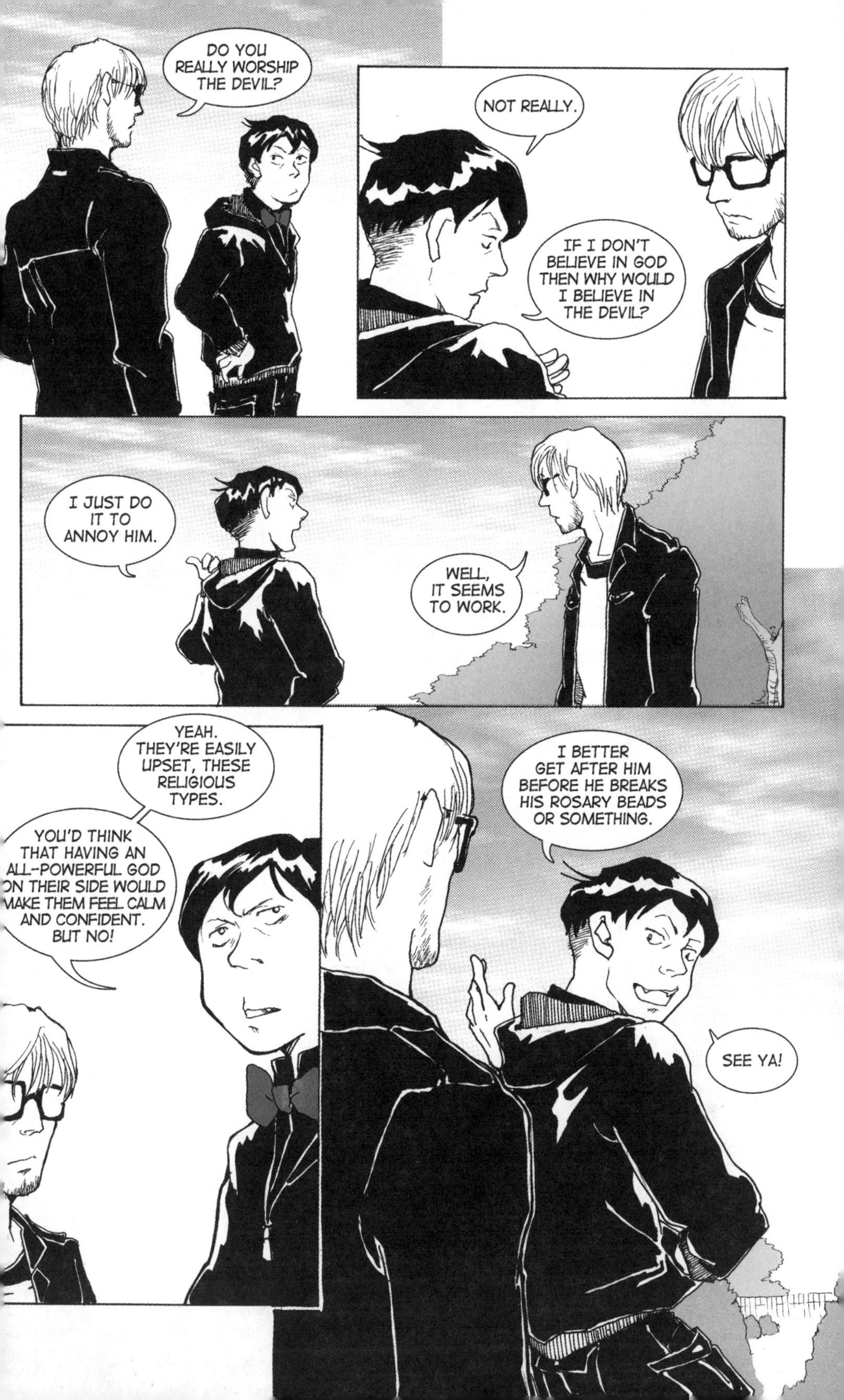
DO YOU REALLY WORSHIP THE DEVIL?
NOT REALLY.
IF I DON'T BELIEVE IN GOD THEN WHY WOULD I BELIEVE IN THE DEVIL?
I JUST DO IT TO ANNOY HIM.
WELL, IT SEEMS TO WORK.
YEAH. THEY'RE EASILY UPSET, THESE RELIGIOUS TYPES.
YOU'D THINK THAT HAVING AN ALL-POWERFUL GOD ON THEIR SIDE WOULD MAKE THEM FEEL CALM AND CONFIDENT. BUT NO!
I BETTER GET AFTER HIM BEFORE HE BREAKS HIS ROSARY BEADS OR SOMETHING.
SEE YA!

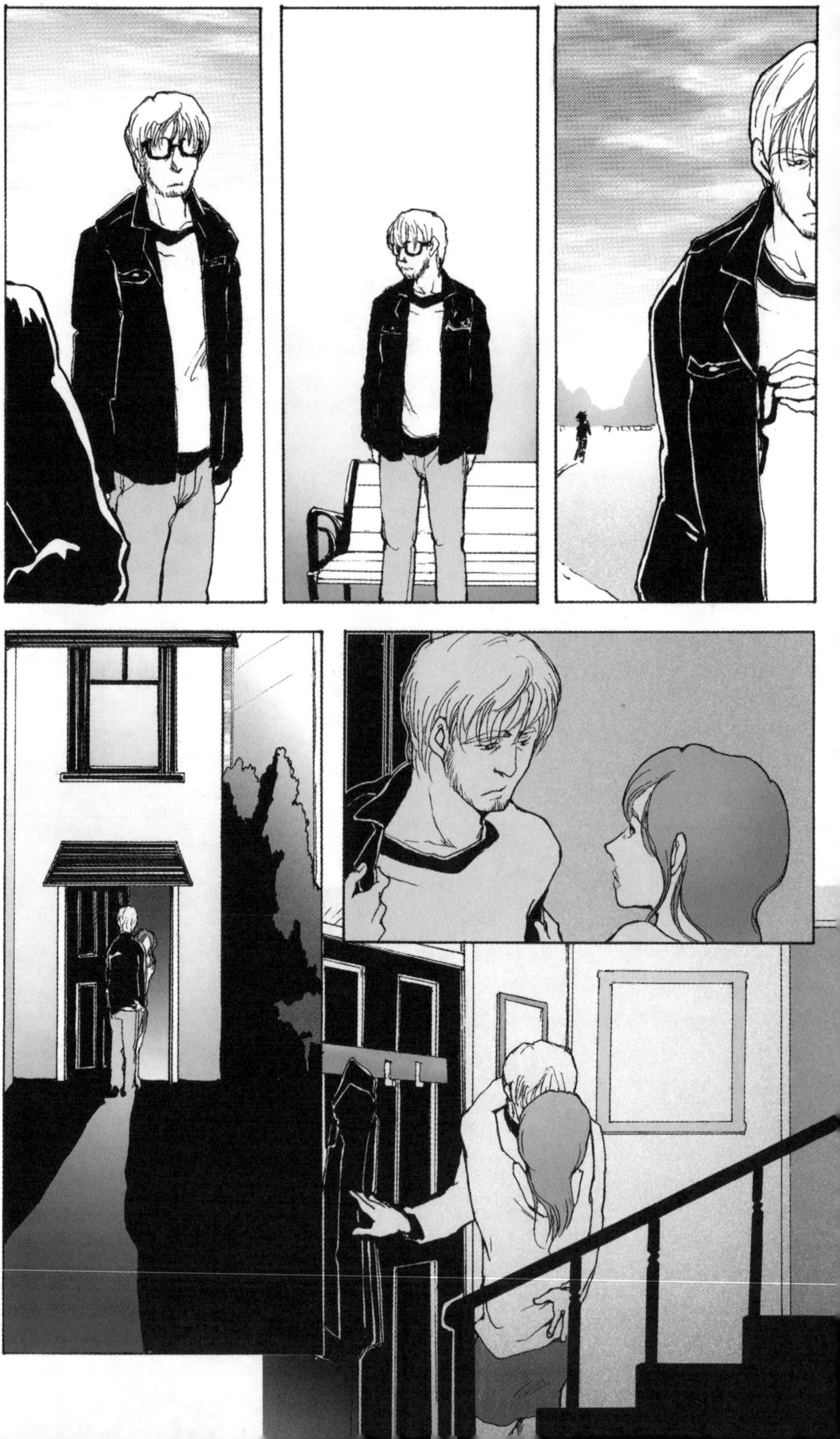

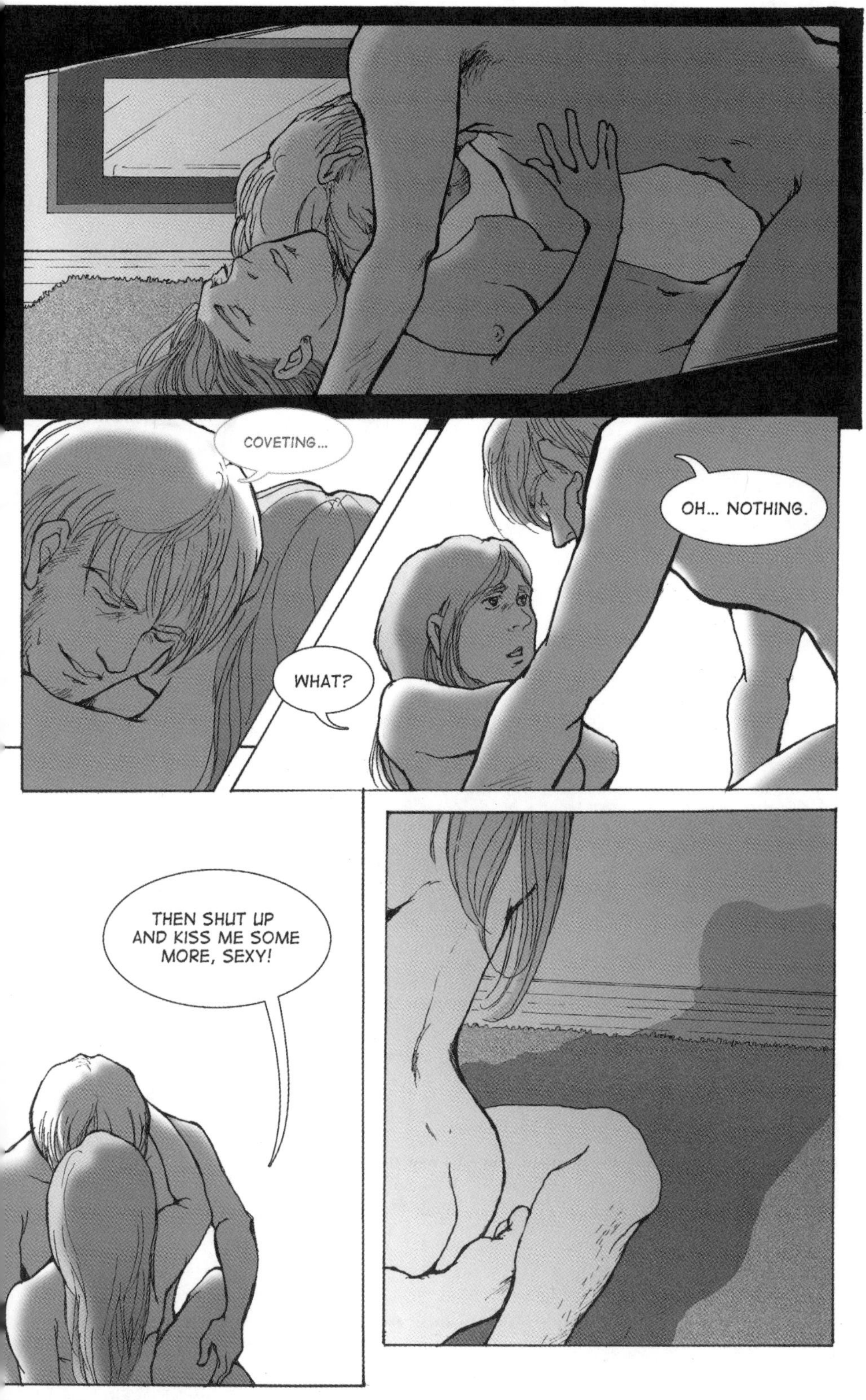
COVETING...
OH... NOTHING.
WHAT?
THEN SHUT UP AND KISS ME SOME MORE, SEXY!

Chapter 4

'Thou shalt not make for yourself a graven image.'

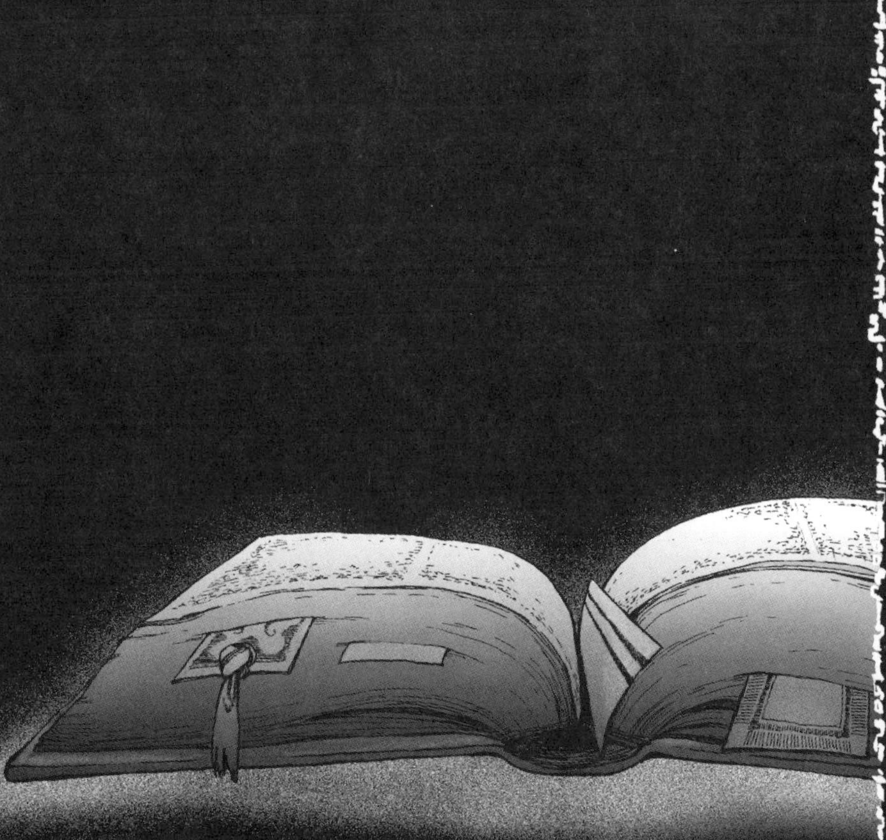

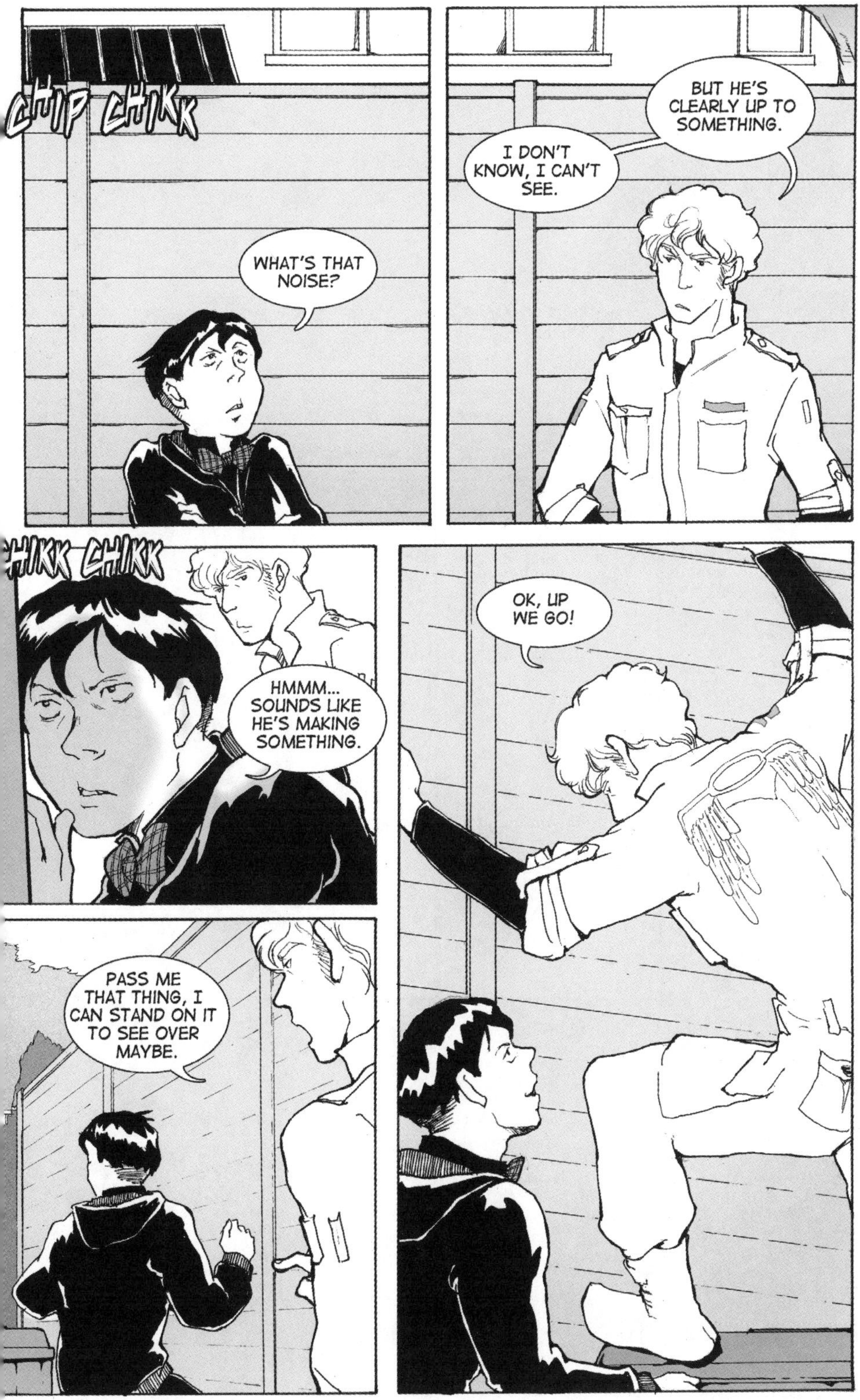
CHIP CHIKK
WHAT'S THAT NOISE?
I DON'T KNOW, I CAN'T SEE.
BUT HE'S CLEARLY UP TO SOMETHING.
CHIKK CHIKK
HMMM... SOUNDS LIKE HE'S MAKING SOMETHING.
OK, UP WE GO!
PASS ME THAT THING, I CAN STAND ON IT TO SEE OVER MAYBE.

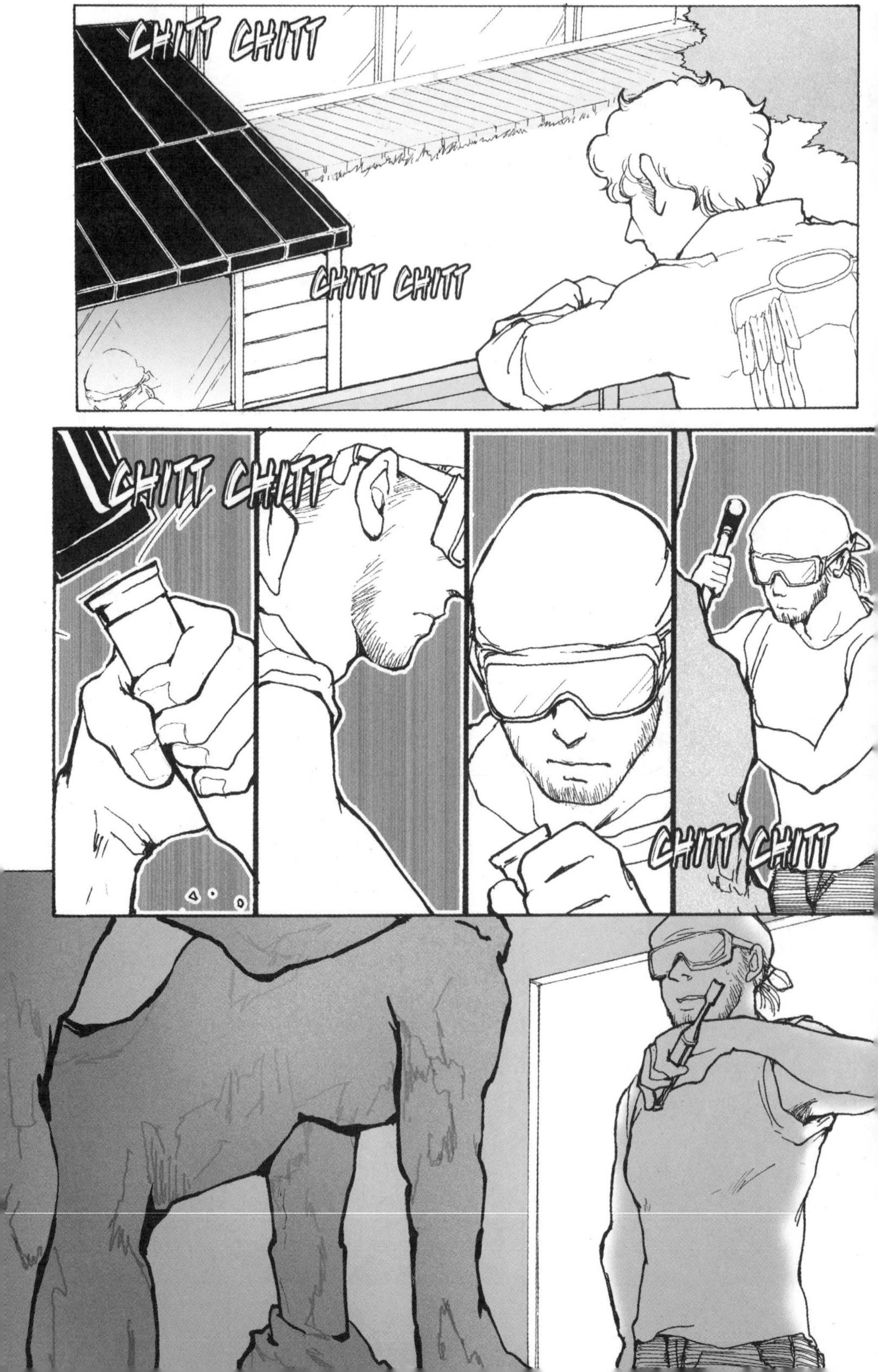
CHITT CHITT
CHITT CHITT
CHITT CHITT
CHITT CHITT

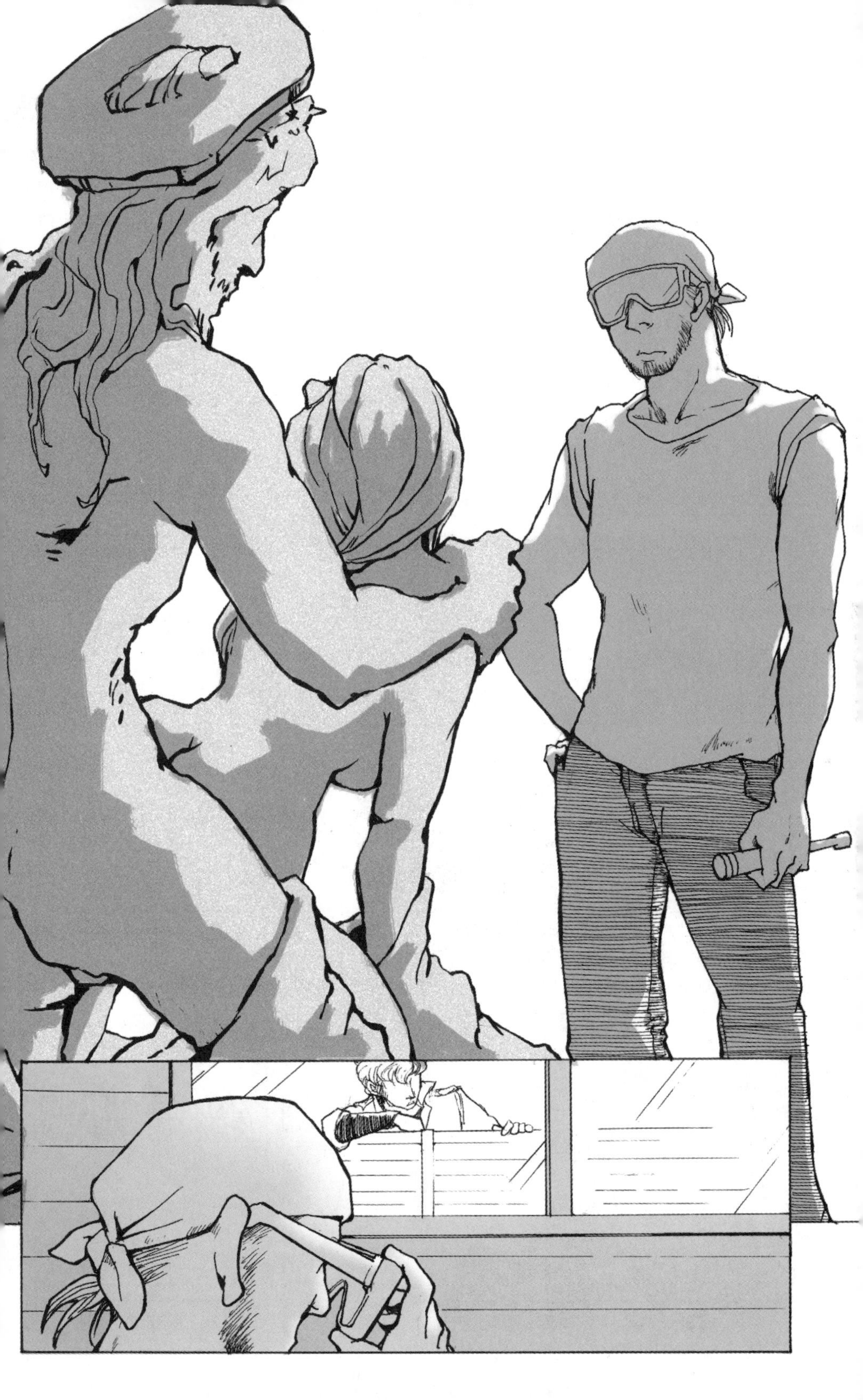

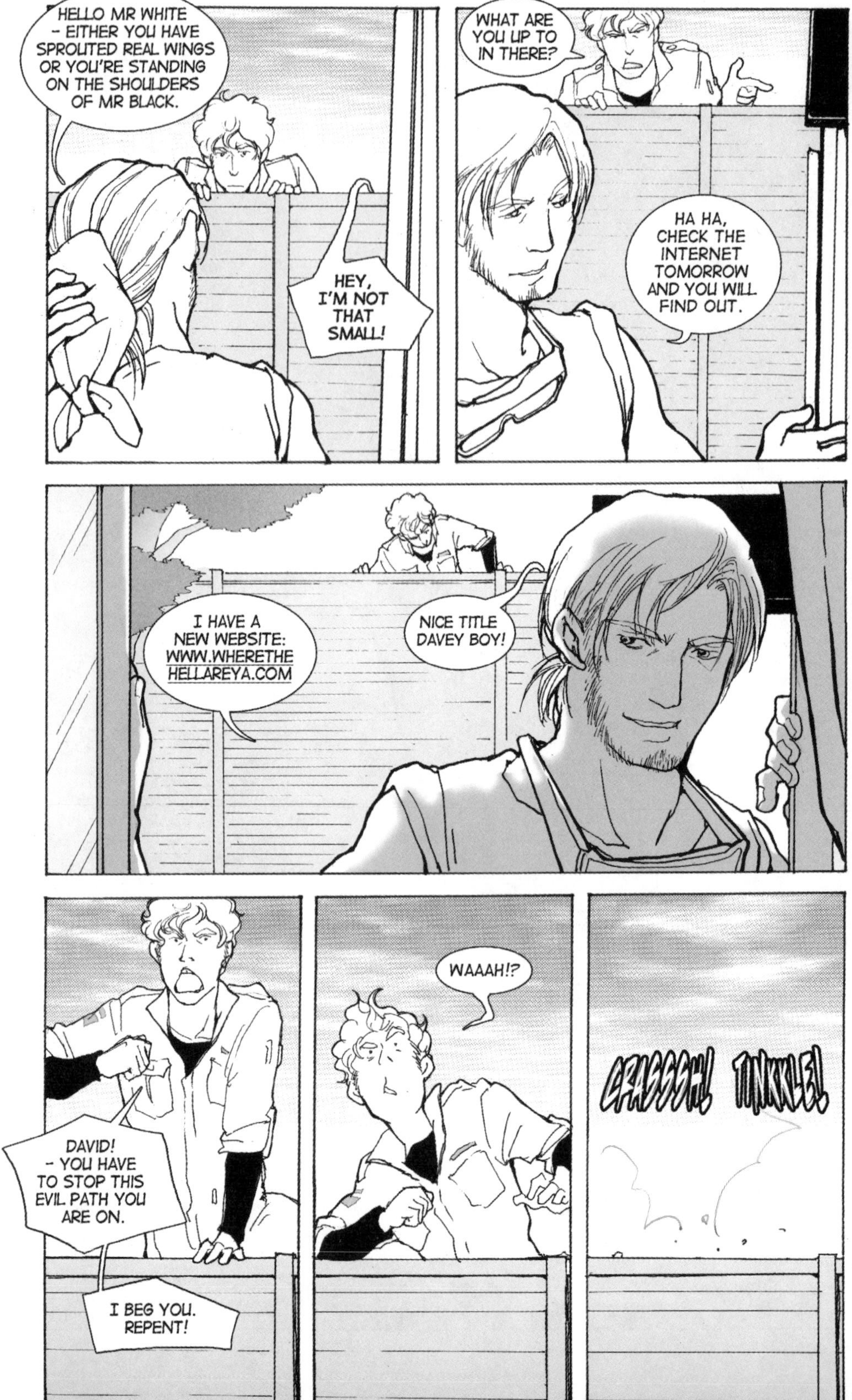
HELLO MR WHITE - EITHER YOU HAVE SPROUTED REAL WINGS OR YOU'RE STANDING ON THE SHOULDERS OF MR BLACK.
HEY, I'M NOT THAT SMALL!
WHAT ARE YOU UP TO IN THERE?
HA HA, CHECK THE INTERNET TOMORROW AND YOU WILL FIND OUT.
I HAVE A NEW WEBSITE: WWW.WHERETHEHELLAREYA.COM
NICE TITLE DAVEY BOY!
DAVID! - YOU HAVE TO STOP THIS EVIL PATH YOU ARE ON.
I BEG YOU. REPENT!
WAAAH!?
CRASSSH! TINKKLE!

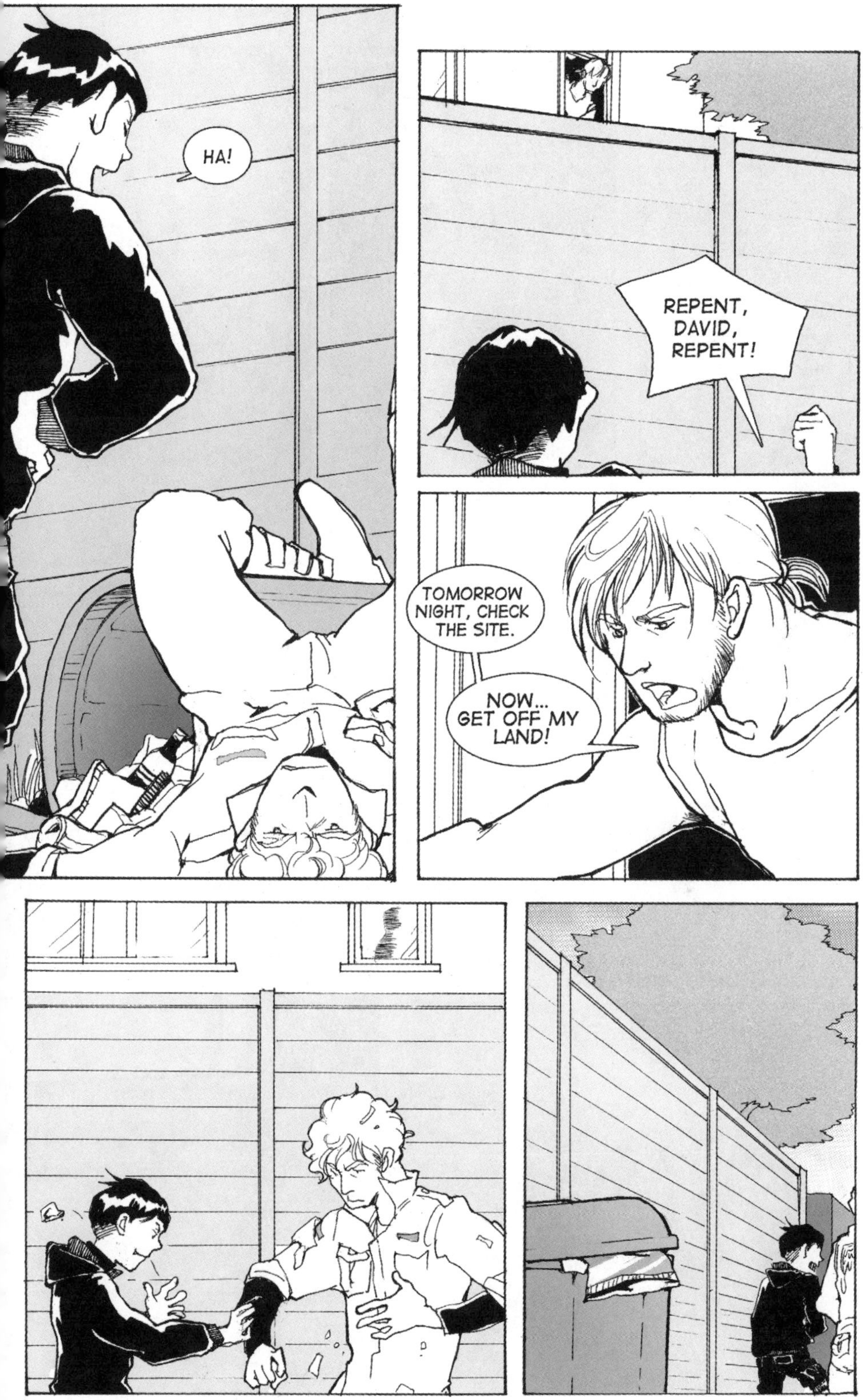
HA!
REPENT, DAVID, REPENT!
TOMORROW NIGHT, CHECK THE SITE.
NOW... GET OFF MY LAND!

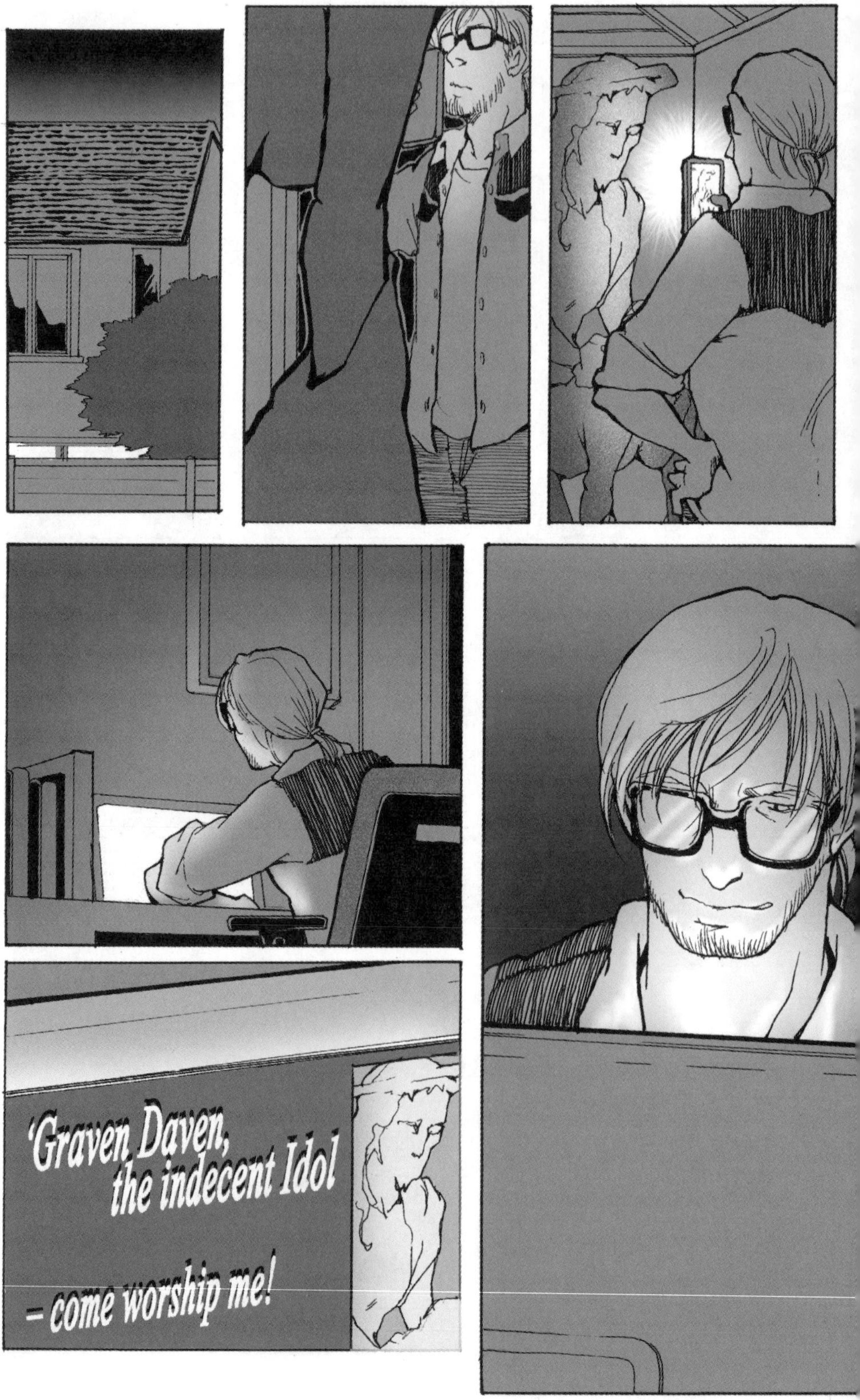
'Graven Daven,
the indecent Idol
– come worship me!

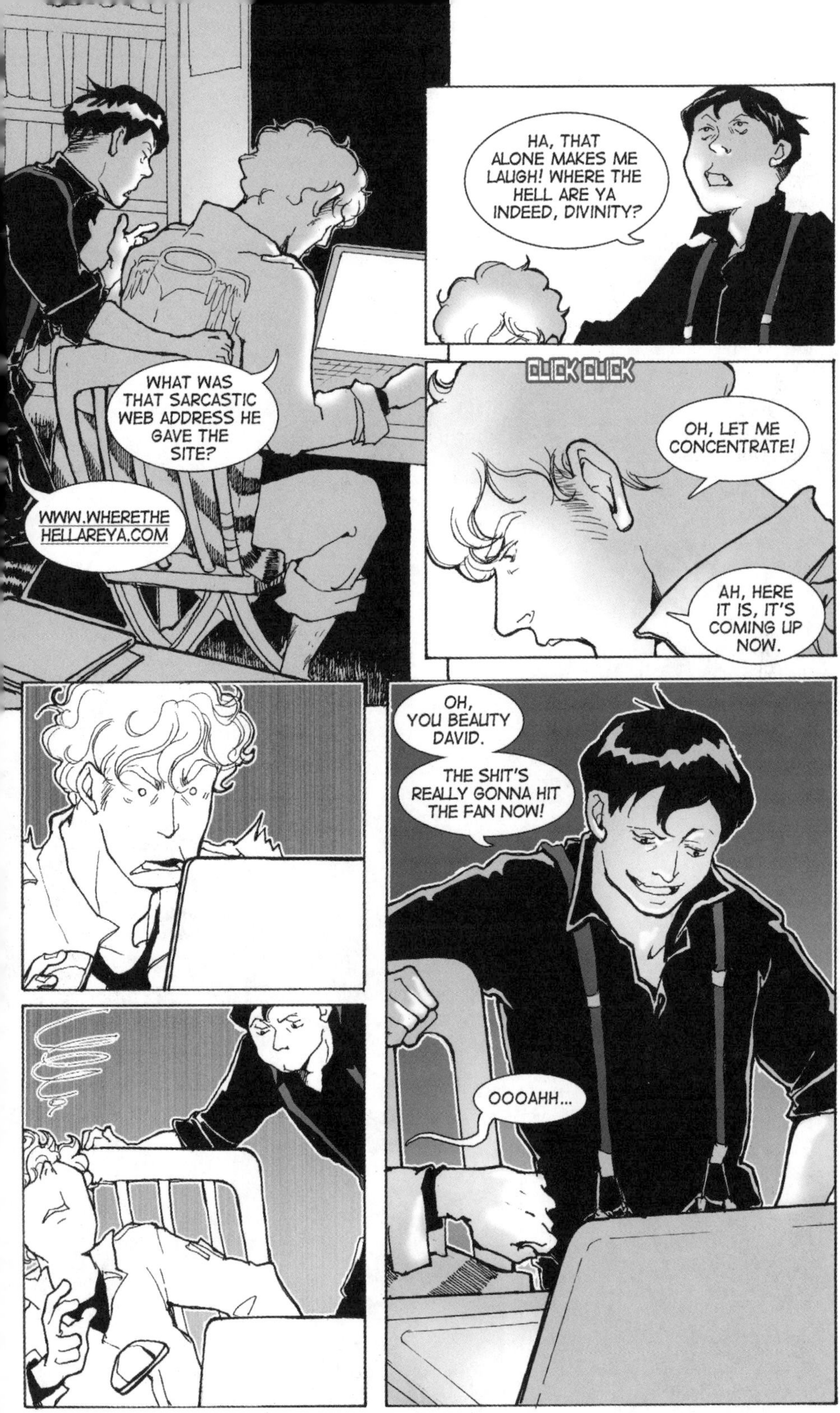
WHAT WAS THAT SARCASTIC WEB ADDRESS HE GAVE THE SITE?
WWW.WHERETHEHELLAREYA.COM
HA, THAT ALONE MAKES ME LAUGH! WHERE THE HELL ARE YA INDEED, DIVINITY?
CLICK CLICK
OH, LET ME CONCENTRATE!
AH, HERE IT IS, IT'S COMING UP NOW.
OH, YOU BEAUTY DAVID.
THE SHIT'S REALLY GONNA HIT THE FAN NOW!
OOOAHH...

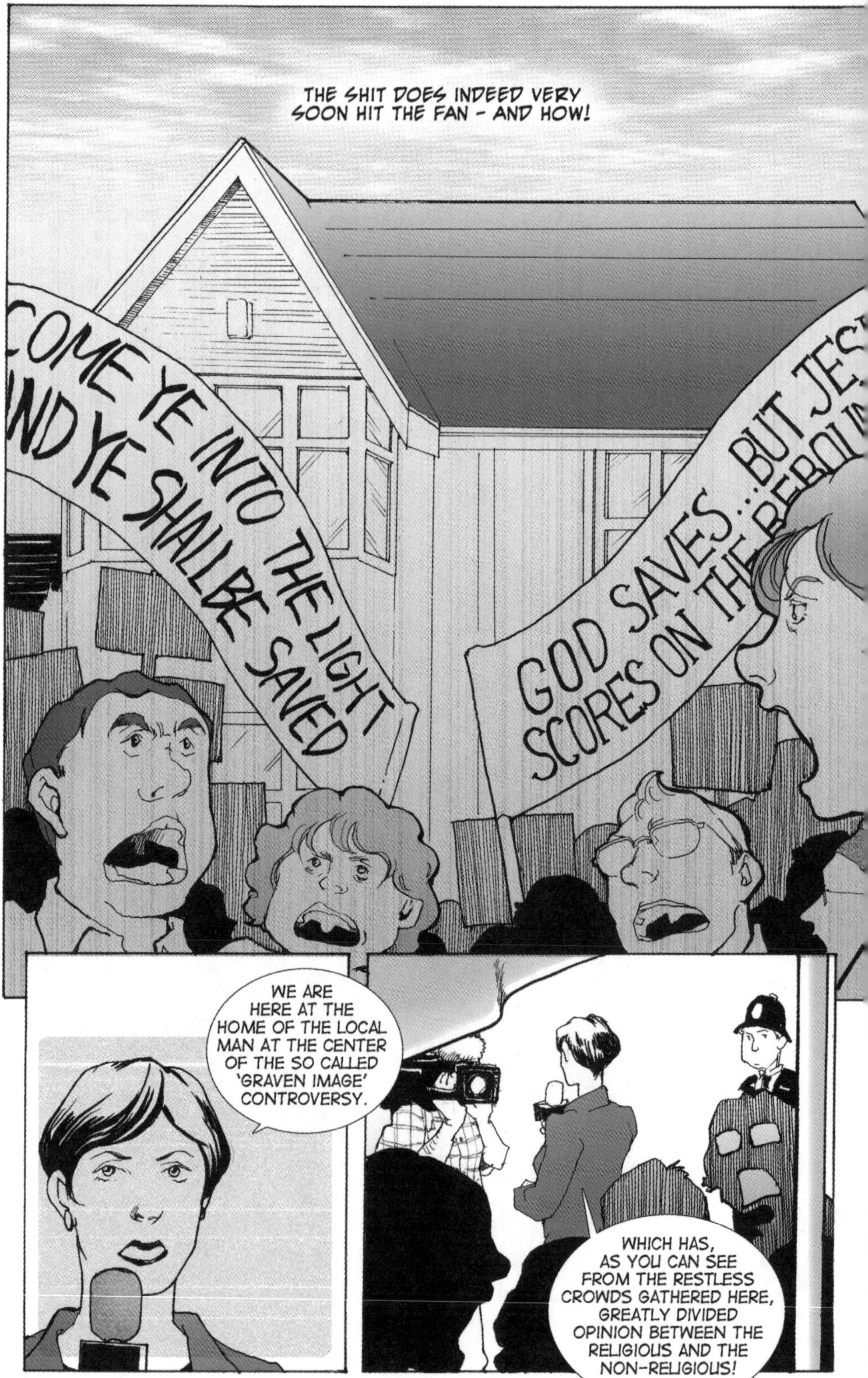

THE SHIT DOES INDEED VERY SOON HIT THE FAN - AND HOW!
COME YE INTO THE LIGHT
YE SHALLBE SAVED
GOD SAVES...
SCORES ON THE
WE ARE HERE AT THE HOME OF THE LOCAL MAN AT THE CENTER OF THE SO CALLED 'GRAVEN IMAGE' CONTROVERSY.
WHICH HAS, AS YOU CAN SEE FROM THE RESTLESS CROWDS GATHERED HERE, GREATLY DIVIDED OPINION BETWEEN THE RELIGIOUS AND THE NON-RELIGIOUS!

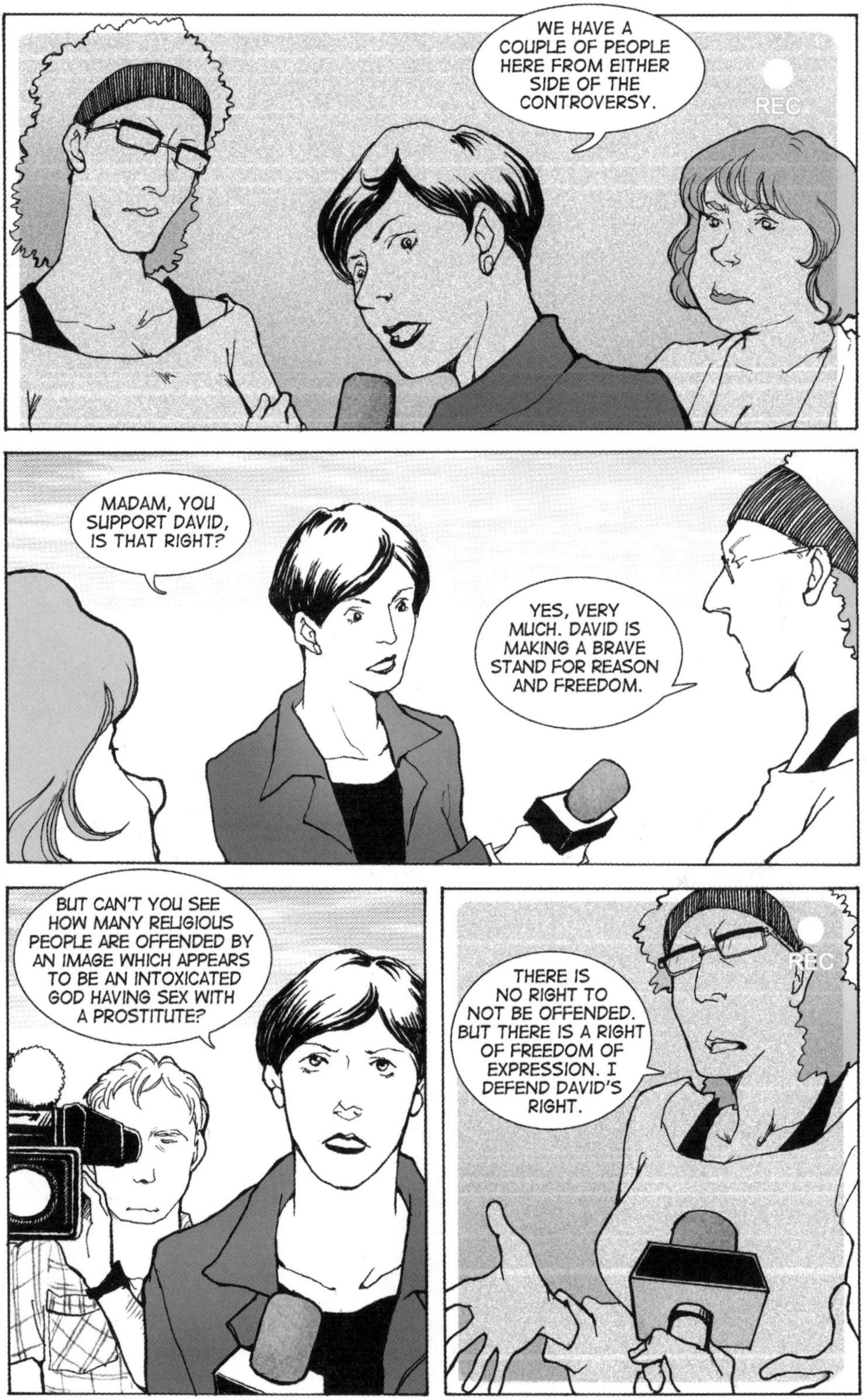
WE HAVE A COUPLE OF PEOPLE HERE FROM EITHER SIDE OF THE CONTROVERSY.
REC
MADAM, YOU SUPPORT DAVID, IS THAT RIGHT?
YES, VERY MUCH. DAVID IS MAKING A BRAVE STAND FOR REASON AND FREEDOM.
BUT CAN'T YOU SEE HOW MANY RELIGIOUS PEOPLE ARE OFFENDED BY AN IMAGE WHICH APPEARS TO BE AN INTOXICATED GOD HAVING SEX WITH A PROSTITUTE?
REC
THERE IS NO RIGHT TO NOT BE OFFENDED. BUT THERE IS A RIGHT OF FREEDOM OF EXPRESSION. I DEFEND DAVID'S RIGHT.

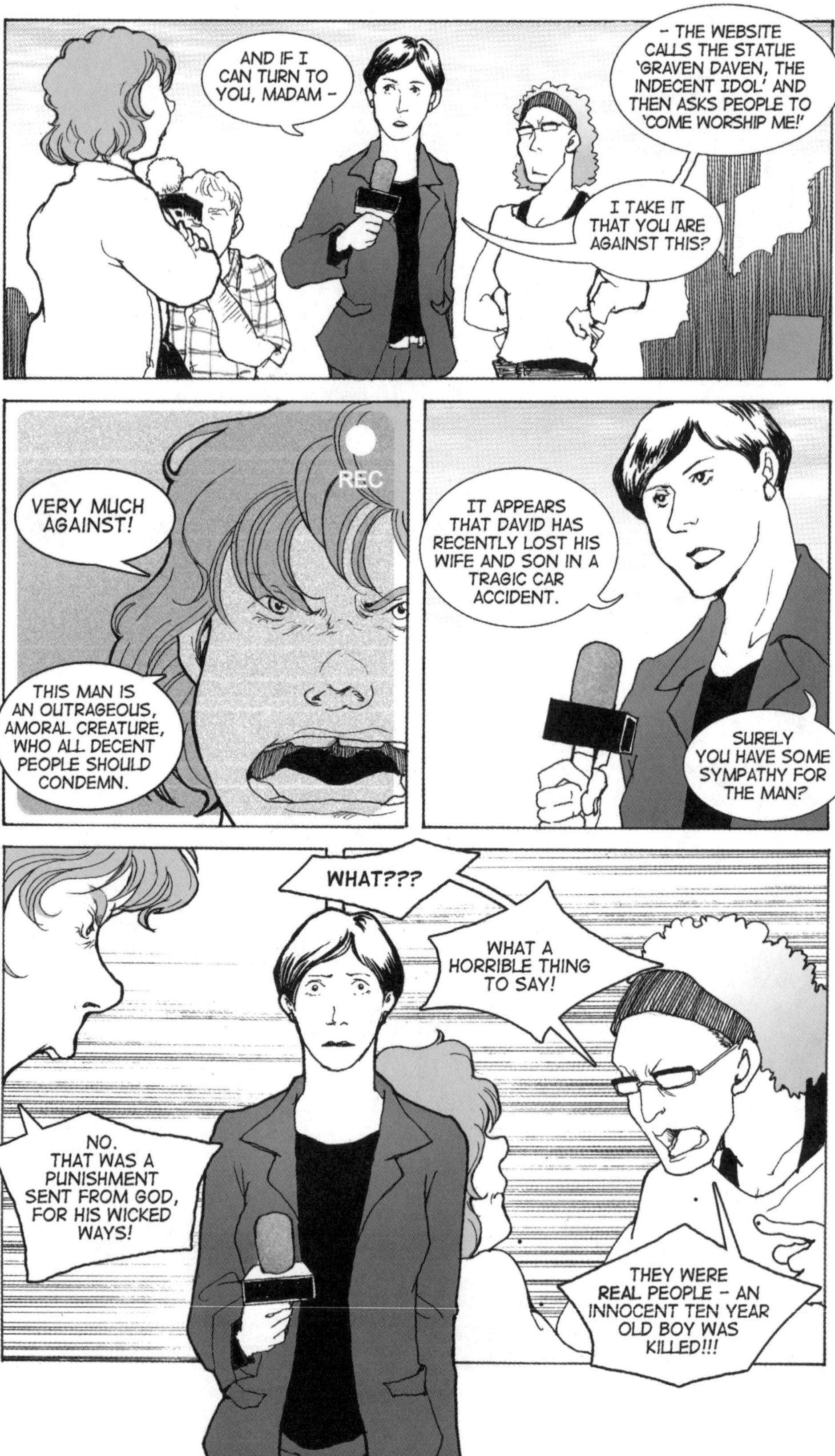
AND IF I CAN TURN TO YOU, MADAM -
- THE WEBSITE CALLS THE STATUE 'GRAVEN DAVEN, THE INDECENT IDOL' AND THEN ASKS PEOPLE TO 'COME WORSHIP ME!'
I TAKE IT THAT YOU ARE AGAINST THIS?
REC
VERY MUCH AGAINST!
THIS MAN IS AN OUTRAGEOUS, AMORAL CREATURE, WHO ALL DECENT PEOPLE SHOULD CONDEMN.
IT APPEARS THAT DAVID HAS RECENTLY LOST HIS WIFE AND SON IN A TRAGIC CAR ACCIDENT.
SURELY YOU HAVE SOME SYMPATHY FOR THE MAN?
WHAT???
WHAT A HORRIBLE THING TO SAY!
NO. THAT WAS A PUNISHMENT SENT FROM GOD, FOR HIS WICKED WAYS!
THEY WERE REAL PEOPLE - AN INNOCENT TEN YEAR OLD BOY WAS KILLED!!!

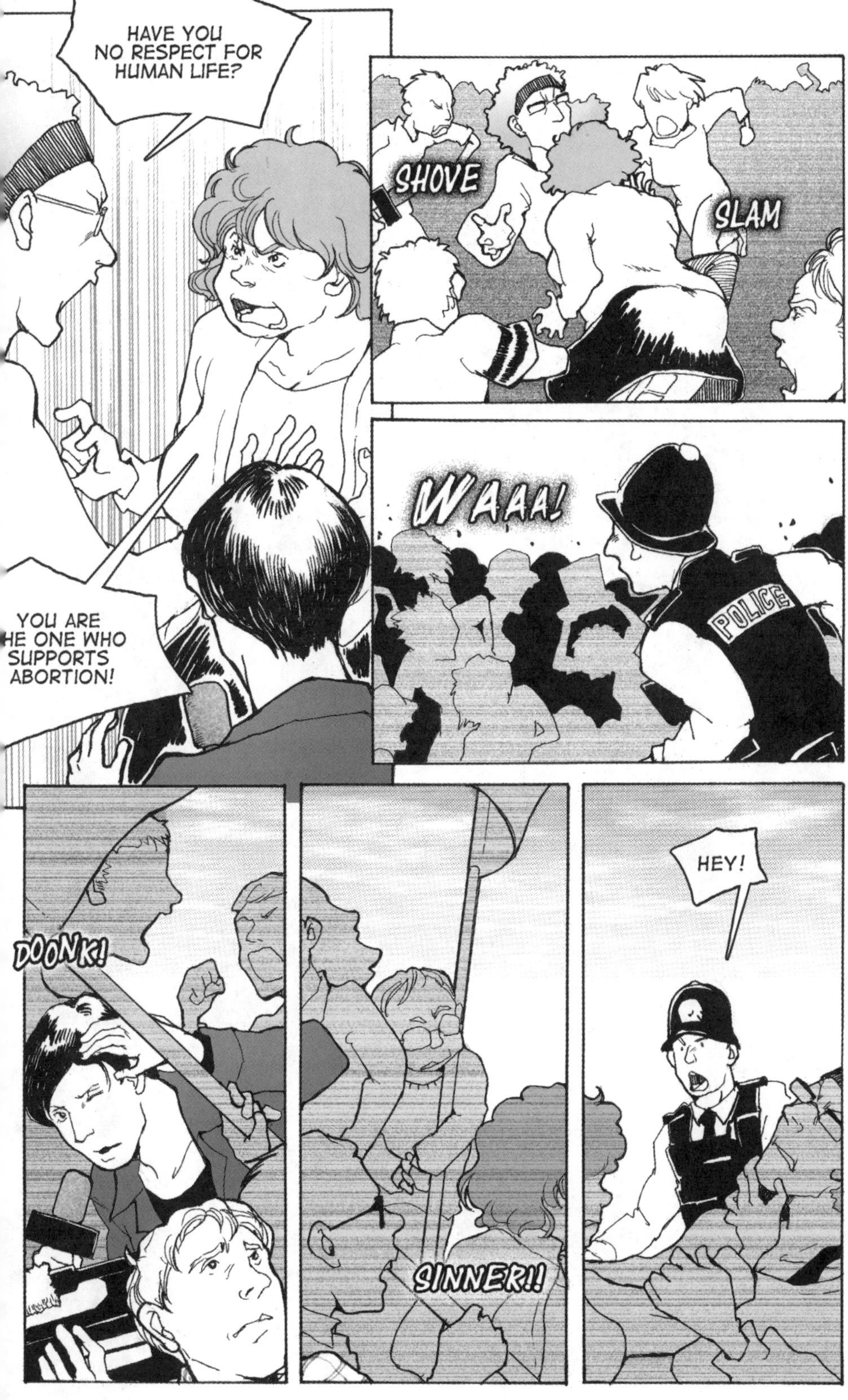
HAVE YOU NO RESPECT FOR HUMAN LIFE?
YOU ARE HE ONE WHO SUPPORTS ABORTION!
SHOVE
SLAM
WAAA!
POLICE
DOONK!
SINNER!!
HEY!

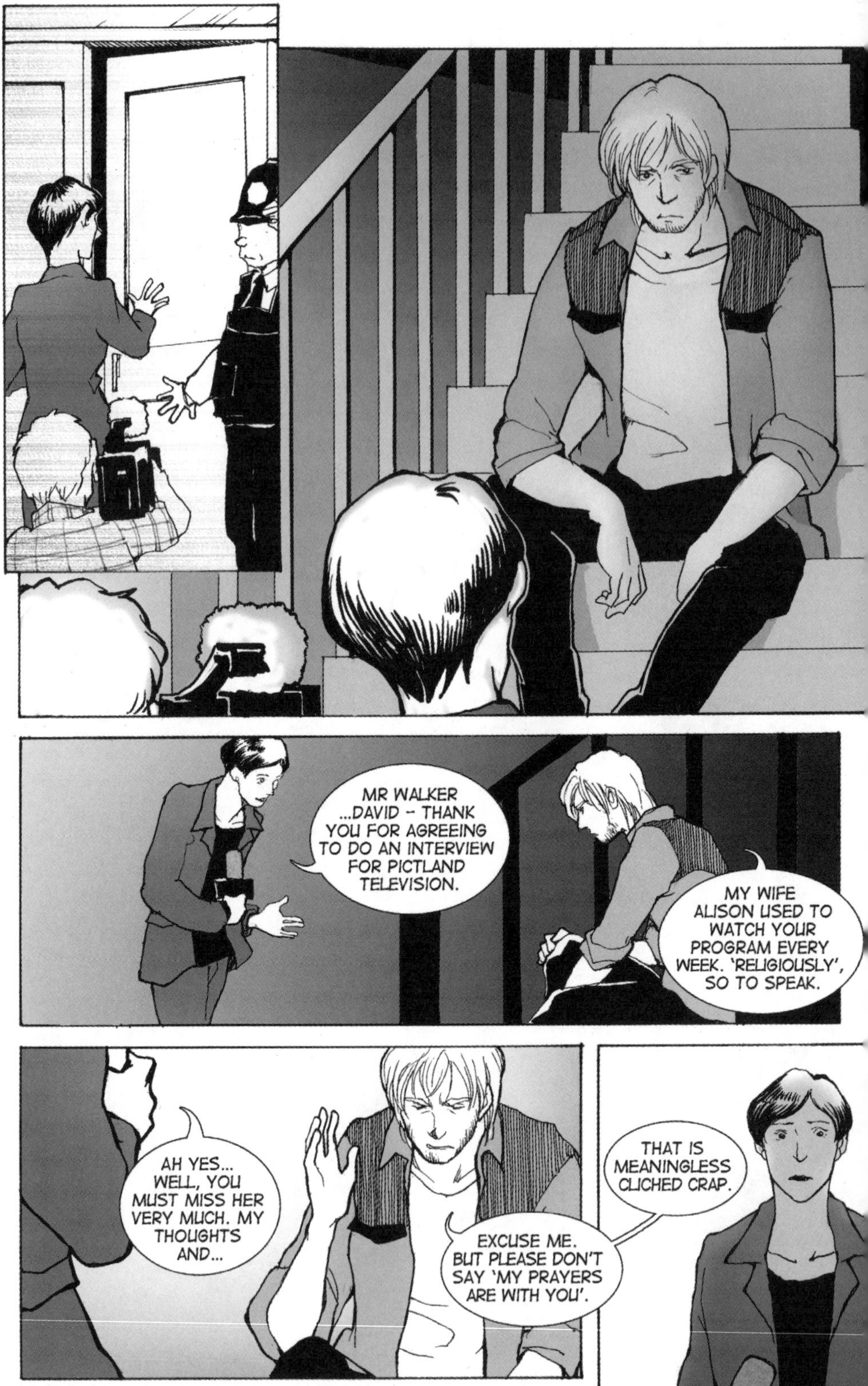
MR WALKER ...DAVID – THANK YOU FOR AGREEING TO DO AN INTERVIEW FOR PICTLAND TELEVISION.
MY WIFE ALISON USED TO WATCH YOUR PROGRAM EVERY WEEK. 'RELIGIOUSLY', SO TO SPEAK.
AH YES... WELL, YOU MUST MISS HER VERY MUCH. MY THOUGHTS AND...
EXCUSE ME. BUT PLEASE DON'T SAY 'MY PRAYERS ARE WITH YOU'.
THAT IS MEANINGLESS CLICHED CRAP.

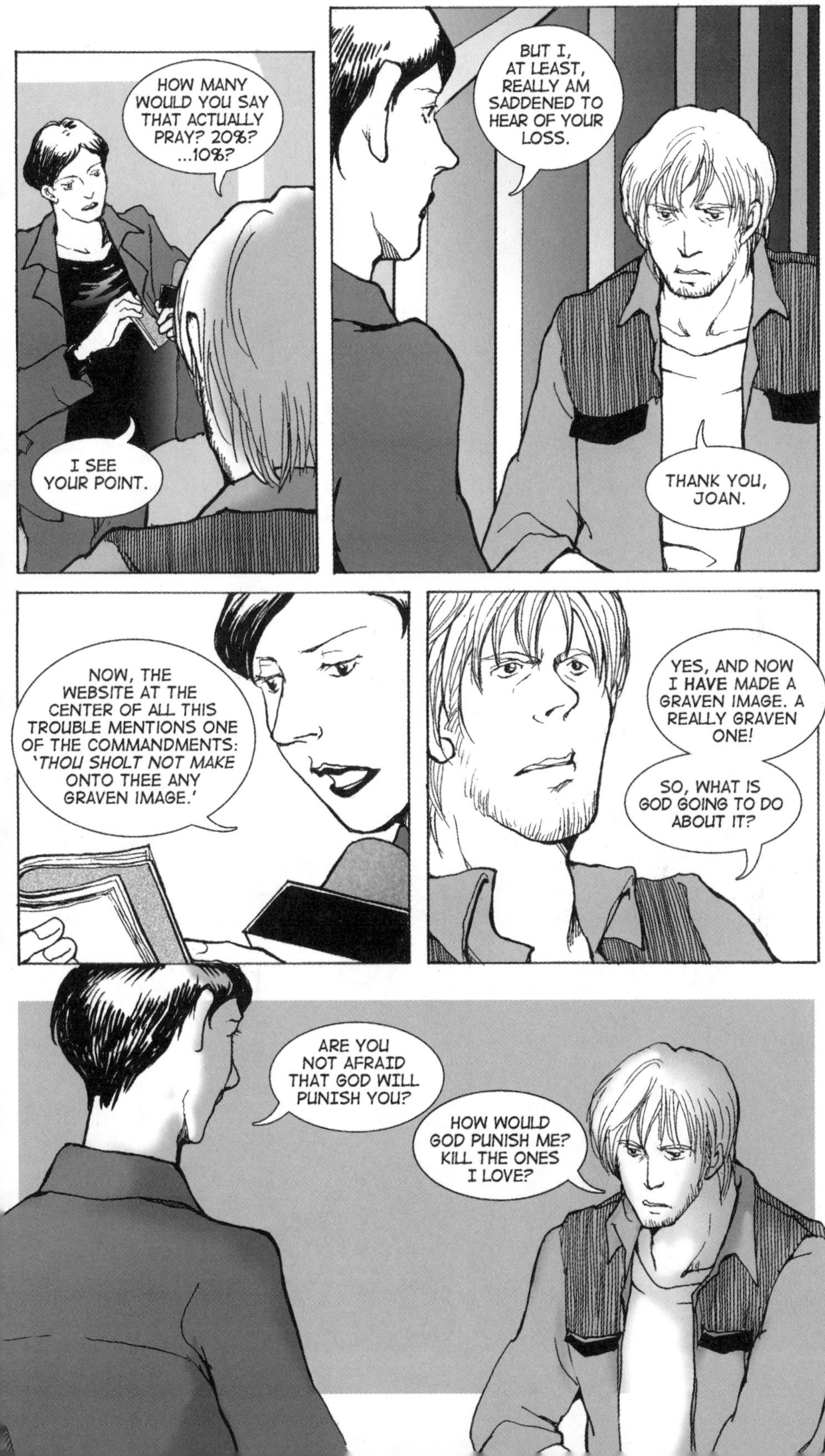
HOW MANY WOULD YOU SAY THAT ACTUALLY PRAY? 20%? ...10%?
I SEE YOUR POINT.
BUT I, AT LEAST, REALLY AM SADDENED TO HEAR OF YOUR LOSS.
THANK YOU, JOAN.
NOW, THE WEBSITE AT THE CENTER OF ALL THIS TROUBLE MENTIONS ONE OF THE COMMANDMENTS: '*THOU SHOLT NOT MAKE ONTO THEE ANY GRAVEN IMAGE.*'
YES, AND NOW I **HAVE** MADE A GRAVEN IMAGE. A REALLY GRAVEN ONE!
SO, WHAT IS GOD GOING TO DO ABOUT IT?
ARE YOU NOT AFRAID THAT GOD WILL PUNISH YOU?
HOW WOULD GOD PUNISH ME? KILL THE ONES I LOVE?

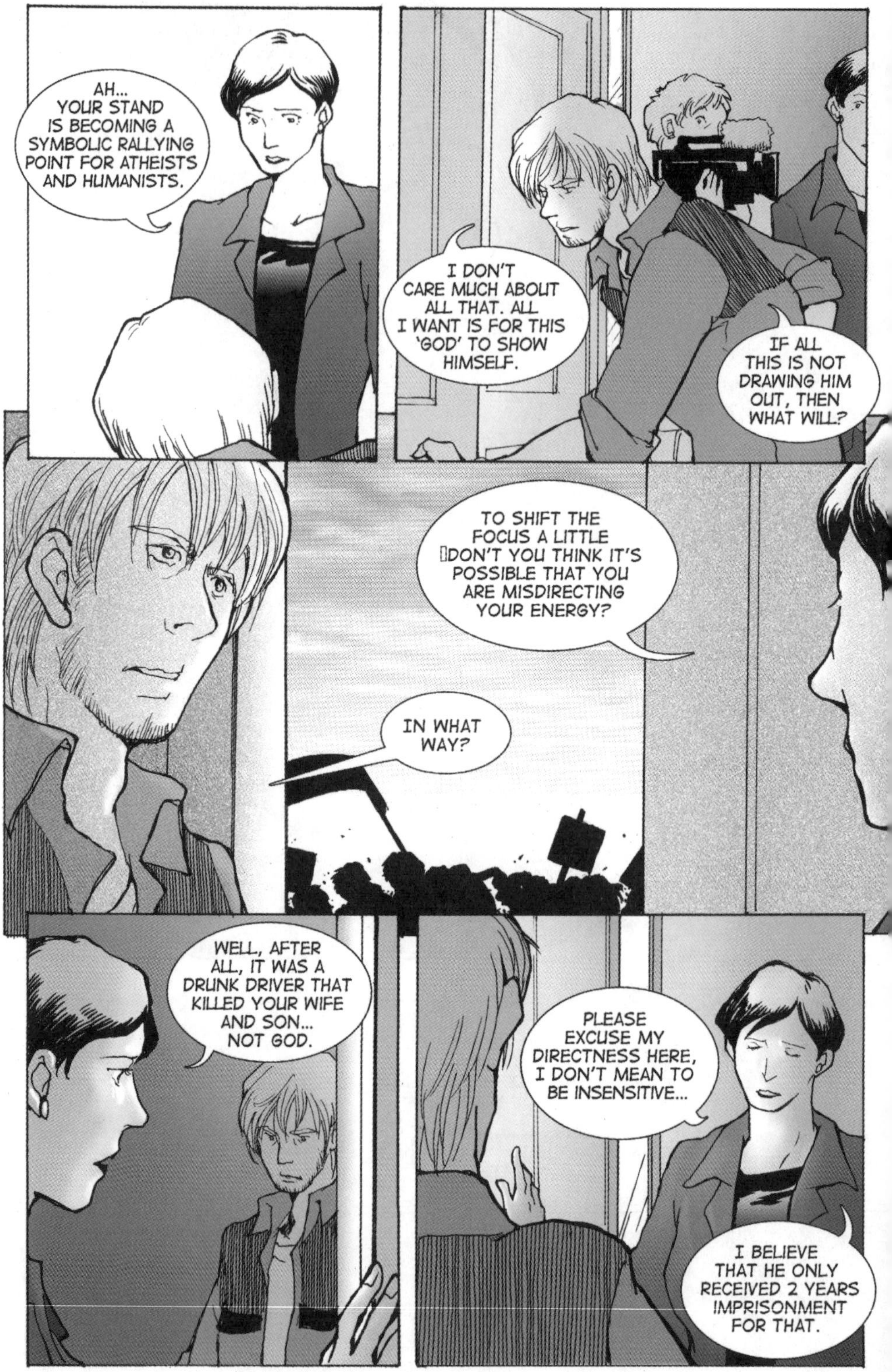
AH... YOUR STAND IS BECOMING A SYMBOLIC RALLYING POINT FOR ATHEISTS AND HUMANISTS.
I DON'T CARE MUCH ABOUT ALL THAT. ALL I WANT IS FOR THIS 'GOD' TO SHOW HIMSELF.
IF ALL THIS IS NOT DRAWING HIM OUT, THEN WHAT WILL?
TO SHIFT THE FOCUS A LITTLE DON'T YOU THINK IT'S POSSIBLE THAT YOU ARE MISDIRECTING YOUR ENERGY?
IN WHAT WAY?
WELL, AFTER ALL, IT WAS A DRUNK DRIVER THAT KILLED YOUR WIFE AND SON... NOT GOD.
PLEASE EXCUSE MY DIRECTNESS HERE, I DON'T MEAN TO BE INSENSITIVE...
I BELIEVE THAT HE ONLY RECEIVED 2 YEARS IMPRISONMENT FOR THAT.

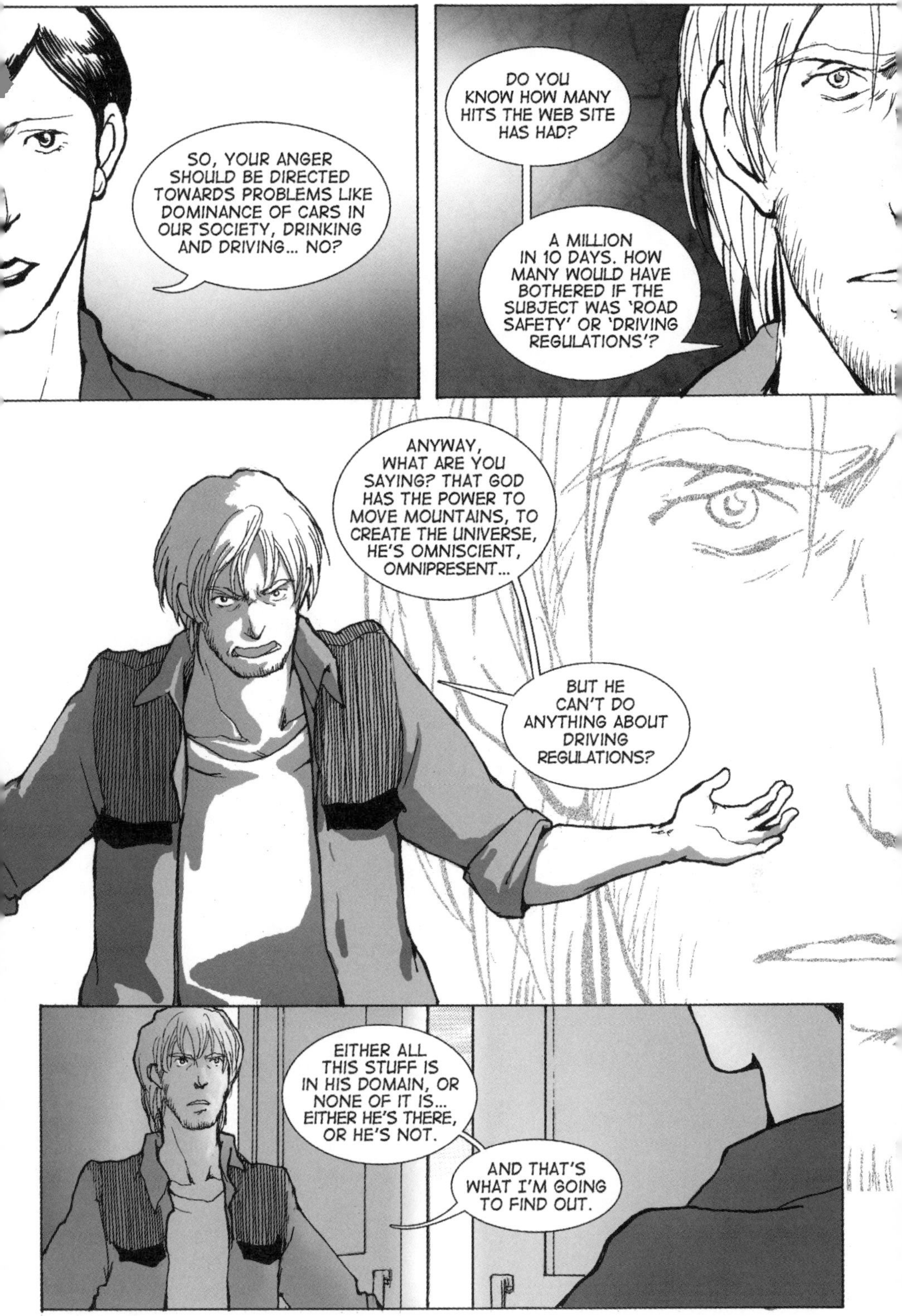

SO, YOUR ANGER SHOULD BE DIRECTED TOWARDS PROBLEMS LIKE DOMINANCE OF CARS IN OUR SOCIETY, DRINKING AND DRIVING... NO?
DO YOU KNOW HOW MANY HITS THE WEB SITE HAS HAD?
A MILLION IN 10 DAYS. HOW MANY WOULD HAVE BOTHERED IF THE SUBJECT WAS 'ROAD SAFETY' OR 'DRIVING REGULATIONS'?
ANYWAY, WHAT ARE YOU SAYING? THAT GOD HAS THE POWER TO MOVE MOUNTAINS, TO CREATE THE UNIVERSE, HE'S OMNISCIENT, OMNIPRESENT...
BUT HE CAN'T DO ANYTHING ABOUT DRIVING REGULATIONS?
EITHER ALL THIS STUFF IS IN HIS DOMAIN, OR NONE OF IT IS... EITHER HE'S THERE, OR HE'S NOT.
AND THAT'S WHAT I'M GOING TO FIND OUT.

Chapter 5

'Thou shalt not bear false witness against your neighbor.'

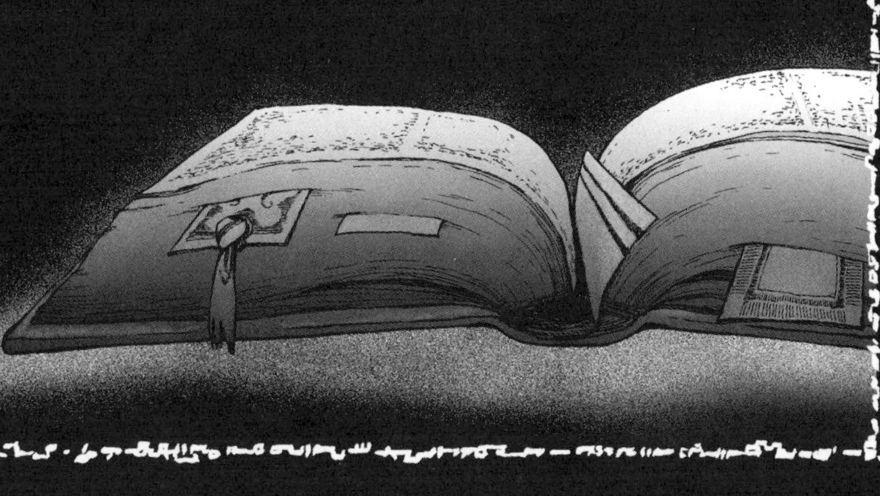

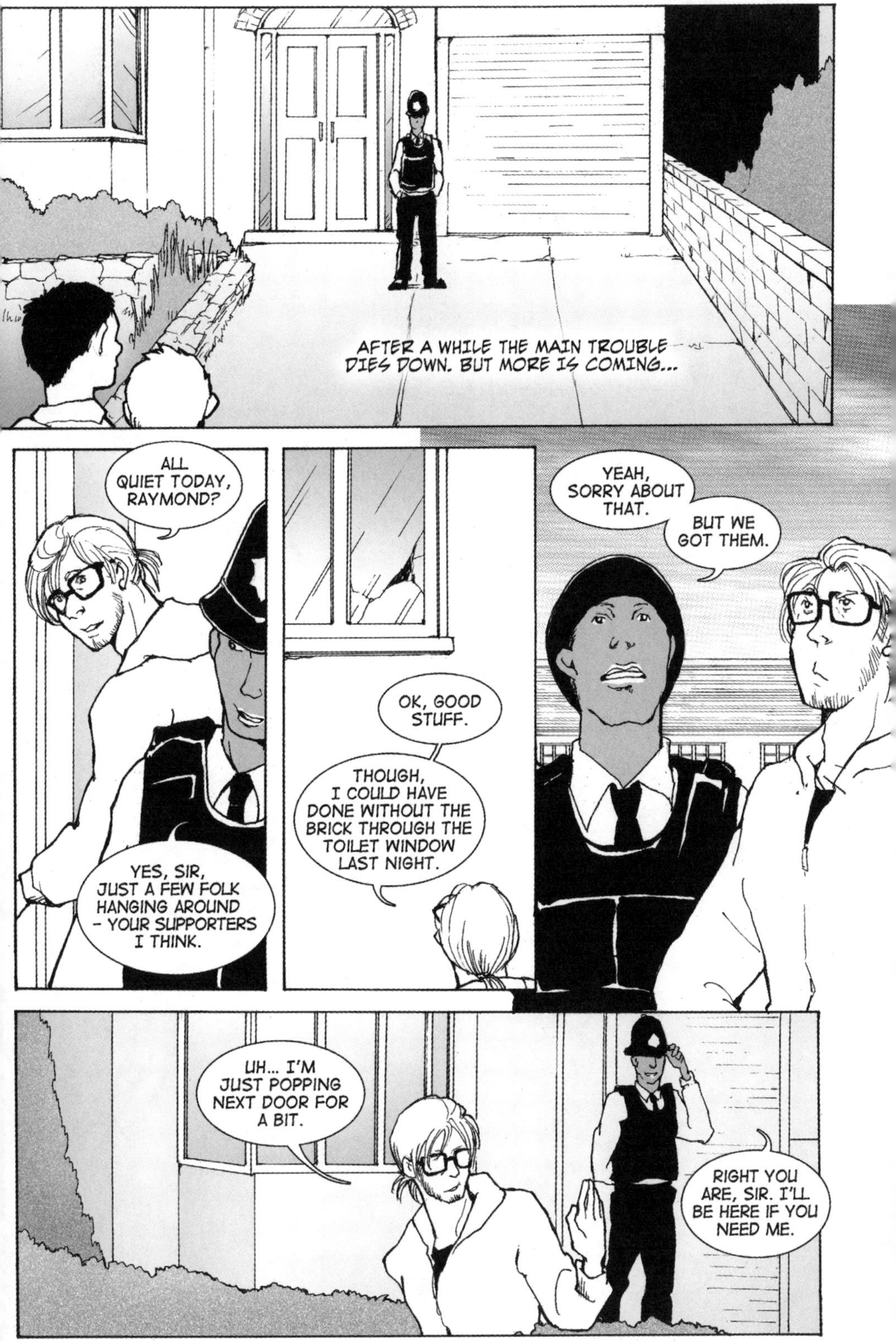
AFTER A WHILE THE MAIN TROUBLE DIES DOWN. BUT MORE IS COMING...
ALL QUIET TODAY, RAYMOND?
YES, SIR, JUST A FEW FOLK HANGING AROUND - YOUR SUPPORTERS I THINK.
OK, GOOD STUFF.
THOUGH, I COULD HAVE DONE WITHOUT THE BRICK THROUGH THE TOILET WINDOW LAST NIGHT.
YEAH, SORRY ABOUT THAT.
BUT WE GOT THEM.
UH... I'M JUST POPPING NEXT DOOR FOR A BIT.
RIGHT YOU ARE, SIR. I'LL BE HERE IF YOU NEED ME.

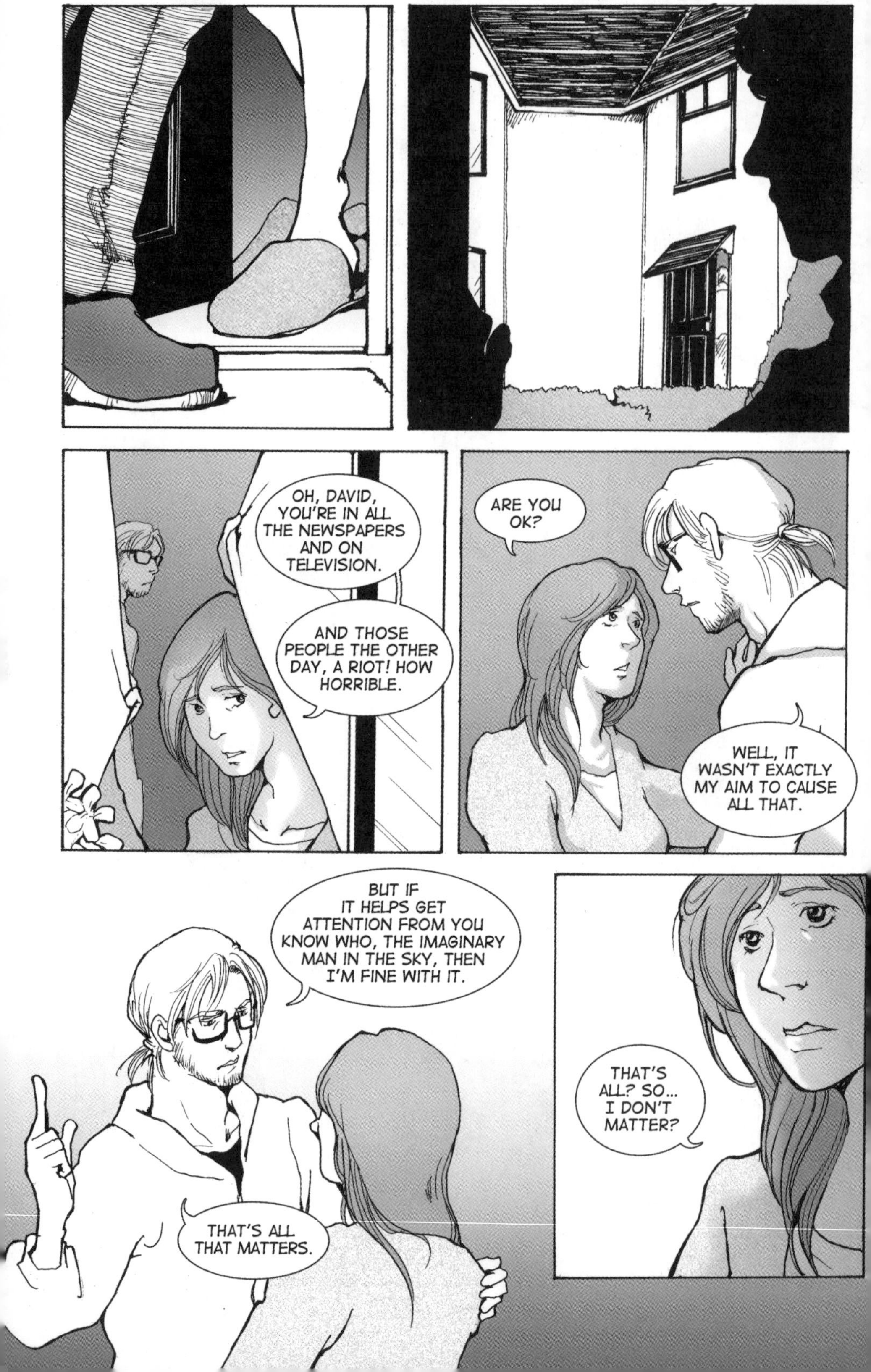
OH, DAVID, YOU'RE IN ALL THE NEWSPAPERS AND ON TELEVISION.
AND THOSE PEOPLE THE OTHER DAY, A RIOT! HOW HORRIBLE.
ARE YOU OK?
WELL, IT WASN'T EXACTLY MY AIM TO CAUSE ALL THAT.
BUT IF IT HELPS GET ATTENTION FROM YOU KNOW WHO, THE IMAGINARY MAN IN THE SKY, THEN I'M FINE WITH IT.
THAT'S ALL THAT MATTERS.
THAT'S ALL? SO... I DON'T MATTER?

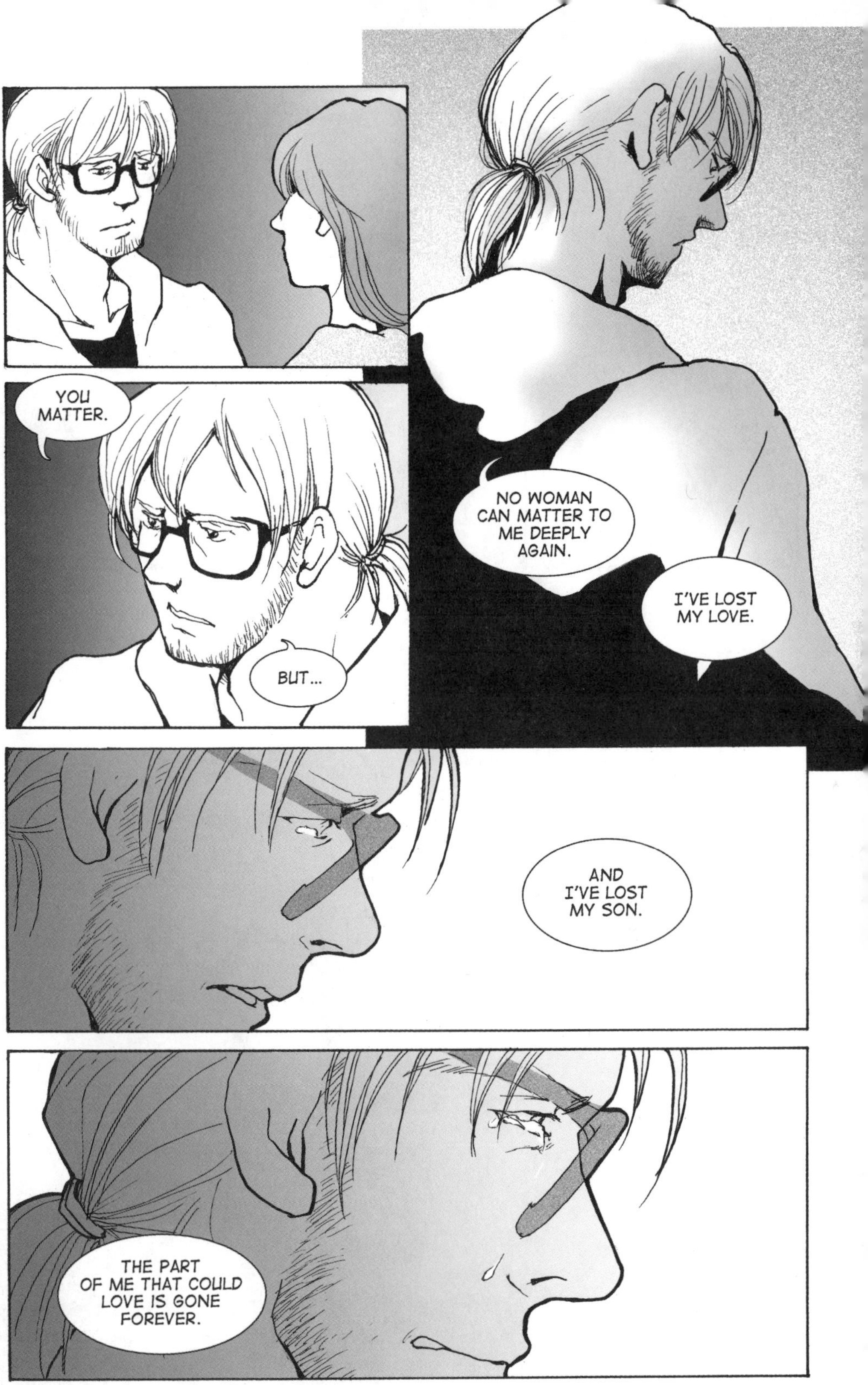
YOU MATTER.
BUT...
NO WOMAN CAN MATTER TO ME DEEPLY AGAIN.
I'VE LOST MY LOVE.
AND I'VE LOST MY SON.
THE PART OF ME THAT COULD LOVE IS GONE FOREVER.

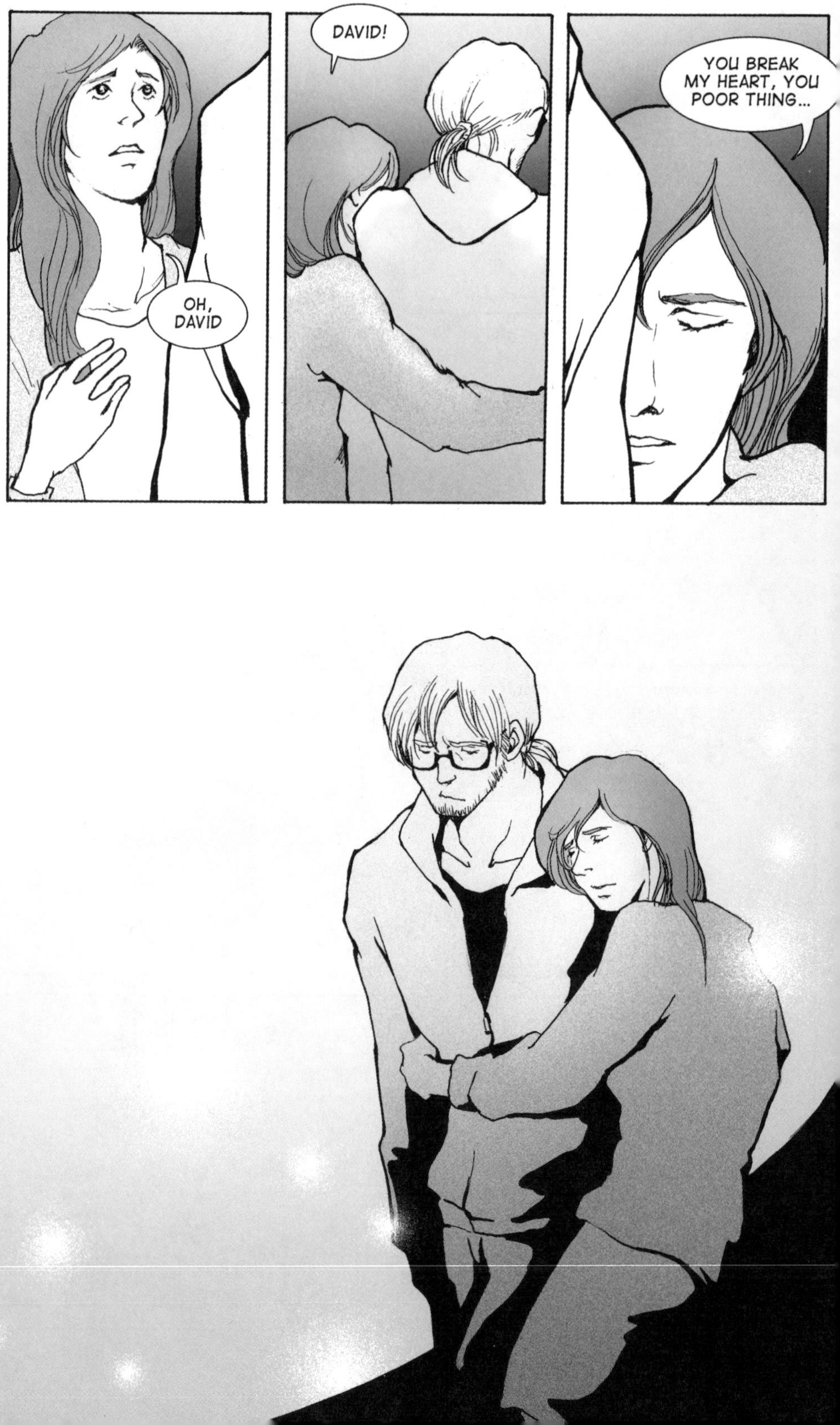
OH, DAVID
DAVID!
YOU BREAK MY HEART, YOU POOR THING...

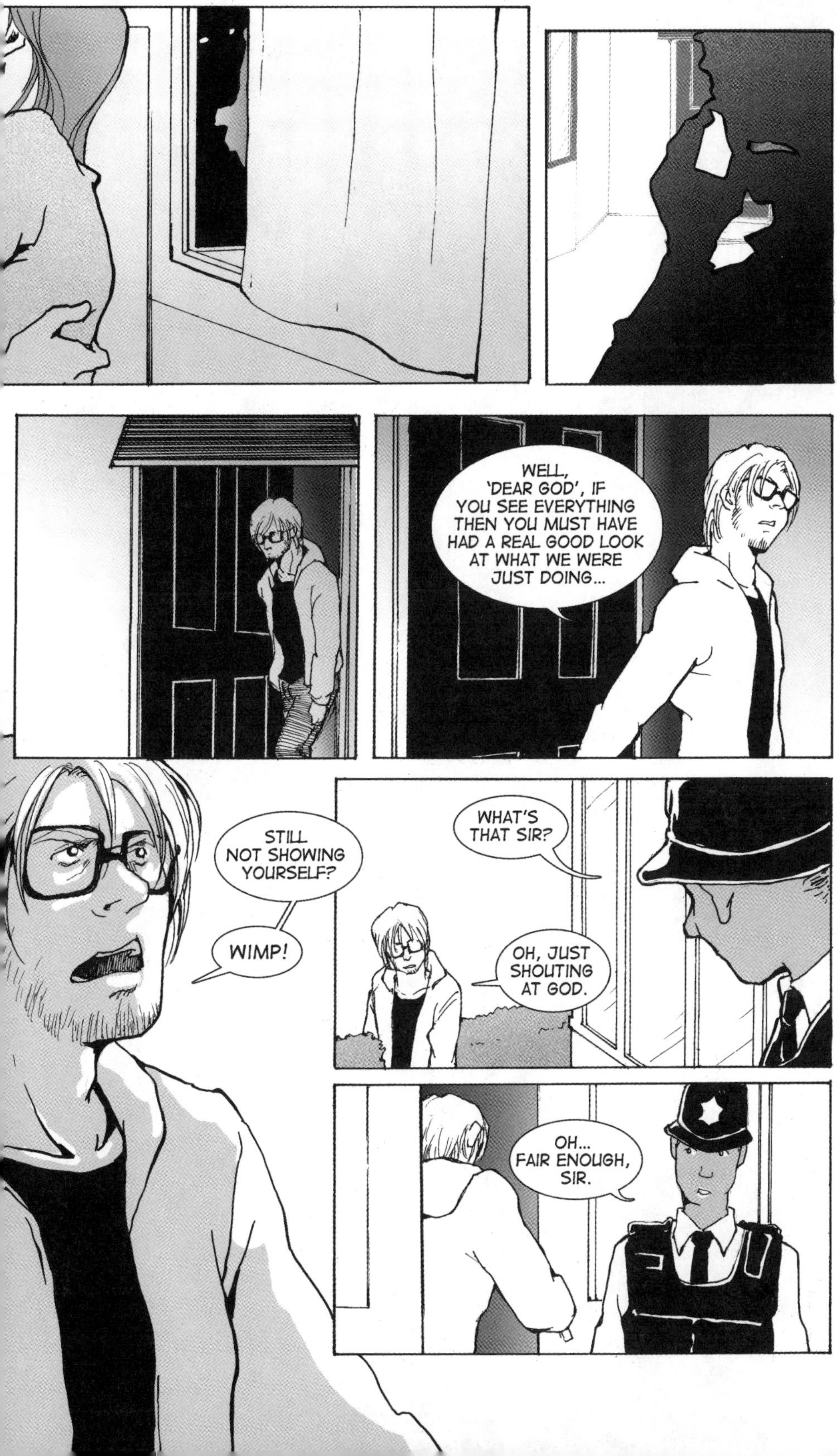

WELL, 'DEAR GOD', IF YOU SEE EVERYTHING THEN YOU MUST HAVE HAD A REAL GOOD LOOK AT WHAT WE WERE JUST DOING...
STILL NOT SHOWING YOURSELF?
WIMP!
WHAT'S THAT SIR?
OH, JUST SHOUTING AT GOD.
OH... FAIR ENOUGH, SIR.

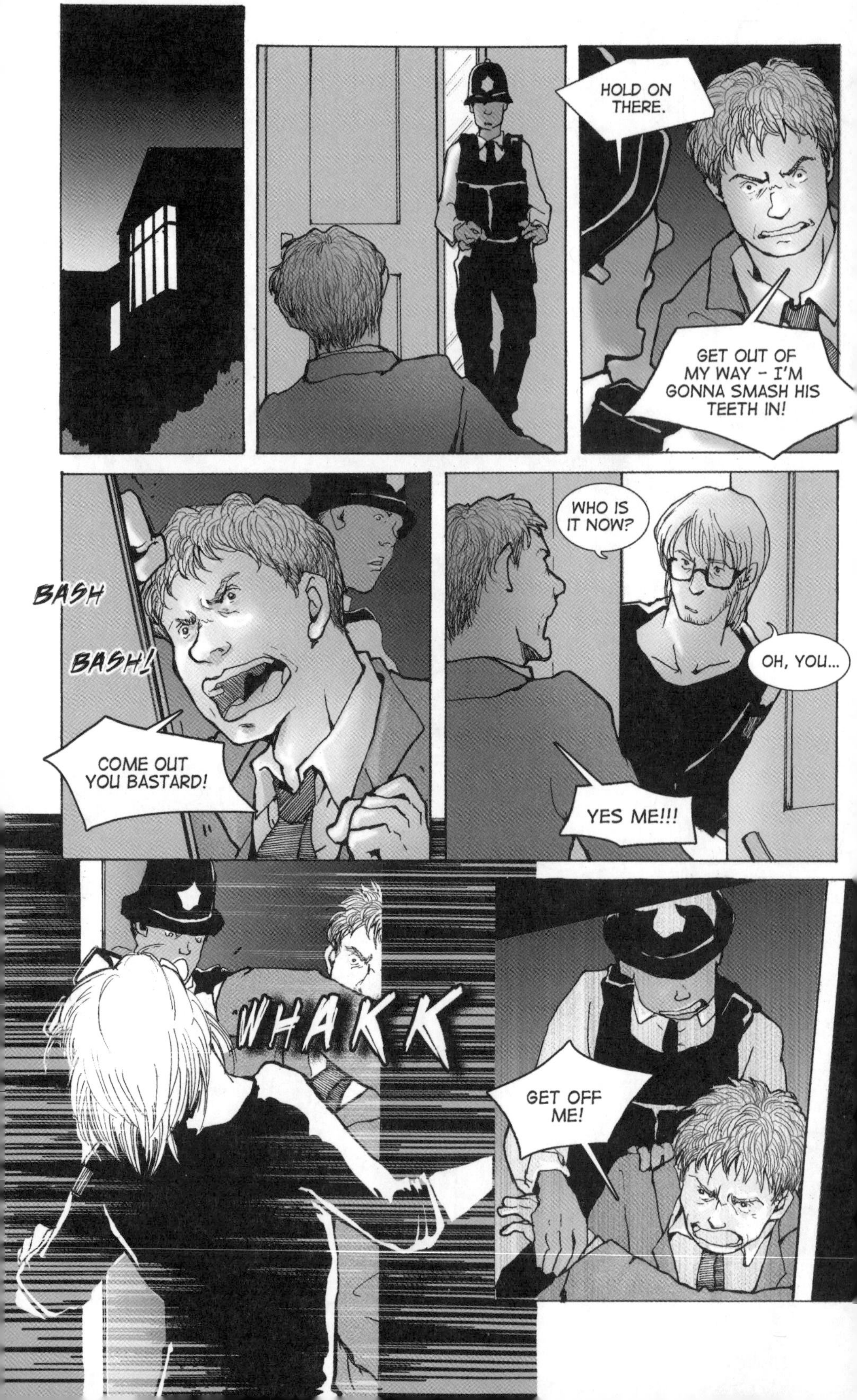
HOLD ON THERE.
GET OUT OF MY WAY - I'M GONNA SMASH HIS TEETH IN!
BASH
BASH!
COME OUT YOU BASTARD!
WHO IS IT NOW?
OH, YOU...
YES ME!!!
WHAKK
GET OFF ME!

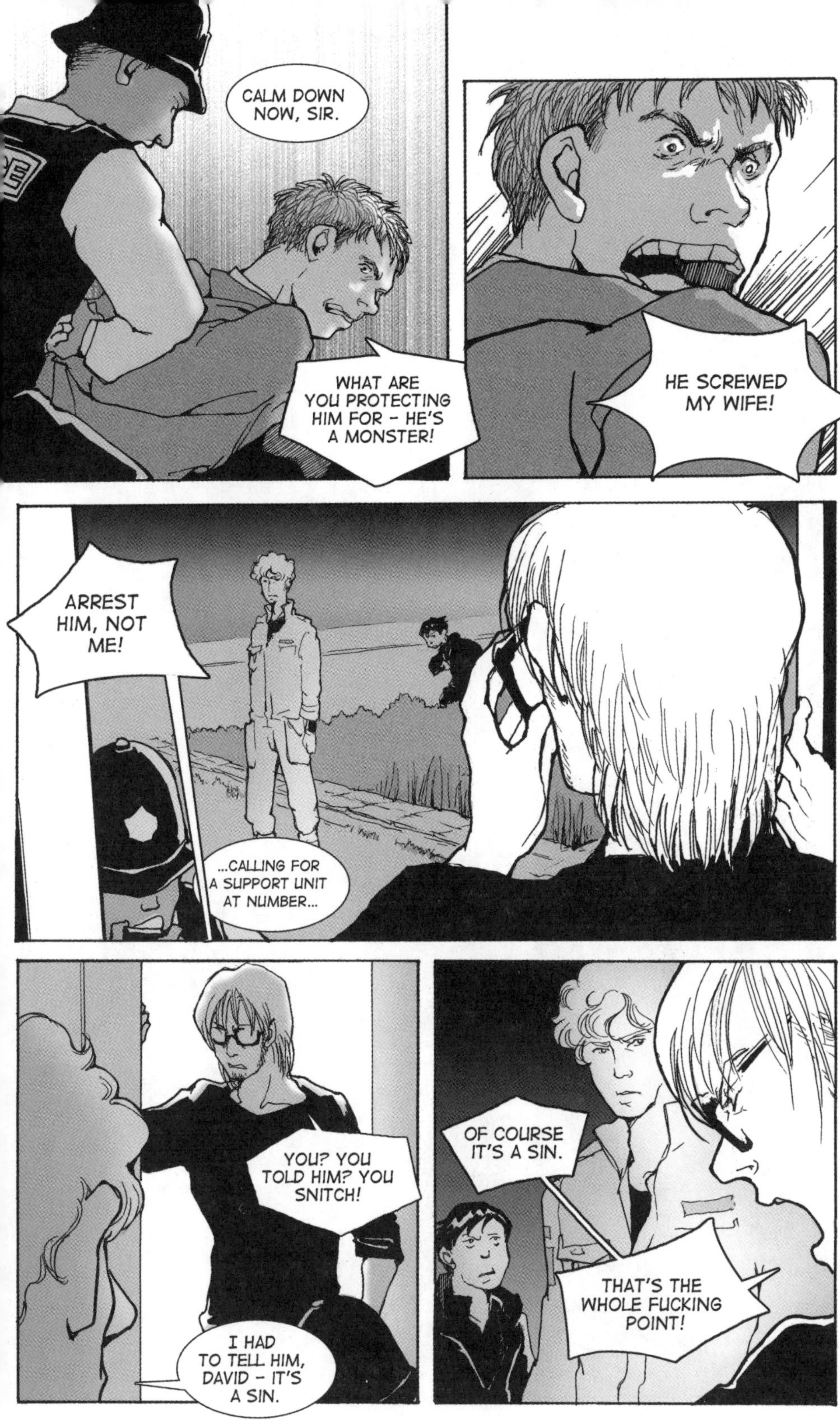
CALM DOWN NOW, SIR.
WHAT ARE YOU PROTECTING HIM FOR - HE'S A MONSTER!
HE SCREWED MY WIFE!
ARREST HIM, NOT ME!
...CALLING FOR A SUPPORT UNIT AT NUMBER...
YOU? YOU TOLD HIM? YOU SNITCH!
I HAD TO TELL HIM, DAVID - IT'S A SIN.
OF COURSE IT'S A SIN.
THAT'S THE WHOLE FUCKING POINT!

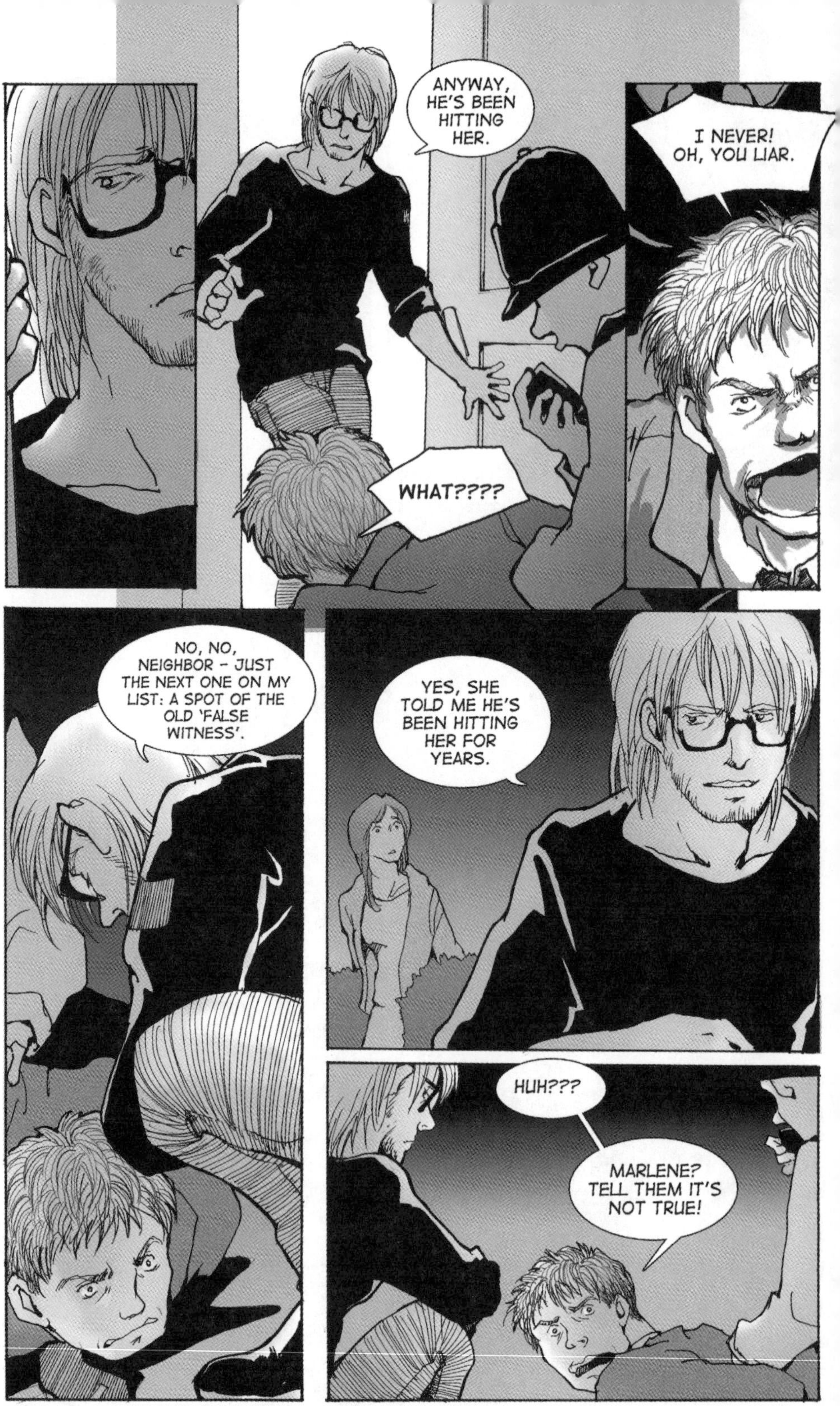

ANYWAY, HE'S BEEN HITTING HER.
WHAT????
I NEVER! OH, YOU LIAR.
NO, NO, NEIGHBOR - JUST THE NEXT ONE ON MY LIST: A SPOT OF THE OLD 'FALSE WITNESS'.
YES, SHE TOLD ME HE'S BEEN HITTING HER FOR YEARS.
HUH???
MARLENE? TELL THEM IT'S NOT TRUE!

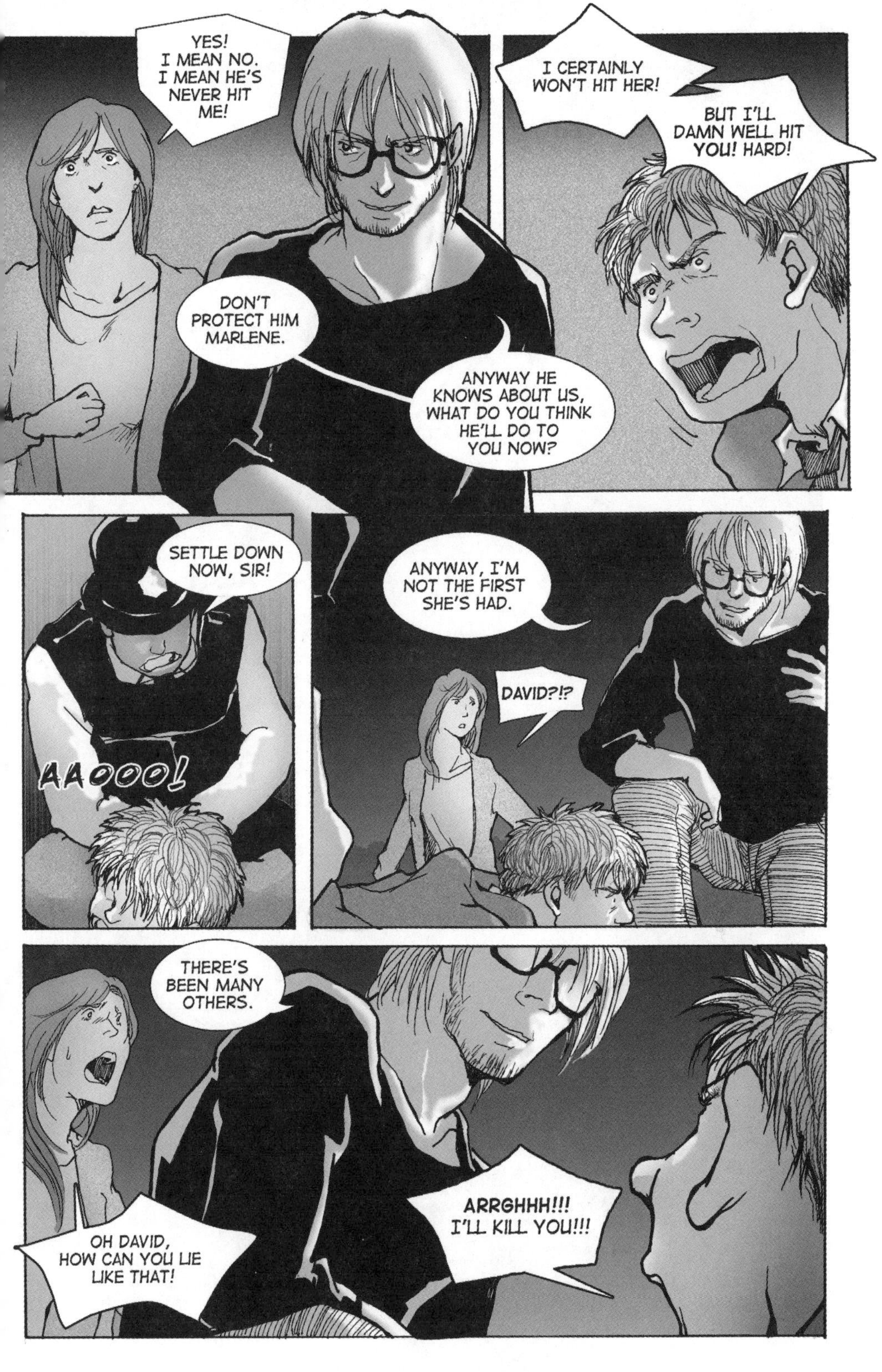
YES! I MEAN NO. I MEAN HE'S NEVER HIT ME!
DON'T PROTECT HIM MARLENE.
ANYWAY HE KNOWS ABOUT US, WHAT DO YOU THINK HE'LL DO TO YOU NOW?
I CERTAINLY WON'T HIT HER!
BUT I'LL DAMN WELL HIT YOU! HARD!
SETTLE DOWN NOW, SIR!
AAOOO!
ANYWAY, I'M NOT THE FIRST SHE'S HAD.
DAVID?!?
THERE'S BEEN MANY OTHERS.
OH DAVID, HOW CAN YOU LIE LIKE THAT!
ARRGHHH!!! I'LL KILL YOU!!!

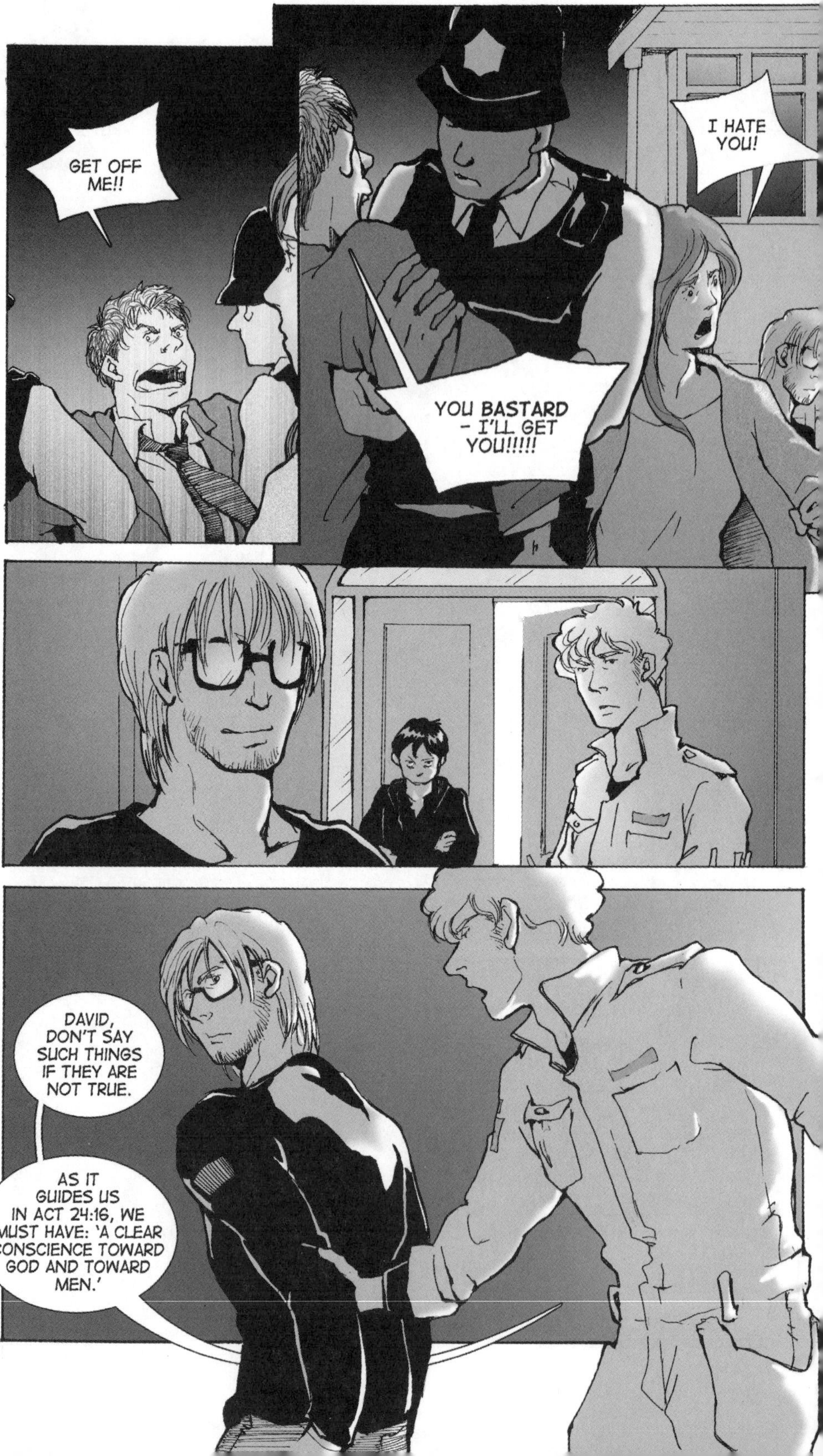
GET OFF ME!!
I HATE YOU!
YOU BASTARD – I'LL GET YOU!!!!!
DAVID, DON'T SAY SUCH THINGS IF THEY ARE NOT TRUE.
AS IT GUIDES US IN ACT 24:16, WE MUST HAVE: 'A CLEAR CONSCIENCE TOWARD GOD AND TOWARD MEN.'

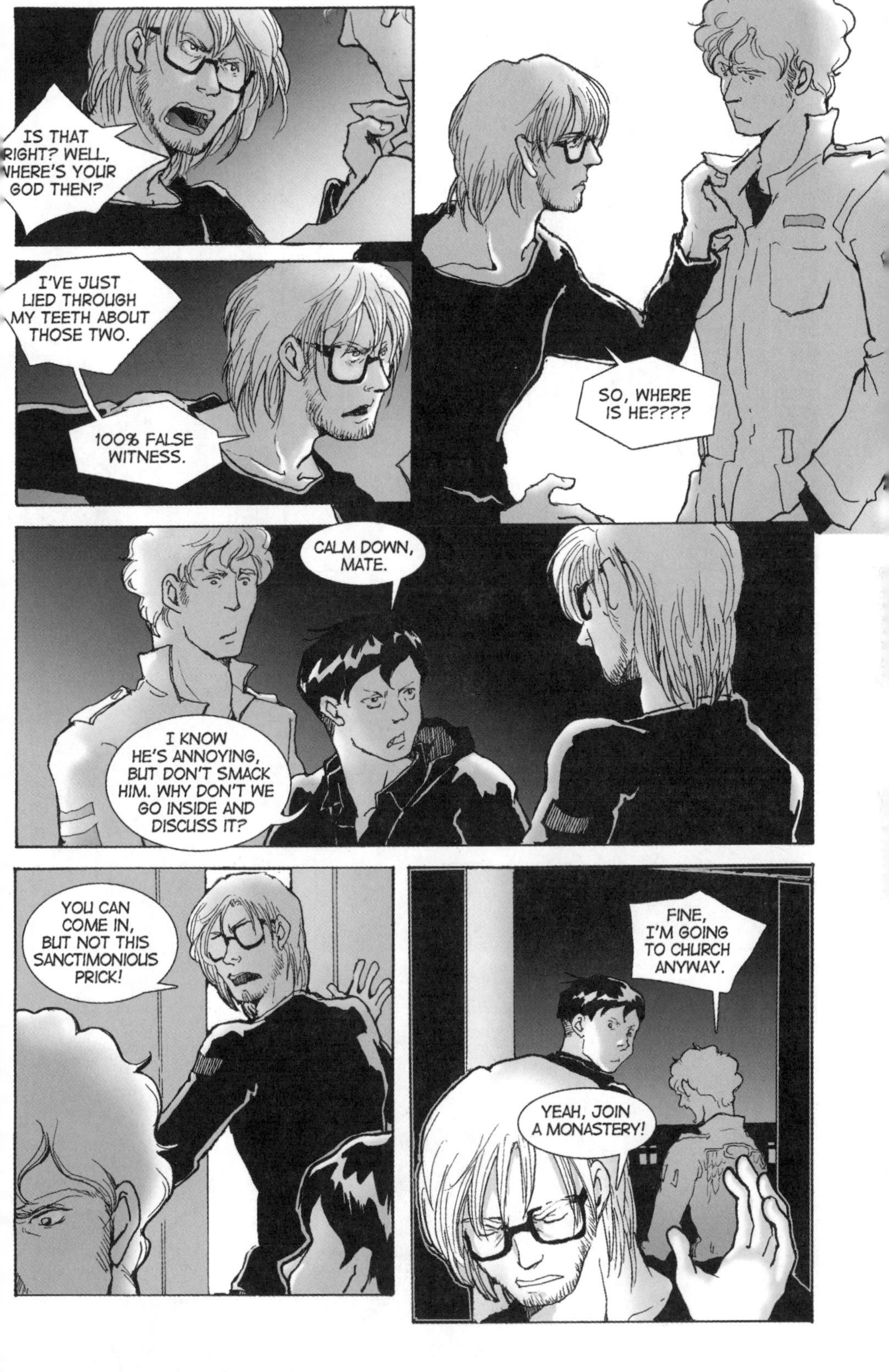

IS THAT RIGHT? WELL, WHERE'S YOUR GOD THEN?
I'VE JUST LIED THROUGH MY TEETH ABOUT THOSE TWO.
100% FALSE WITNESS.
SO, WHERE IS HE????
CALM DOWN, MATE.
I KNOW HE'S ANNOYING, BUT DON'T SMACK HIM. WHY DON'T WE GO INSIDE AND DISCUSS IT?
YOU CAN COME IN, BUT NOT THIS SANCTIMONIOUS PRICK!
FINE, I'M GOING TO CHURCH ANYWAY.
YEAH, JOIN A MONASTERY!

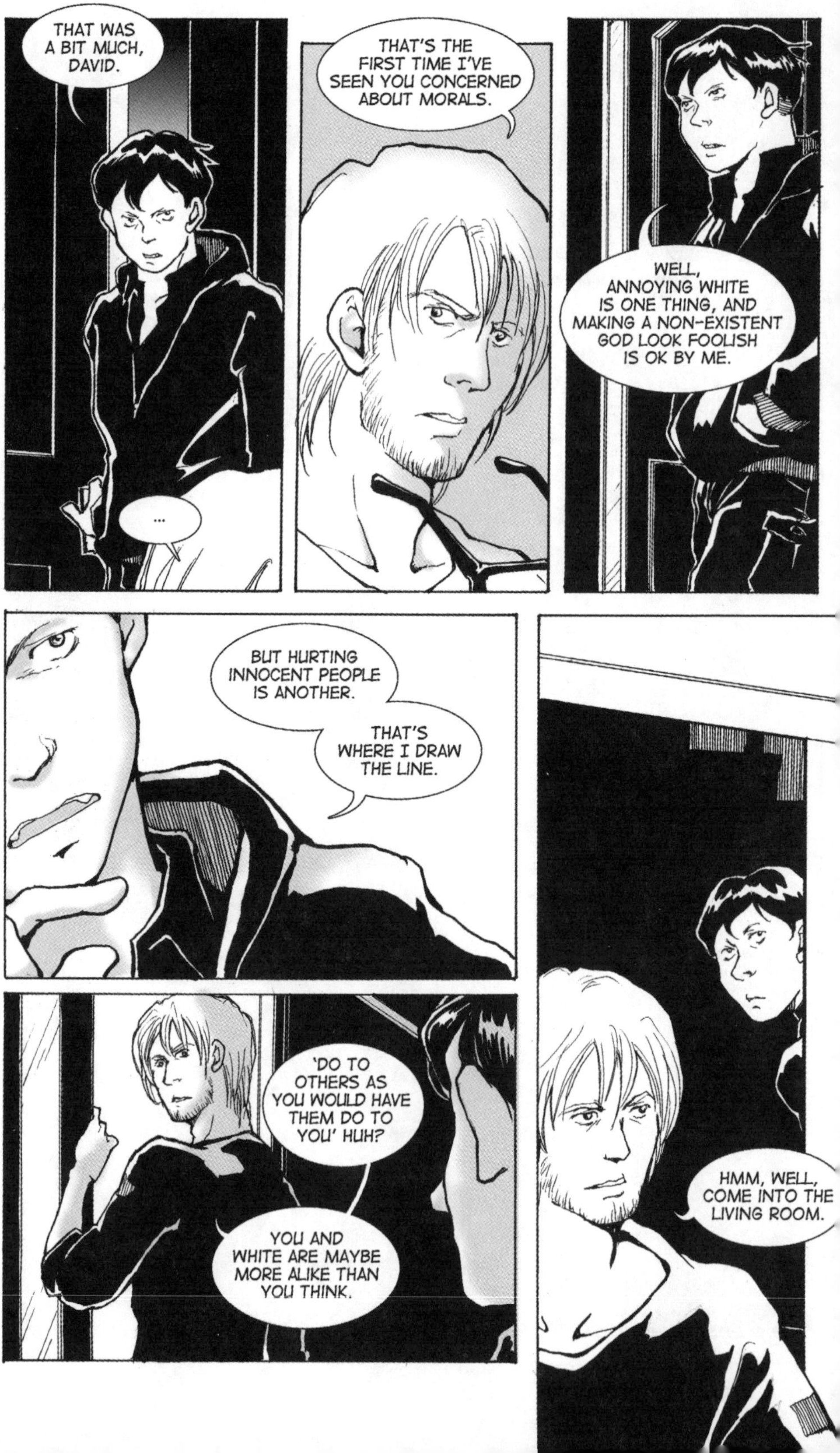
THAT WAS A BIT MUCH, DAVID.
...
THAT'S THE FIRST TIME I'VE SEEN YOU CONCERNED ABOUT MORALS.
WELL, ANNOYING WHITE IS ONE THING, AND MAKING A NON-EXISTENT GOD LOOK FOOLISH IS OK BY ME.
BUT HURTING INNOCENT PEOPLE IS ANOTHER.
THAT'S WHERE I DRAW THE LINE.
'DO TO OTHERS AS YOU WOULD HAVE THEM DO TO YOU' HUH?
YOU AND WHITE ARE MAYBE MORE ALIKE THAN YOU THINK.
HMM, WELL, COME INTO THE LIVING ROOM.

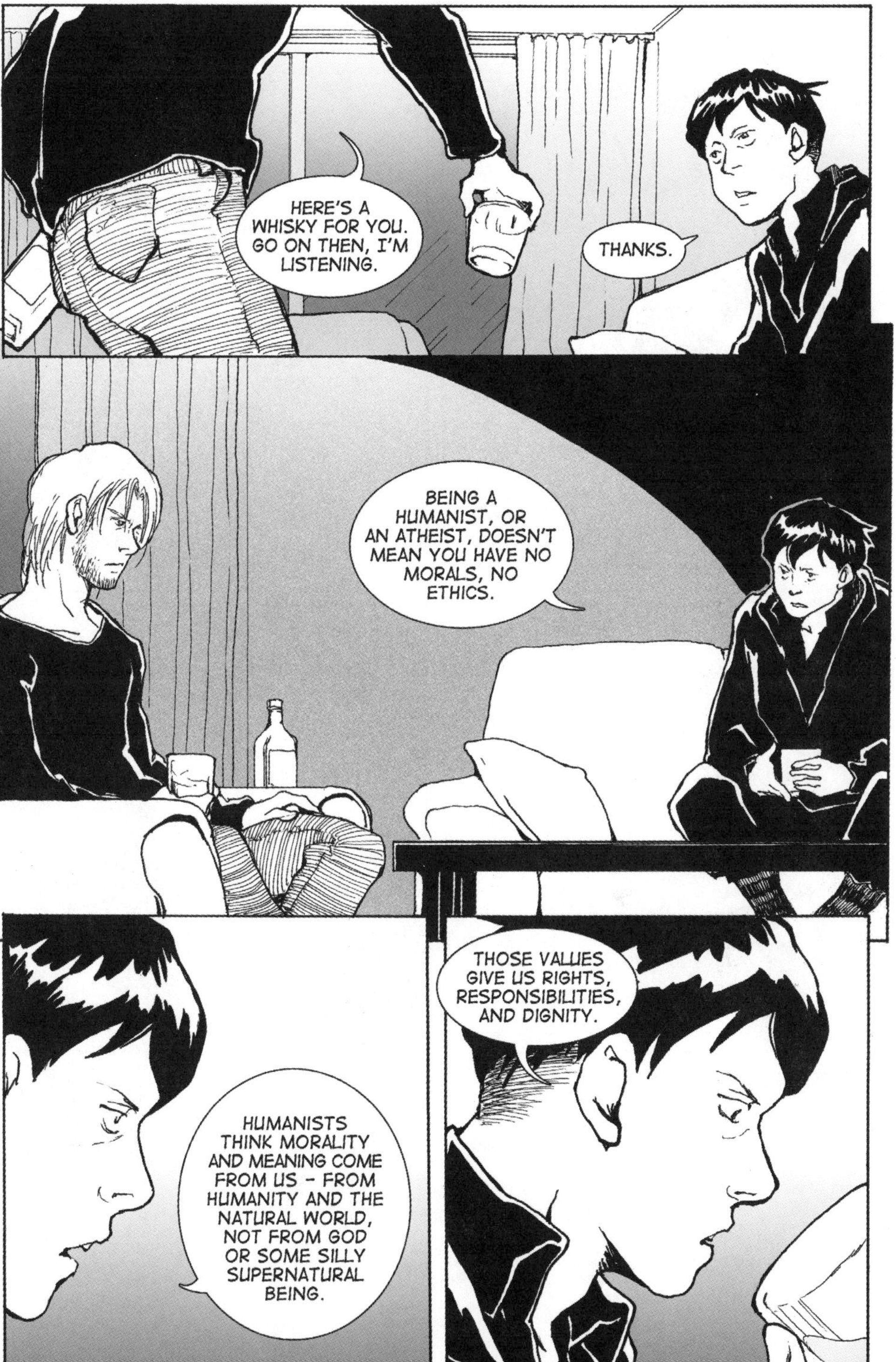
HERE'S A WHISKY FOR YOU. GO ON THEN, I'M LISTENING.
THANKS.
BEING A HUMANIST, OR AN ATHEIST, DOESN'T MEAN YOU HAVE NO MORALS, NO ETHICS.
HUMANISTS THINK MORALITY AND MEANING COME FROM US - FROM HUMANITY AND THE NATURAL WORLD, NOT FROM GOD OR SOME SILLY SUPERNATURAL BEING.
THOSE VALUES GIVE US RIGHTS, RESPONSIBILITIES, AND DIGNITY.

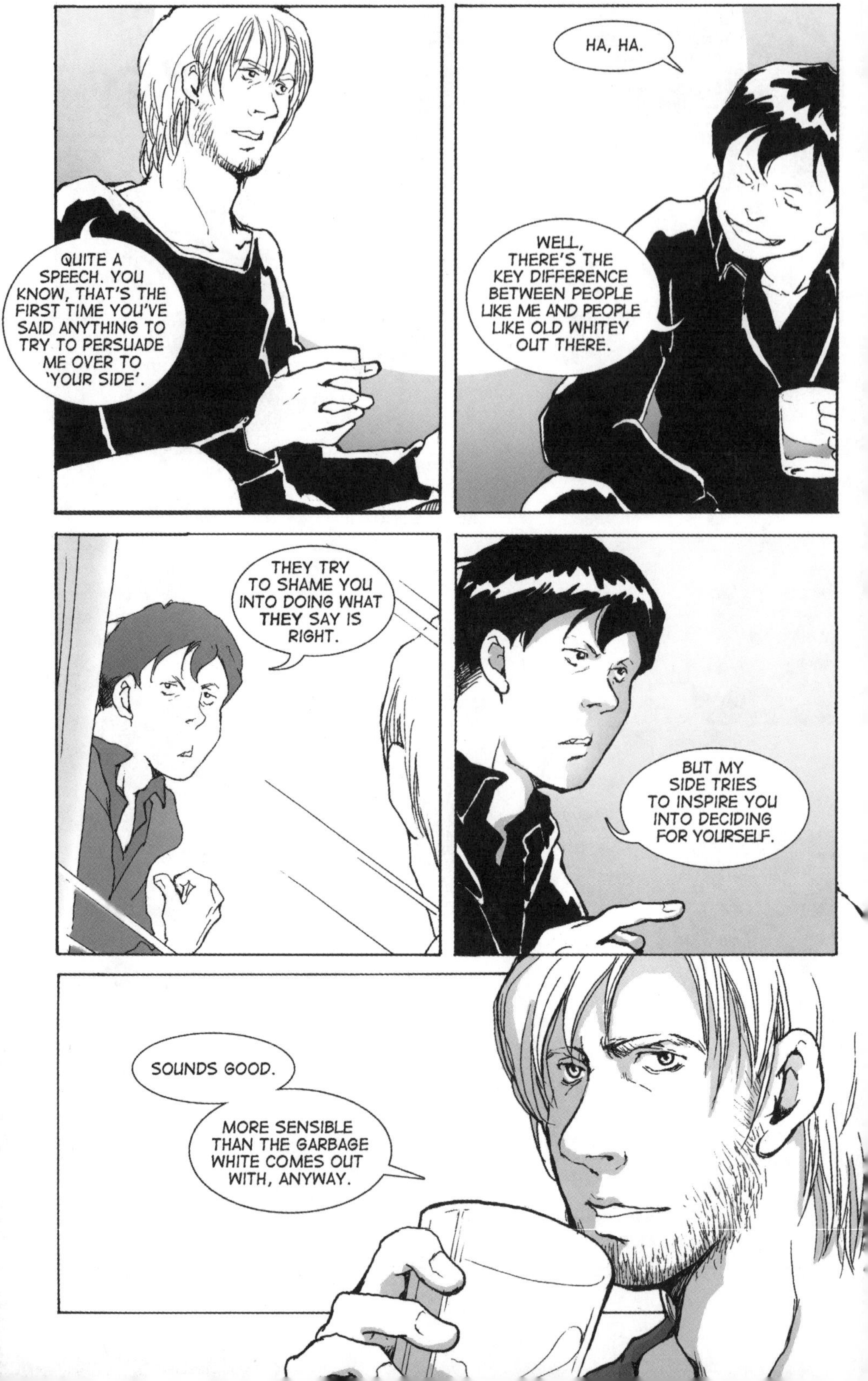
QUITE A SPEECH. YOU KNOW, THAT'S THE FIRST TIME YOU'VE SAID ANYTHING TO TRY TO PERSUADE ME OVER TO 'YOUR SIDE'.
HA, HA.
WELL, THERE'S THE KEY DIFFERENCE BETWEEN PEOPLE LIKE ME AND PEOPLE LIKE OLD WHITEY OUT THERE.
THEY TRY TO SHAME YOU INTO DOING WHAT THEY SAY IS RIGHT.
BUT MY SIDE TRIES TO INSPIRE YOU INTO DECIDING FOR YOURSELF.
SOUNDS GOOD.
MORE SENSIBLE THAN THE GARBAGE WHITE COMES OUT WITH, ANYWAY.

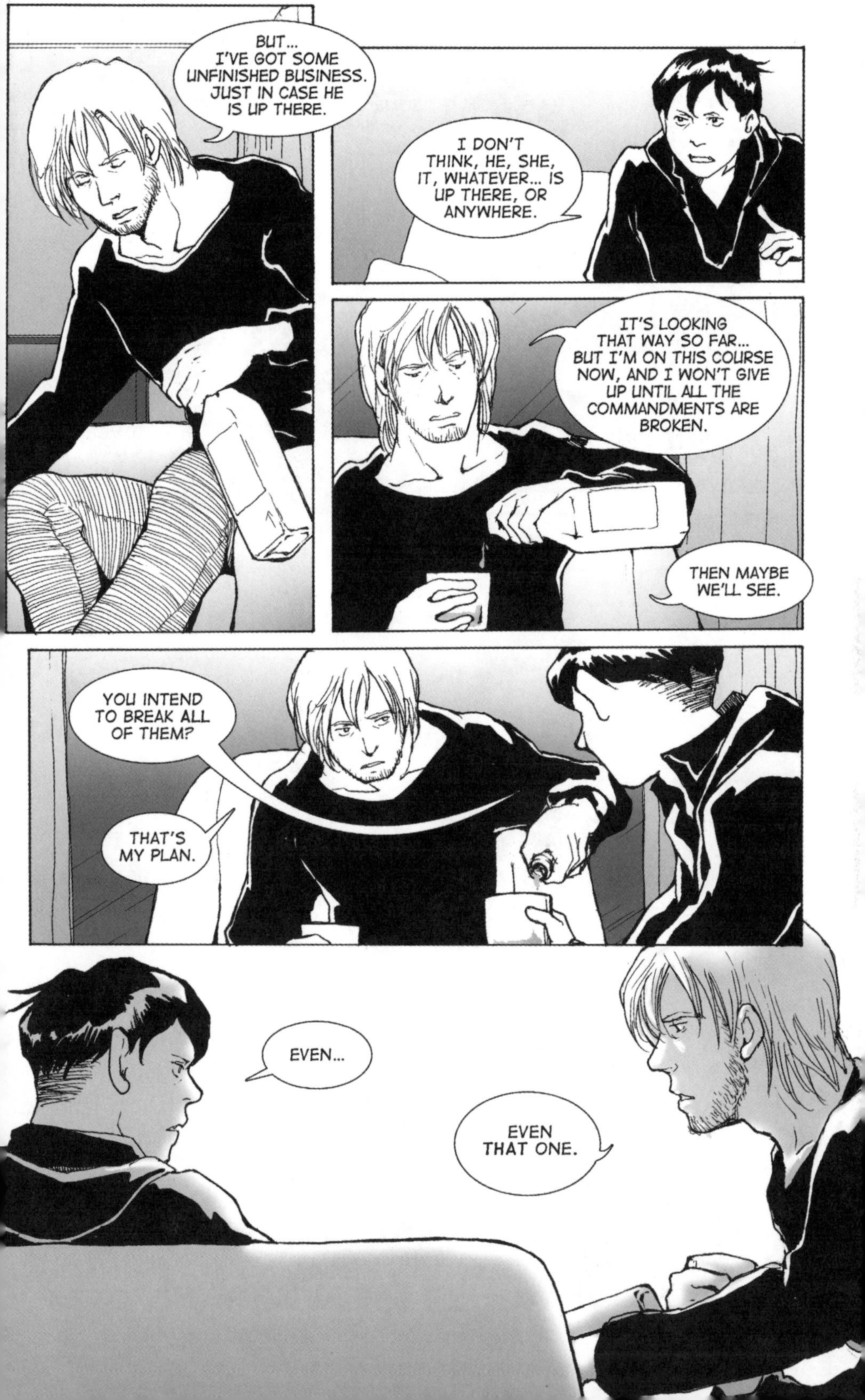
BUT... I'VE GOT SOME UNFINISHED BUSINESS. JUST IN CASE HE IS UP THERE.
I DON'T THINK, HE, SHE, IT, WHATEVER... IS UP THERE, OR ANYWHERE.
IT'S LOOKING THAT WAY SO FAR... BUT I'M ON THIS COURSE NOW, AND I WON'T GIVE UP UNTIL ALL THE COMMANDMENTS ARE BROKEN.
THEN MAYBE WE'LL SEE.
YOU INTEND TO BREAK ALL OF THEM?
THAT'S MY PLAN.
EVEN...
EVEN THAT ONE.

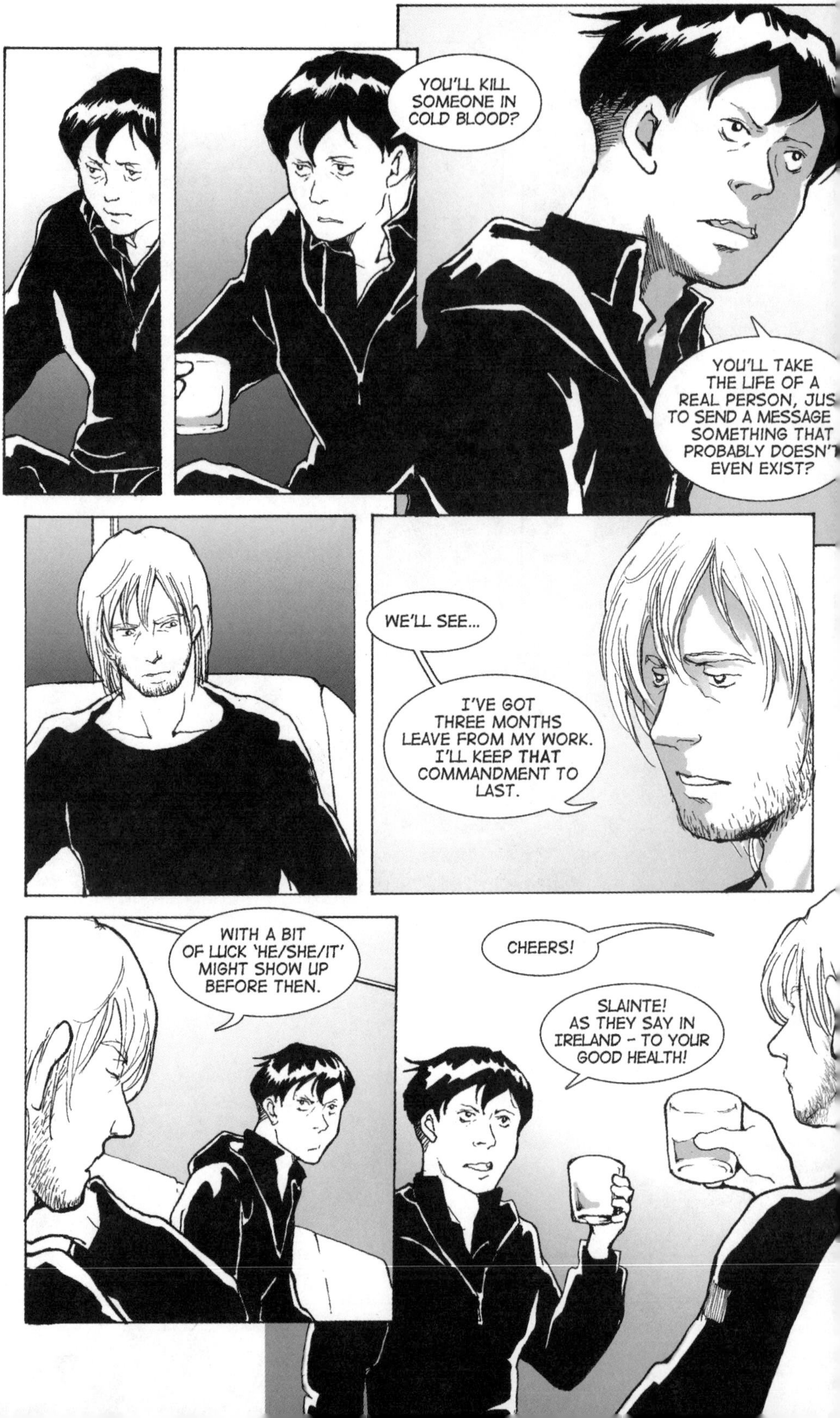
YOU'LL KILL SOMEONE IN COLD BLOOD?
YOU'LL TAKE THE LIFE OF A REAL PERSON, JUS TO SEND A MESSAGE SOMETHING THAT PROBABLY DOESN'T EVEN EXIST?
WE'LL SEE...
I'VE GOT THREE MONTHS LEAVE FROM MY WORK. I'LL KEEP THAT COMMANDMENT TO LAST.
WITH A BIT OF LUCK 'HE/SHE/IT' MIGHT SHOW UP BEFORE THEN.
CHEERS!
SLAINTE! AS THEY SAY IN IRELAND - TO YOUR GOOD HEALTH!

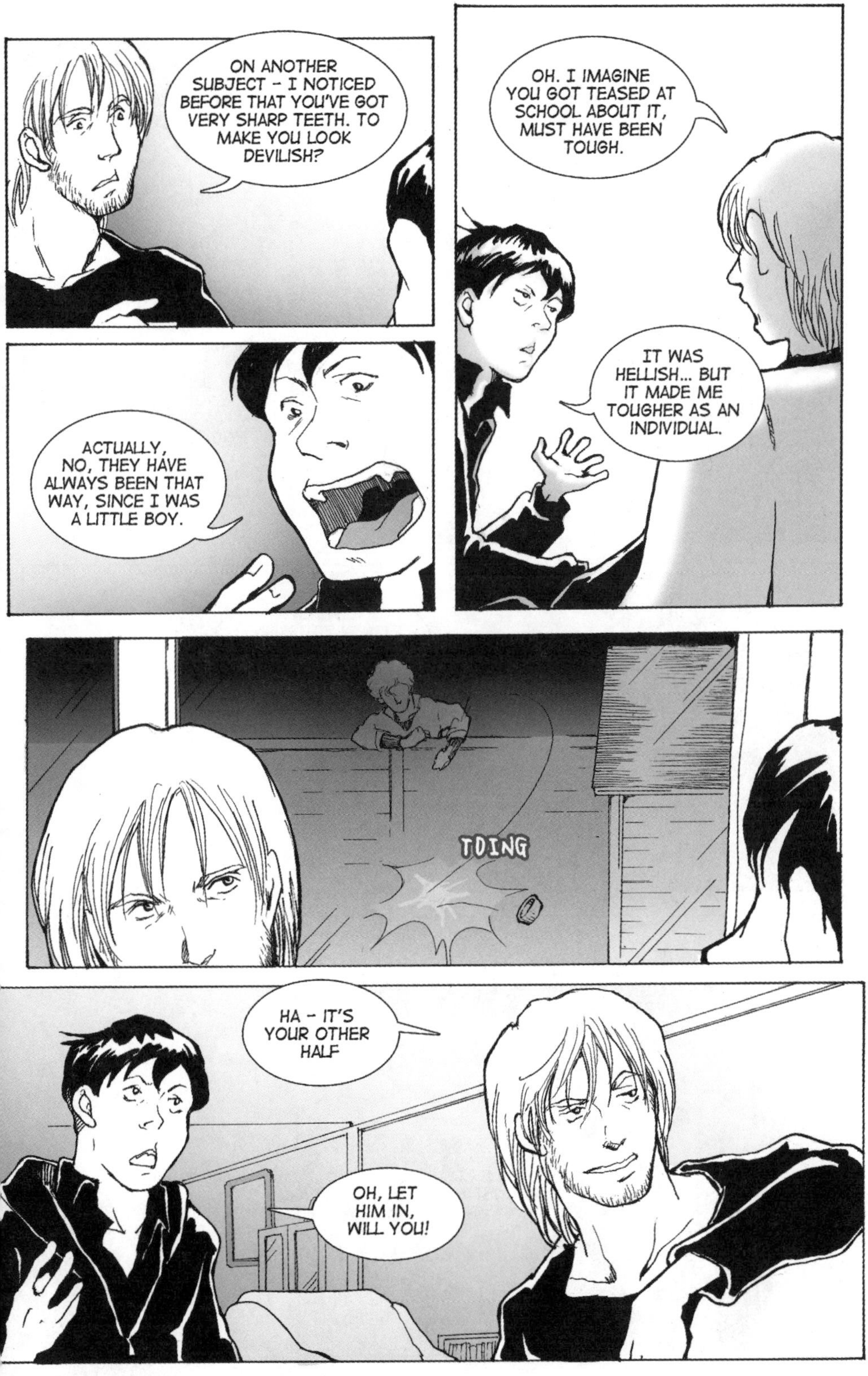

ON ANOTHER SUBJECT - I NOTICED BEFORE THAT YOU'VE GOT VERY SHARP TEETH. TO MAKE YOU LOOK DEVILISH?
ACTUALLY, NO, THEY HAVE ALWAYS BEEN THAT WAY, SINCE I WAS A LITTLE BOY.
OH. I IMAGINE YOU GOT TEASED AT SCHOOL ABOUT IT, MUST HAVE BEEN TOUGH.
IT WAS HELLISH... BUT IT MADE ME TOUGHER AS AN INDIVIDUAL.
TDING
HA - IT'S YOUR OTHER HALF
OH, LET HIM IN, WILL YOU!

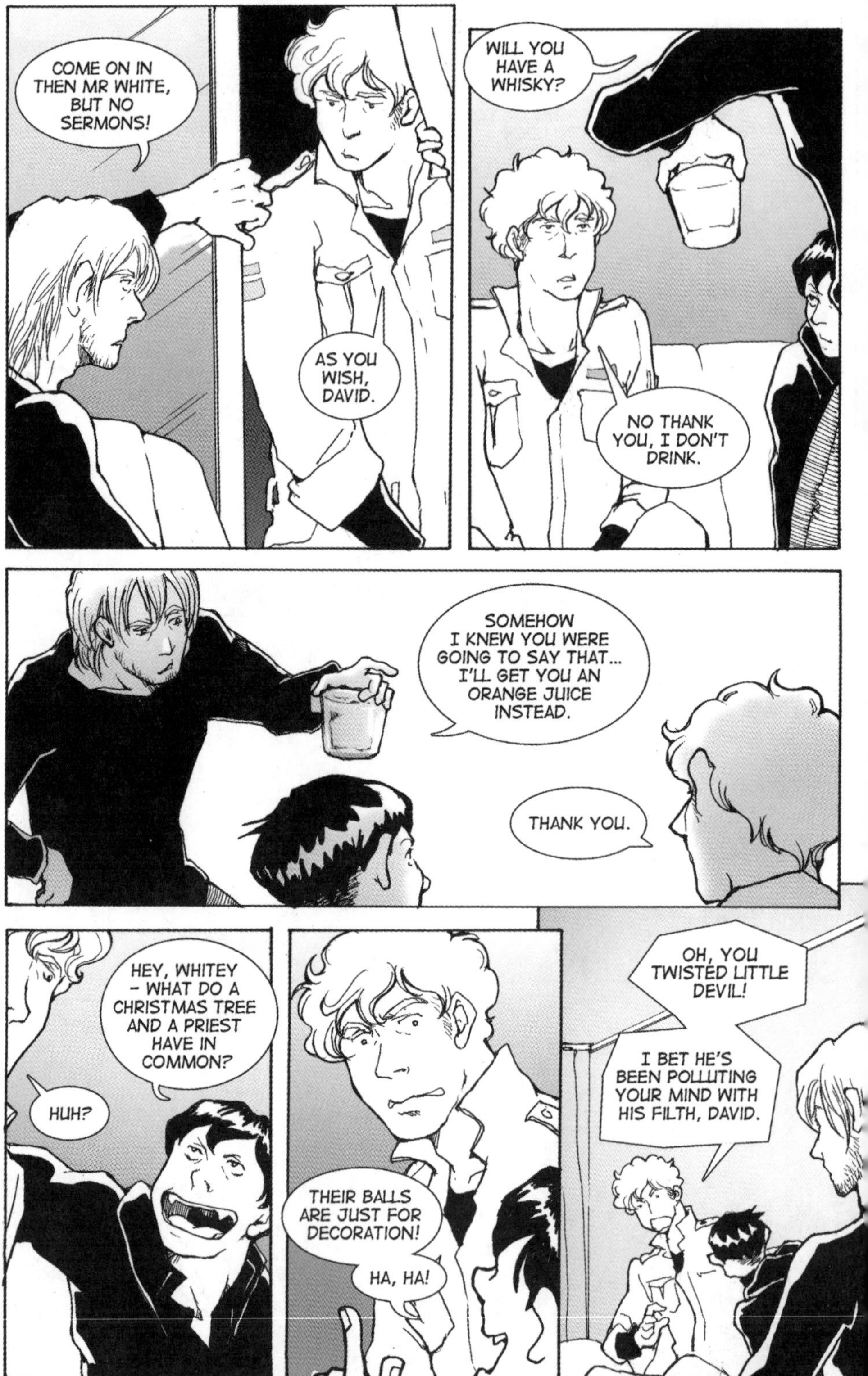
COME ON IN THEN MR WHITE, BUT NO SERMONS!
AS YOU WISH, DAVID.
WILL YOU HAVE A WHISKY?
NO THANK YOU, I DON'T DRINK.
SOMEHOW I KNEW YOU WERE GOING TO SAY THAT... I'LL GET YOU AN ORANGE JUICE INSTEAD.
THANK YOU.
HEY, WHITEY - WHAT DO A CHRISTMAS TREE AND A PRIEST HAVE IN COMMON?
HUH?
THEIR BALLS ARE JUST FOR DECORATION!
HA, HA!
OH, YOU TWISTED LITTLE DEVIL!
I BET HE'S BEEN POLLUTING YOUR MIND WITH HIS FILTH, DAVID.

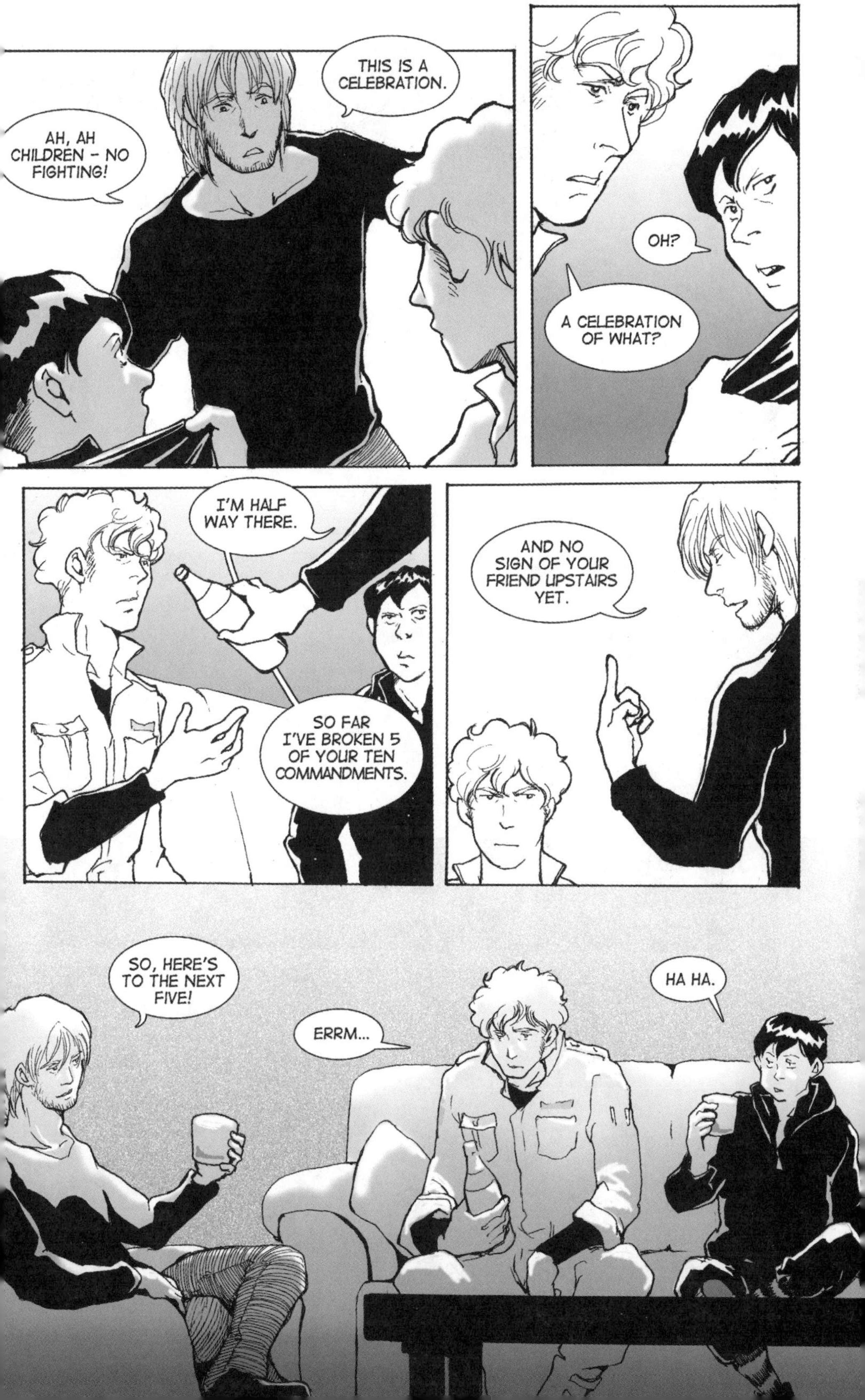
THIS IS A CELEBRATION.
AH, AH CHILDREN - NO FIGHTING!
OH?
A CELEBRATION OF WHAT?
I'M HALF WAY THERE.
SO FAR I'VE BROKEN 5 OF YOUR TEN COMMANDMENTS.
AND NO SIGN OF YOUR FRIEND UPSTAIRS YET.
SO, HERE'S TO THE NEXT FIVE!
ERRM...
HA HA.

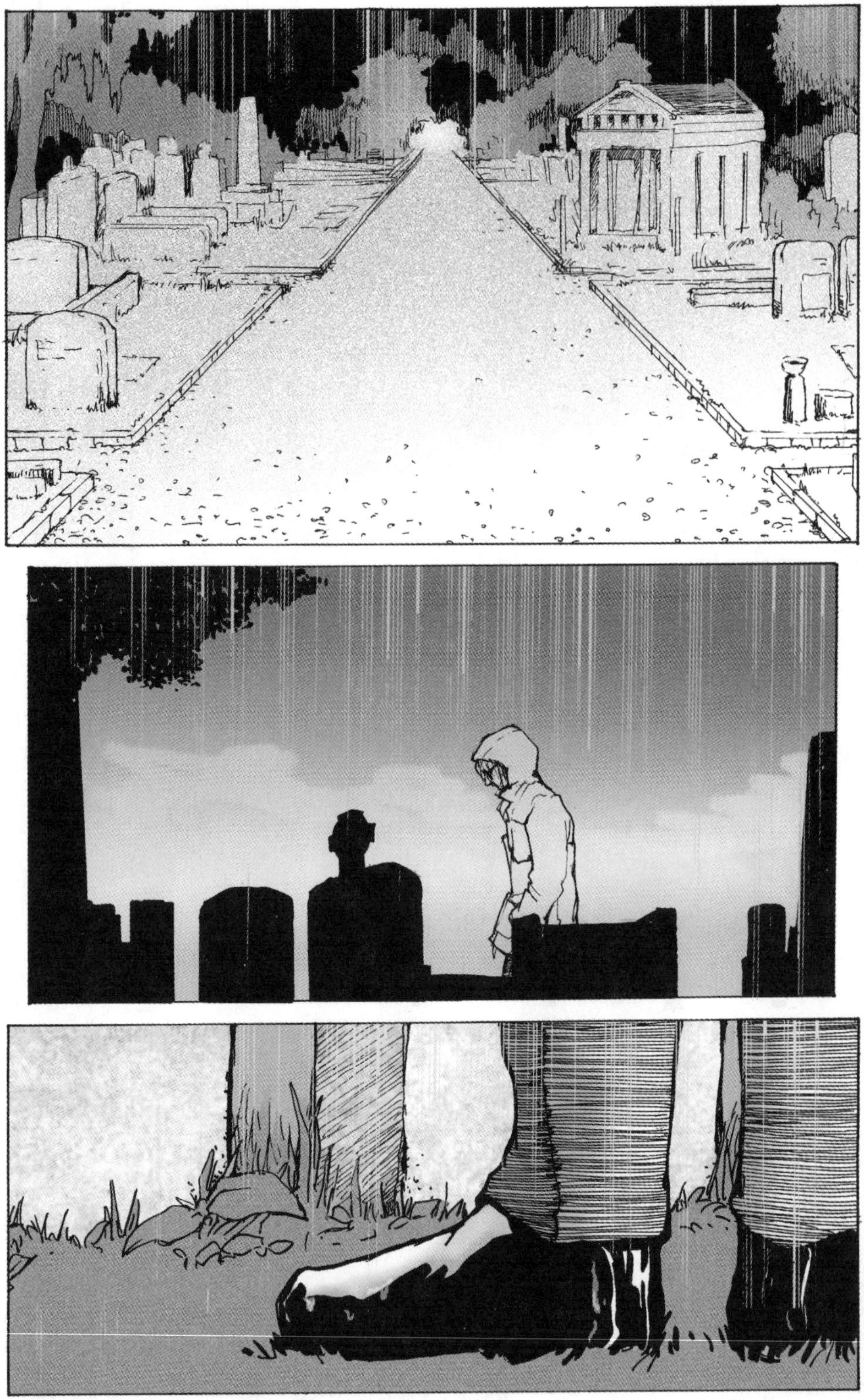

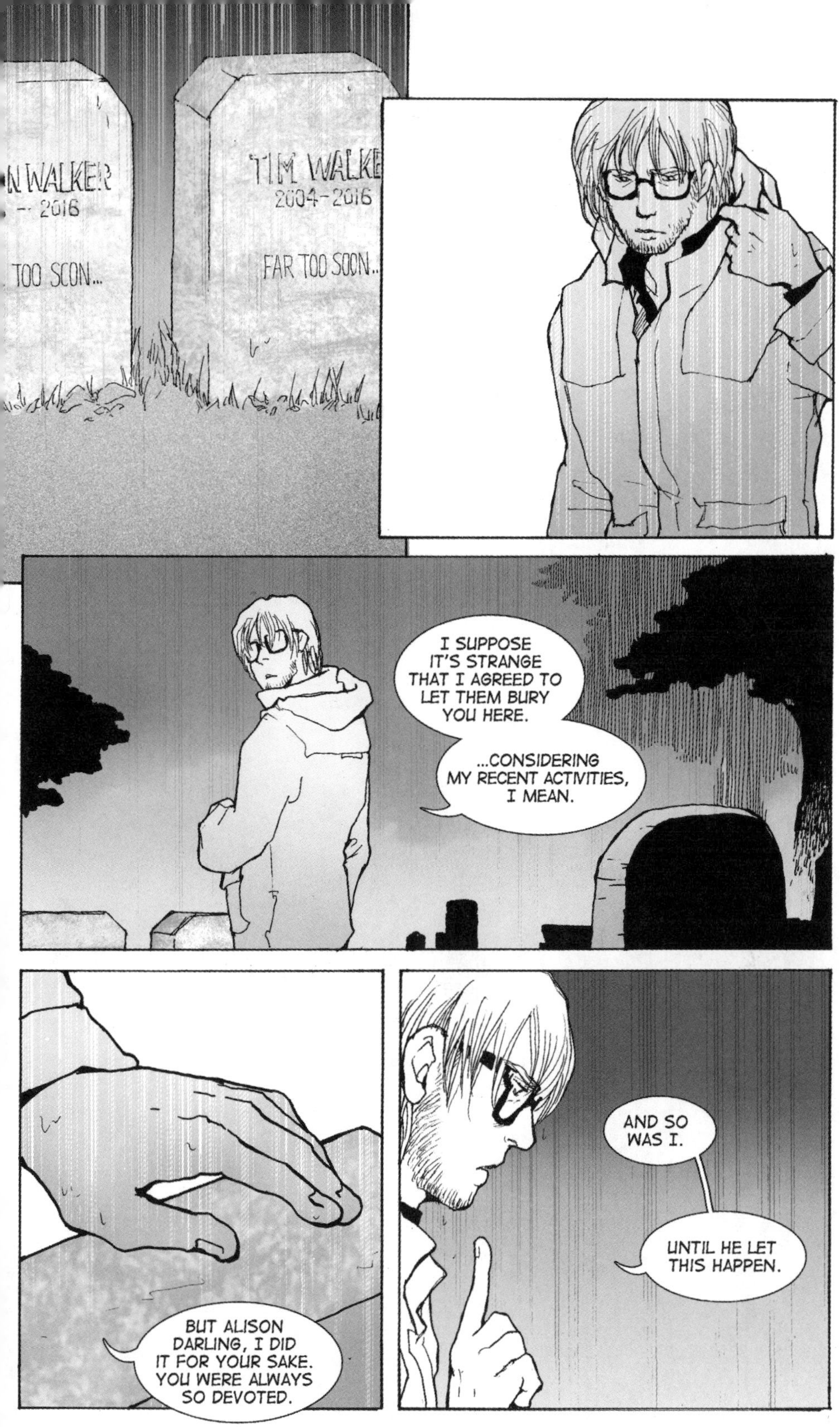
TIM WALKE
2004-2016
FAR TOO SOON...
I SUPPOSE IT'S STRANGE THAT I AGREED TO LET THEM BURY YOU HERE.
...CONSIDERING MY RECENT ACTIVITIES, I MEAN.
BUT ALISON DARLING, I DID IT FOR YOUR SAKE. YOU WERE ALWAYS SO DEVOTED.
AND SO WAS I.
UNTIL HE LET THIS HAPPEN.

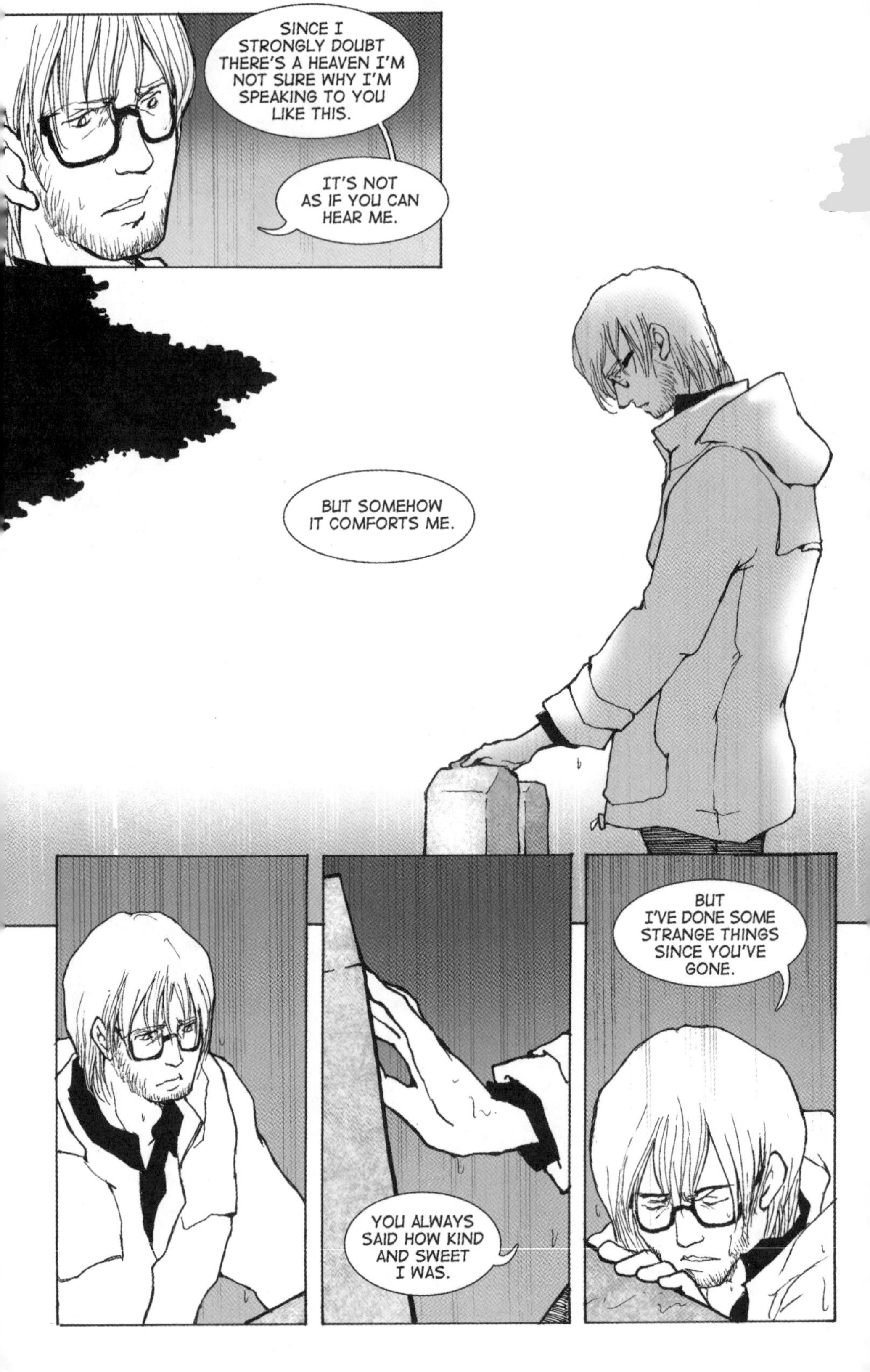
SINCE I STRONGLY DOUBT THERE'S A HEAVEN I'M NOT SURE WHY I'M SPEAKING TO YOU LIKE THIS.
IT'S NOT AS IF YOU CAN HEAR ME.
BUT SOMEHOW IT COMFORTS ME.
YOU ALWAYS SAID HOW KIND AND SWEET I WAS.
BUT I'VE DONE SOME STRANGE THINGS SINCE YOU'VE GONE.

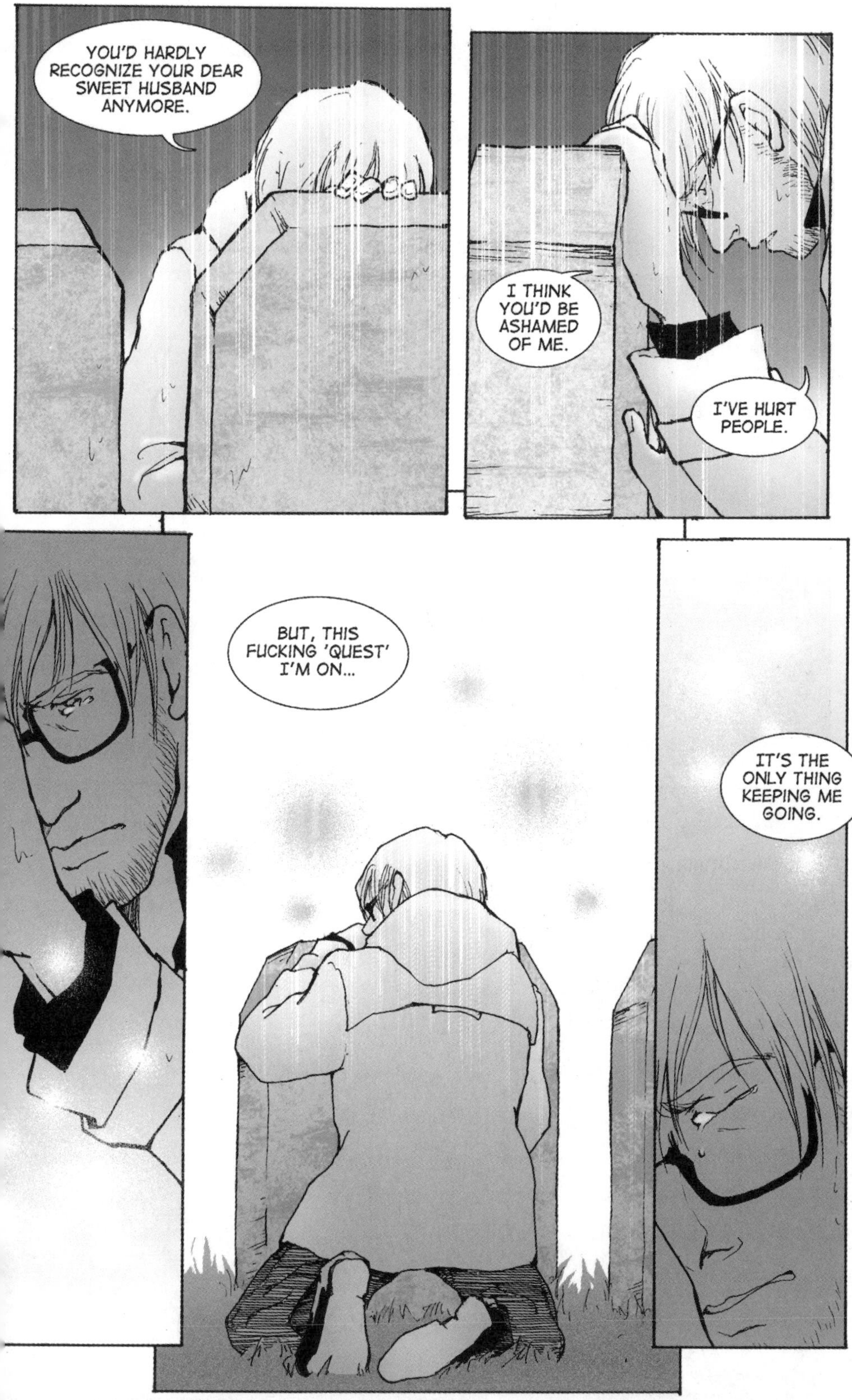
YOU'D HARDLY RECOGNIZE YOUR DEAR SWEET HUSBAND ANYMORE.
I THINK YOU'D BE ASHAMED OF ME.
I'VE HURT PEOPLE.
BUT, THIS FUCKING 'QUEST' I'M ON...
IT'S THE ONLY THING KEEPING ME GOING.

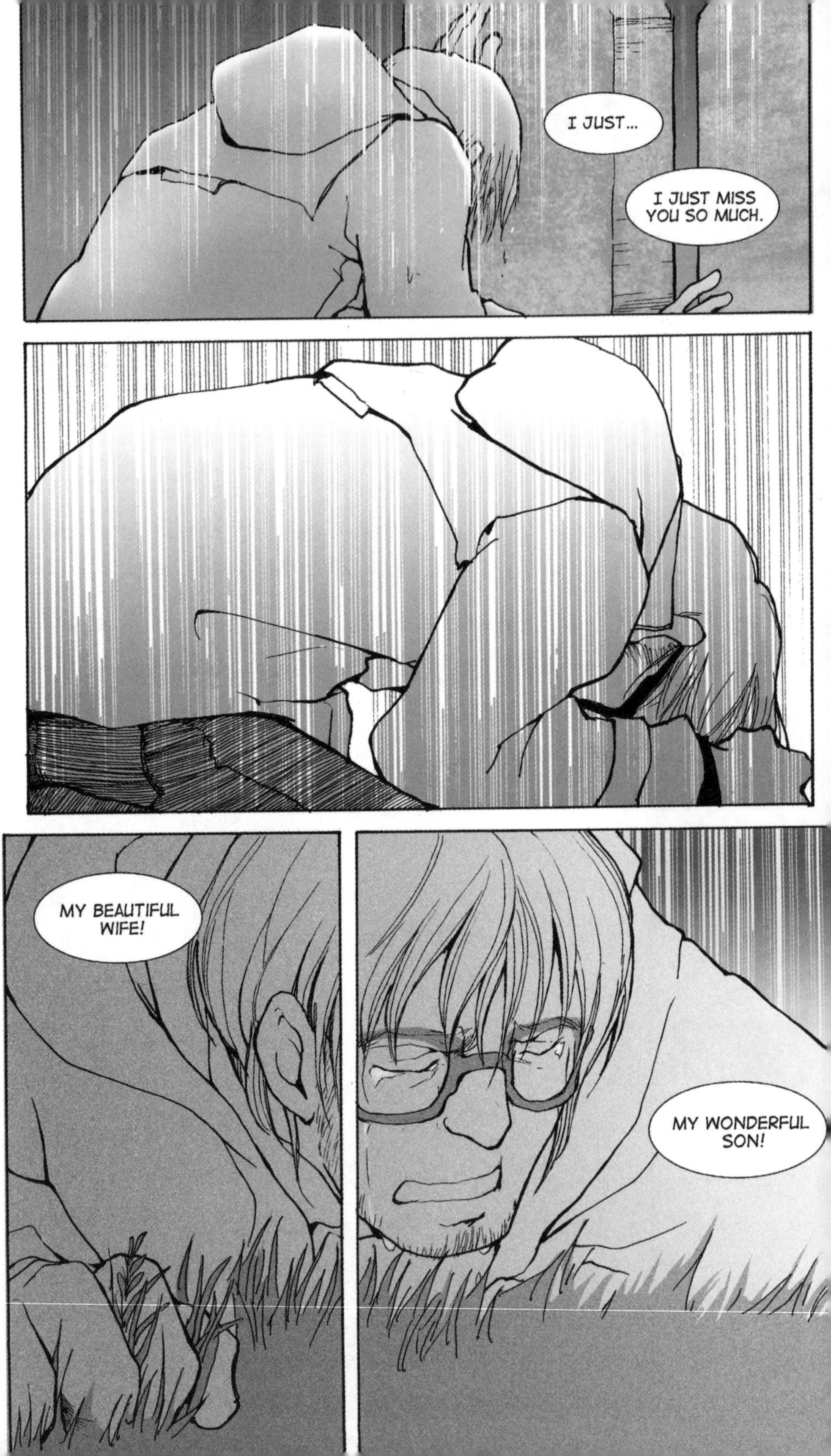
I JUST...
I JUST MISS YOU SO MUCH.
MY BEAUTIFUL WIFE!
MY WONDERFUL SON!

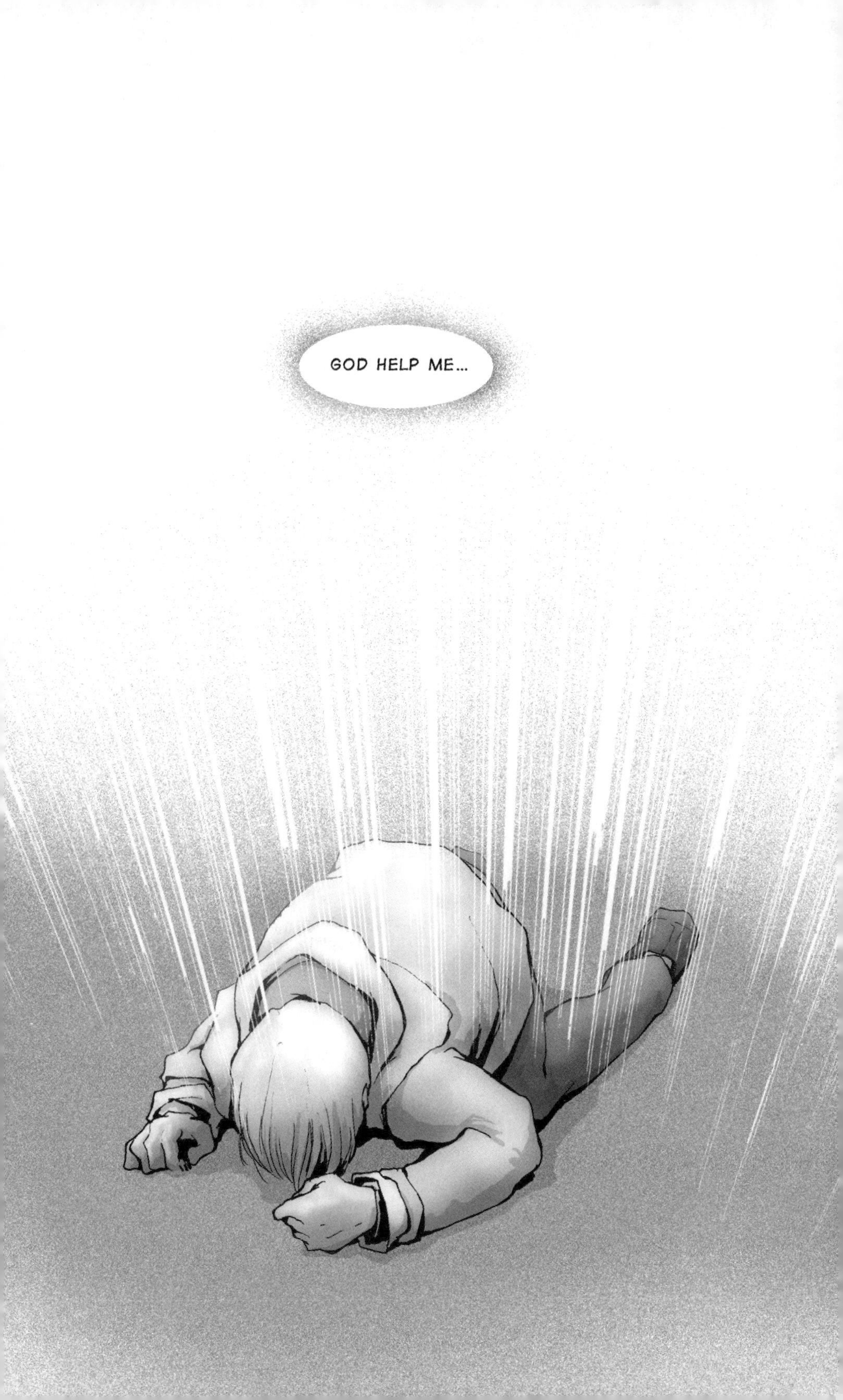
GOD HELP ME...

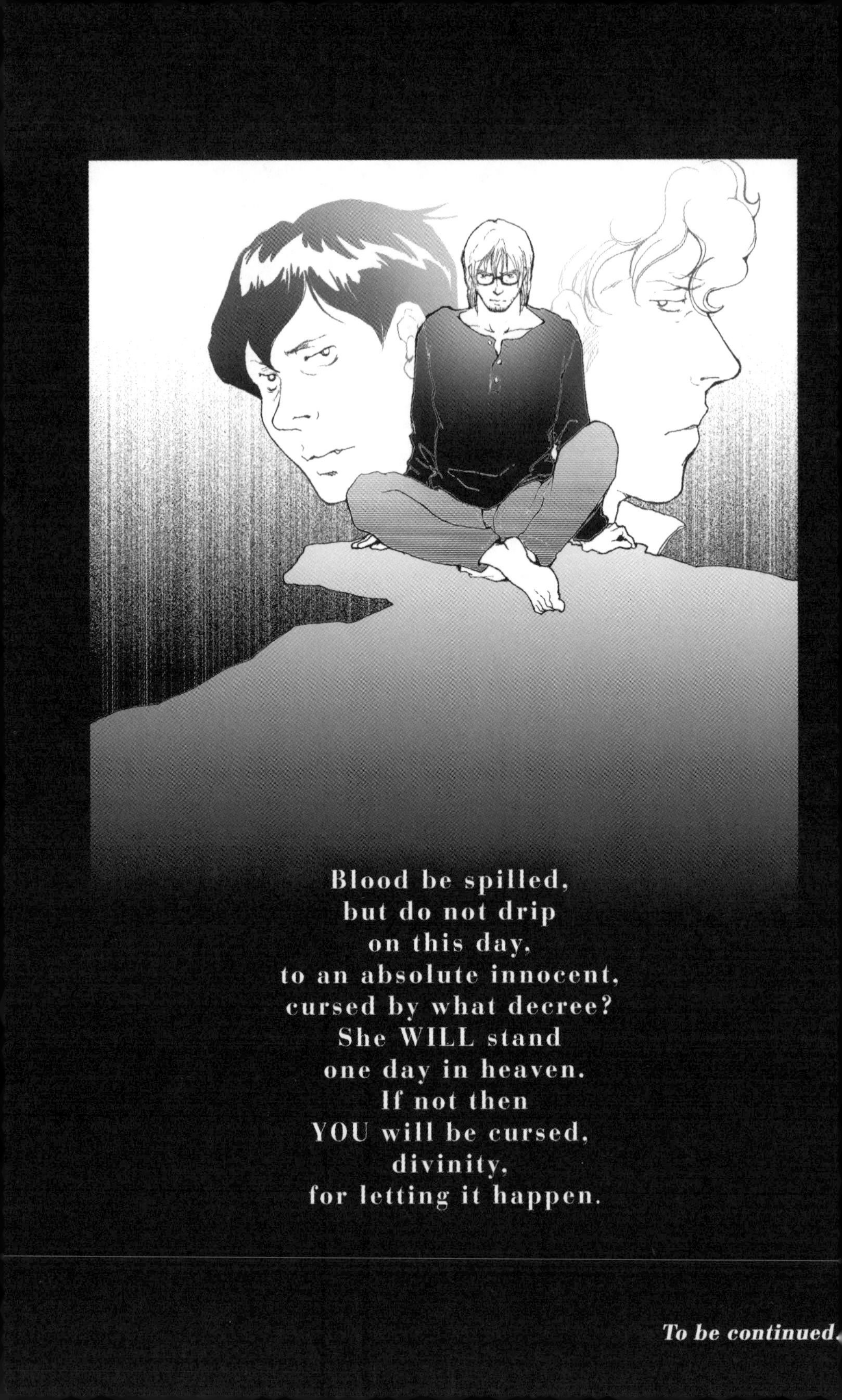

Blood be spilled,
but do not drip
on this day,
to an absolute innocent,
cursed by what decree?
She WILL stand
one day in heaven.
If not then
YOU will be cursed,
divinity,
for letting it happen.

To be continued.

Also by Wilson from NBM:
The Story of Lee, vols.1, 2 (trade pb., e-books)
"Made me feel warm and fuzzy. [The authors'] familiarity with the turf wars gives this unpretentious East-meets-West, boy-meets girl story an easy, breezy sense of verisimilitude."
-Scripps Howard News Service

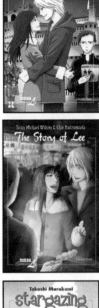

Other manga from ComicsLit:
Stargazing Dog by Murakami
"Perhaps the best compliment I can pay Murakami is to acknowledg just how much Stargazing Dog moved me." -Manga Critic
In the Louvre collection:
Rohan at the Louvre by Araki
"A must read! A truly unique reading experience."
-Ain't it Cool News
Guardians of the Louvre by Taniguchi
Publishers Weekly Top Ten Graphic Novel
for Spring '16

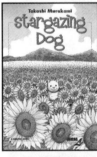

We have over 200 titles.

See our complete list, Wilson's blog and order at:
NBMPUB.COM

NBM Graphic Novels
160 Broadway, Suite 700, East Wing,
New York, NY 10038
Catalog available by request

The Story of Lee

The Story of Lee

Takashi Murakami
stargazing Dog

Rohan at the Louvre
Hirohiko Araki

GUARDIANS OF THE LOUVRE

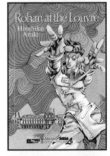

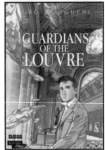